DIARY OF AN ALCOHOLIC HOUSEWIFE

DIARY OF AN ALCOHOLIC HOUSEWIFE

Brenda Wilhelmson

HAZELDEN®

Hazelden
Center City, Minnesota 55012
hazelden.org

Library of Congress Cataloging-in-Publication Data

Wilhelmson, Brenda.
Diary of an alcoholic housewife / Brenda Wilhelmson.
p. cm.
ISBN 978-1-61649-086-7 (softcover) — ISBN 978-1-61649-000-3 (e-book)
1. Wilhelmson, Brenda. 2. Women alcoholics—United States—Diaries. 3. Alcoholics—Rehabilitation—United States. I. Title.
HV5293.W54A3 2011
362.292092—dc22
[B]

2010051679

Editor's note
Some names, details, and circumstances have been changed to protect the privacy of those mentioned in this publication.

The Big Book (*Alcoholics Anonymous*) is a registered trademark of Alcoholics Anonymous World Services, Inc.

14 13 12 11 3 4 5 6

Cover design by Theresa Jaeger Gedig
Interior design by Cathy Spengler
Typesetting by BookMobile Design and Publishing Services

If you have a drinking problem,
or love someone who does,
this book is for you.
Peace.

CONTENTS

ACKNOWLEDGMENTS

Big thanks to my beautifully imperfect family and friends. If we were perfect, we wouldn't need each other—or be very interesting. Thank you, Sarah Karon, for reading this book, asking Paul to take it to Hazelden, and being a kick-ass friend. Paul Karon, thank you for putting my book in front of the editorial powers that be. Sid Farrar, big thanks for believing in this book and making me a published author. Amy Krouse-Rosenthal, thank you for turning me on to Amy Rennert. Amy Rennert, my contract navigator, thank you. To my mother, Sally, and husband, Charlie, thank you for your unflinching support. And to my Higher Power, thank you for the amazing ride.

INTRODUCTION

One of the many nights I left a recovery meeting wondering if I really belonged there, I drove to a bookstore and pulled every drinking-related memoir I could find off the shelves. I didn't want to read a depraved story about how low a person could go. I wanted verification that someone like me was a drunk and needed to stop drinking. I left the store empty handed and bummed. As I lay in bed that night, the thought *Write that book* flew into my head.

I bought a notebook the next day and began my first journal entry with the evening I got blackout-wasted and woke up the next morning knowing I needed to quit. I don't know why that episode was the lynchpin. I'd had countless drunks and hangovers just like it. I believe it was just the accumulation of so many shit-faced nights and sick mornings.

I kept writing journal entries for fifteen months as I worked to stay sober. During that time, I worried about my family and friends, the people who were appearing in its pages. Many were not going to like what they saw. I didn't come off well either. If I wasn't honest, if I didn't accurately report the way the world appeared through my lens, however, my book would be trash, useless to other high-functioning alcoholics I wanted to connect with. I changed the names and identities of my friends so that only the people themselves, or others who already saw them as I did, would know who I was writing about. But my family wasn't as fortunate. If you know me, you know my family. They were stuck.

I finished my last journal entry on February 8, 2003. I walked over to a chest of drawers in my bedroom, opened the drawer where I kept the other nine notebooks I'd filled with journal entries, threw it in, and closed the drawer. My journals sat there untouched for about a year and a half. I didn't want to look at them or deal with them until the day (and I don't remember what day it was) I felt compelled to start typing my journal entries into my computer. I began rewriting and editing. I'd work then stop, work then stop. Sometimes I'd stop for days, weeks, or months because life got busy or difficult, or the journal entries I was looking at were uncomfortable. I'd begin again when I felt an internal urge to get back to it.

Three and a half years later, I completed the manuscript for *Diary of an Alcoholic Housewife*. On December 26, 2008, I began blogging it. Two months after the blog was up, I was vacationing in Puerto Rico with my husband and woke up in the middle of the night thinking, *What the hell am I doing? I'm putting myself and my loved ones out there in a big way and people are going to be hurt and hate me.* I considered killing the blog when I got home, but people were reading it, and I figured I was helping them. "If *Diary* ends up being no more than a helpful blog, I'm good with that," I decided. That spring, after hearing from people with drinking problems who contacted me through my blog, I started looking for an agent. That summer, my friend, Sarah Karon, urged me to let her husband, Paul, take my book to Hazelden, and Hazelden liked it. So here's my book.

• • •

DIARY ENTRIES

[Friday, December 6]

Shook up a vodka martini and stirred my beef bourguignon. I like my martinis like James Bond's: straight up, dry, and with a twist, except my martini glasses—artfully etched with small decorative rectangles—are triple size. My husband, Charlie, poured himself a scotch on the rocks.

This afternoon I took our sons—Max, ten, and Van, two—to my parents' for the weekend because we're partying. The O'Brians, high school friends of Charlie's, are coming for dinner tonight, and tomorrow Charlie and I are going to the Wendts' because it's their turn to host the Bacchanal Dinner Club I started.

The doorbell rang. I stopped stirring the bourguignon, walked through the living room, and waved at Mary and Pat through the leaded glass door of our 100-year-old arts and crafts bungalow. A bit of martini sloshed over the rim of my glass as I pulled the door open. A blast of cold air blew in with Mary and Pat. Their sleeping car-seat-cradled infant dangled from Pat's arm. He set the baby down on the living room floor, and Charlie went off to pour Pat a scotch and shake a martini for Mary.

"I love your artwork," Mary cooed, taking her martini from Charlie and roaming from living room to TV room to dining room.

"Thanks," I said, pointing out a few impressionistic cocktail party scenes. "Martha painted those."

"Charlie's mom was so talented," Mary sighed.

"Yes, she was."

Charlie's mom, Martha, died of lung cancer three months ago. Her memorial service was held at a Chicago art gallery that sold her work, and Mary had attended.

"I really miss her," I said. I lifted my martini toward one of her paintings. "To you, Martha," I said and sipped my drink. I looked at Mary. "She was a hell of a lot of fun."

"I miss my grandmother, too," Mary said. "She was a ballet dancer. Loved to entertain. Didn't bother picking up before her guests arrived—which drove my mother nuts. She'd move laundry off furniture as people needed to sit down. She always opened the door with a martini in her hand. You reminded me of her."

"Here's to your grandmother," I said. We clinked glasses and drank. The phone rang, and I headed for the kitchen.

I picked up the phone and heard my friend Kelly, one of my regular drinking buddies, giggle. "Hey Bren," she said.

"Hey Kel," I said, throwing ice cubes into my martini shaker.

"Whatchya drinkin'?" she asked

"Martinis," I said, pouring vodka over the crackling cubes.

"Don't forget you're partying with us tomorrow."

"Are you checking up on me?" I laughed. I shook the shaker and watched it grow frosty in my hands.

"I want to make sure you're not overdoing it," Kelly said.

"You *are* checking on me. That's sweet, but I gotta go. See ya tomorrow."

I returned to Mary with the shaker and freshened her martini. The phone rang again.

"God, who's calling now?" I said and returned to the kitchen to pick it up.

"This is totally stupid," Liv said, "but Kelly made me call you." Liv started cackling. "Kelly wanted me to tell you not to drink too much." Liv's voice cut out and cut back in. "God, I can't believe it. Call waiting. It's Kelly making sure I'm calling you."

Charlie walked into the kitchen and uncorked a bottle of cabernet. "I think we should serve dinner pretty soon," he said. Charlie opened the martini shaker, dumped the ice down the sink, and gave me a fatherly you've-had-enough-martinis look.

"Sure," I said.

I finished my martini and served up the beef bourguignon along with homemade blue-cheese-and-apple coleslaw, bakery baguettes, and wine. For dessert I served lemon tarts. I was pretty buzzed by the time I dished up dessert and decided to mention I had freeze-dried psychedelic mushrooms in our basement freezer. I'd purchased the mushrooms two summers ago from Ralph, a whack job who impregnated my friend Rachel. Charlie and I had the unhappy couple over for a barbecue and while Charlie was grilling chicken, Ralph informed me that AIDS was a government conspiracy begun to get rid of Rock Hudson and Andy Warhol. He told me the white lines trailing airplanes were evidence that the government was dumping toxic waste on us. Later, Ralph casually mentioned he had mushrooms for sale. I hadn't tripped in more than thirteen years and felt a little giddy. I told Charlie about the mushrooms, but he didn't think buying an ounce was a good idea. I purchased the mushrooms anyway.

I kept the mushrooms on a high shelf in a little-used kitchen cabinet and waited for the right occasion to eat them.

After they'd been up there a few months, I took them down for an inspection and noticed they were sprouting mold. I threw them into the deep freeze and hadn't looked at them since.

"Why don't we go down and take a look at them?" Pat offered. I took him downstairs and pulled the 'shrooms out from under a large frozen turkey. Pat turned the baggie over in his hands a couple of times, opened it, and popped one into his mouth. "They're fine," he said. I laughed and popped a mushroom, too.

Either Pat or I suggested going for a walk to look at Christmas lights. Charlie and Mary declined so Pat and I threw on coats and left. I teetered down snowy sidewalks on four-inch stiletto-heeled boots and, on the way back, slipped and fell hard on my ass. I remember Pat helping me up, and the next thing I remember is sitting on the living room couch uncorking another bottle of wine. Charlie was glaring at me. It was three o'clock in the morning.

[Saturday, December 7]

Strips of sunshine beamed on my face as the sun streamed through loosely closed bedroom window blinds. I opened my eyes and pressed my hands to my puffy face. My cheekbones ached. I lifted my head off the pillow and the room started spinning. I lowered my head back on the pillow. I was still drunk. Charlie kissed me and started tugging at my pajama bottoms. I started to cry.

"I can't do this anymore," I blubbered. "I'm a wreck. I've got to stop drinking." Charlie rubbed my arm sympathetically.

I really didn't want to stop drinking, I wanted to control my drinking. But I couldn't control it. I kept getting plastered.

Once, when I was thirty years old and Max was two, I was sitting alone on the back deck of my house in Chicago drinking my third vodka on the rocks when I thought, *I'm going to wind up in a program for addicts if I keep this up.* Then I laughed and thought, *At least I'll get out of the house and socialize again.* Then I walked into the kitchen and poured myself another stiff cocktail.

I married Charlie when I was twenty-seven and had Max at twenty-eight. I was an artsy, 115-pound freelance journalist who drank like a 250-pound guy. I wrote for the *Chicago Reader* and the *Chicago Tribune,* and covered the television commercial industry for *Creativity* magazine. I got wined and dined a lot while interviewing advertising people and commercial directors, but I stopped interviewing them in person after Max was born. My interviews were now done over the phone as I ping-ponged between Max and my computer. Some days I never got out of my pajamas.

Charlie and I moved from a relatively hip apartment in Chicago's Ravenswood neighborhood to a house we could afford in a safe, blue-collar neighborhood. The neighborhood was in the new Little Italy area by Belmont and Harlem. It was peppered with Italian delis, shady social clubs, and homes with gaudy lamps and plastic-sheathed couches in front of big picture windows. Much of the landscape gleamed with bright white stones and tiny manicured shrubs. Elmwood Park was next door. Whenever a mafioso got whacked, chances were he lived in Elmwood Park.

Five days a week Charlie took the train downtown to an office where he edited a trade magazine about telephone directories. I worked at home, took Max to parks and museums, and felt guilty about whatever I was doing. When I was writing, I felt guilty about not playing with Max. When I was playing with Max, I felt guilty about not writing. Mountains of dirty laundry piled up. The kitchen sink brimmed with dirty dishes. There was a layer of dust everywhere. When I reached my filth limit I'd clean, all the while muttering expletives about having to waste my precious time on banal tasks.

I started having a glass of wine or two when I cooked dinner. It was my treat for pulling off another day. Soon I was drinking two, three, four glasses of wine, and Charlie would come home and we'd finish off the bottle I started and uncork another.

My cousin, Mike, began coming over and hanging out with me in the afternoons. Mike lived fifteen minutes away and was working on his doctoral dissertation in economics. His days went something like this: lumber out of bed around ten thirty, ease the hangover with greasy eggs and bacon, work on his dissertation until four, and drive to my house for cocktails. Mike wasn't a wine drinker and I wasn't a beer and bourbon drinker, so we compromised on vodka.

I drank vodka martinis when I ate out and went clubbing because I thought they gave me a Bette Davis kind of glamour, plus the buzz was great. They soon became my at-home drink. Mike and I would polish off half a bottle to three-quarters of a bottle of vodka. Charlie would come home and find us dancing with Max to Concrete Blonde, or lolling in the backyard baby pool, or laughing our asses off about something stupid. Charlie would shoot me dirty looks and I'd ignore him.

Max and I went to a Moms & Tots class on Tuesday and Thursday mornings. We'd sit in a circle on the floor, and Miss Lisa, eyes painted in frosted blue, stretchy stirrup pants on her legs, would start with calendar time. Max would squirm out of my lap, I'd lasso him back, and this went on and on through story time. Miss Lisa would pop in a cassette tape, and we'd all attempt to dance and sing "The Hokey Pokey." I'd shake Max's left foot, jiggle him about; he'd never do it on his own. Then Max and I would sit at a junior-sized table for art. The moms would cut and paste together Halloween bats, Santa heads, and apple trees, and coax their children to scribble on them.

"Max made this?" Charlie would ask when he saw an art project hanging on the refrigerator.

"Uh, yeah, sorta."

One night, while I was cooking, Mike was sitting on a bar stool at my kitchen island when he noticed my Moms & Tots class photo tucked behind a candy dish. He started laughing. "All these domestic-looking moms and then there's you. Here comes trouble."

The picture was taken a few weeks into the Moms & Tots session. Most of the moms were wearing Bermuda shorts and crisp blouses or dowdy T-shirts, and they were holding smiling children. I was wearing frayed cut-offs, a Banana Republic tank, and balancing a crying Max on my hip.

Marie, a pretty Brooklyn native with enormous auburn hair, was someone I'd targeted as a possible friend at Moms & Tots because she was funny as hell. We were coloring fall leaves at our tiny art tables one day when Marie griped, "I can't tell the difference between my canned tomatoes and store-bought ones, but Sal won't eat gravy with store-bought." A wave of commiseration went up, and I learned most of the other moms were preserving homegrown tomatoes in their summer kitchens: second kitchens in their basements where they baked lasagnas and eggplant parmesans all summer long so they wouldn't heat up the house.

"My husband once tasted a pot of sauce I was making and threw it out the back door because I was using store-bought," Tina said.

I scanned the faces of the women to see if they were joking, and they were nodding their heads except for Vicky, a pretty Puerto Rican, who shot me a thank-God-we're-not-them look.

Vicky and I got to be chummy. She invited Charlie and me to her New Year's Eve party and I gladly accepted. Charlie and

I pulled up in front of Vicky's modest ranch house and parked. "This is it?" Charlie asked with a chuckle. Every square inch of their snowy lawn was covered with light-up Santas, reindeer, giant snowmen, candy canes, carolers, and gingerbread men. It looked like they'd cleaned out every hardware store in the area. The house next door was the same. We shielded our eyes from the bright lights and rang the bell. Vicky's husband, Lou, answered. He was a butcher and body builder. He pumped Charlie's hand up and down. "Did you see the lawn next door?" he asked, shaking his head. "Every time we put a decoration out, that guy puts another one up. It's like it's a contest or something." Lou led us to the basement. The basement floor was carpeted in a lush deep-pile. The heads of timber wolves, mountain lions, and bear looked out from dark wood paneling.

"Wow!" I gasped.

Lou clapped Charlie on the back and led him from a snarling bobcat to a stately buck. Vicky grabbed my arm. "Do you know what it's like to have to vacuum and dust down here? It's a nightmare."

The four of us padded across the expensive carpet to the bar. Five muscle men in tight-fitting shirts were sitting there with their pretty women. Lou introduced us and poured us stiff drinks. The men continued talking about their BMWs and Mercedes. Lou slapped one on the back and laughed. "Alex here's got a house in Barrington the size of an airplane hangar. Better watch it, mafioso."

Alex smiled sheepishly. He turned his doughy face to his blond glamour girl, and she shot him a cold smile.

Charlie and I drank heavily. We rang in the New Year and quickly left.

• • •

Spring approached, and by that time Mike and I'd been partying for almost a year. Charlie finally reached his limit.

"This is not what I want," he blurted one night after Mike left. "I don't want to come home to a tanked wife. Your cousin is here all the time." Charlie flicked his hand disgustedly at the door. "You have to do something."

I could see Charlie's point, but what a buzz kill. I'd already had my backyard epiphany. My hangovers were getting hellish, so I nodded in agreement. When Mike called the next afternoon, I told him about my conversation with Charlie and suggested cutting our happy hours down to once or twice a week. Mike wasn't thrilled, but what could he do?

I began drinking in moderation by myself. When Mike showed up, we hit the booze hard. One morning, after Mike had been over, I woke up feeling like I'd done serious damage to myself. Every molecule in my body was vibrating, and it felt like someone had split my skull with an ax. I couldn't think. Charlie's friend, Sean, had recently gone to a posh rehab out west and sobered up with an aging rock star. He went to meetings, took up running, and looked great. Jim, another alcoholic high school buddy of Charlie's, had been sober ten years. I didn't want to spend money on rehab or tell my insurance company I was an alcoholic, so I picked up the Yellow Pages, sat down at my kitchen island, and dialed a number for recovery meetings. A woman answered and I began blubbering.

"Ma'am," the woman said. "Ma'am, this is the answering service. If you just give me your name and number, I'll have someone call you back."

I choked out my phone number and hung up. Ten minutes later, the phone rang.

"Hi, this is Maggie—from the recovery program," a woman said. I started crying again. "Did you call the program?"

"Yes," I croaked.

“Do you think you might have a drinking problem?”

“Uh-huh.”

“If you want, I could tell you a little about myself.”

“Okay.”

“My husband died and I was left with four small children,” Maggie began. “This was a number of years ago. I felt very sorry for myself, very, very sorry for myself for having to raise four children on my own. That’s when I started drinking.”

“You had good reason,” I sniffed.

“I didn’t know how I was going to raise those kids,” Maggie continued. “I didn’t want to think about it, so I started drinking as soon as I woke up and kept it up until I went to bed. I wasn’t cooking, wasn’t cleaning. The kids were taking care of themselves. My oldest son was getting everybody off to school. He hated me. Then somebody, I think it was a neighbor, called the Department of Children and Family Services.”

I stopped connecting with Maggie and thought, *Rotten mother. Loser.*

“Blah, blah, blah,” went Maggie. “That was twenty years ago and I’ve been sober since.”

“I don’t drink during the day,” I told Maggie. “And my drinking doesn’t interfere with my work or being a good mother. So, I don’t know.”

“There’s a meeting tonight at the United Methodist Church,” Maggie said. “I could meet you there.”

“Uh, okay,” I said. I wrote down directions and hung up. “Shit!” I said and sat at my kitchen counter staring off into space. I called my father at work. He answered the phone and I began blubbering again.

“I called a recovery program.”

“You did what? Well. Good for you.”

One of my dad’s nicknames for me was Bernice. Bernice was my fall-off-the-barstool alcoholic aunt. I called my dad

Norman. Norman was Bernice's mean-as-a-snake alcoholic husband. My dad and I partied a lot together. When I was twenty, I quit college for a year to figure out what I wanted to do with my life and went to work for my dad thinking I'd, perhaps, take over his printing company. I packed up my stuff at Northern Illinois University and moved back into my parents' house near Chicago. Every morning my dad and I would get into his car, pick up his friend Jack, who worked in the same building, and drive downtown. At the end of the day, we'd hop back in the car and stop for happy hour at a rib joint named Bones. We'd hook up with one or two of my dad's customers or suppliers, and my dad and his buddies would down manhattans like kids drinking Kool-Aid. I'd drink Heineken and do my best to keep up. Holding your liquor was a badge of honor with these guys. Thank God there was a large buffet table of hors d'oeuvres.

"If you're gonna drink, you gotta eat," my father told me. "Your grandfather always said that. You gotta lay a foundation. The skinny drunks who don't eat, the booze kills 'em."

My grandfather died of a stroke when I was twenty. One day he fell in the bathroom and my grandmother couldn't get him up. An ambulance whisked him to Illinois Masonic Hospital in a coma-like state. My grandfather, hooked up to a ventilator for the next several days, swatted at invisible spiders and rats in delirium tremens. A week or so later, he died.

My father handed me a cocktail rye he'd smeared with chopped liver. He popped one into his mouth and said, "One more drink and we'll go."

My friend Ecklund, whom I'd been partying with since high school, called me one post-happy-hour evening and started yelling at me. "What the hell, Brenda?" he ranted. "The last few times I've called you, you've been wasted by six thirty!"

I was hung over all the time. One morning, as we drove to work, my father had to stop the car three times so I could vomit on the side of the road.

"You drank too much yesterday," he said sternly.

"I've got a little bug," I said, wiping my lips. "I'll be fine."

After a year, I enrolled at Roosevelt University's School of Journalism in Chicago. I moved into an apartment with my friend Audrey, waited tables part time, and, for the most part, saved getting loaded for the weekends.

• • •

At that moment, on the phone with my dad, I told him, "I don't think I have the guts to meet Maggie and go to that meeting tonight."

"You want me to go with you?"

"You'd go with me?"

"Probably wouldn't hurt," he said. "I don't need it, but I'll go with you."

My dad picked me up and parked his car by the side door of the church. A woman with graying hair was standing next to it, smoking.

"Are you Brenda?" she asked as my dad and I walked up.

I introduced my father to Maggie and the three of us walked downstairs to a lounge area where roughly fifteen people were seated in a circle. All of the dilapidated chairs were occupied. Someone got us metal folding chairs, and my father and I sat next to each other. Maggie took a chair directly opposite us. A thin, older woman with reading glasses perched at the end of her beaky nose rang a bell. "Is this anyone's first time at a meeting?" she asked. My father and I raised our hands. "Welcome," she said, and everyone clapped. People took turns reading out of a recovery book, and the chairwoman announced that the members were going to take turns telling their addiction stories for the benefit of my dad and me. The first woman to speak had burned down her house in a drunken stupor. The man sitting next to her had gone to prison for vehicular homicide while driving drunk. A guy sitting a little further down went on benders and regularly woke up in a pool of his own urine.

"Hi, I'm Jerry," my dad said. "I probably drink too much, but I run a successful business and my drinking doesn't interfere with my work." He patted my knee. "I'm here for my daughter."

"Hi," I said nervously. "I'm Brenda. I've been drinking too much. That's why I'm here. But I'm just going to listen tonight." Maggie had told me I could say that if I didn't want to speak.

After the meeting I thanked Maggie, and she asked me to meet her at another meeting the following night. Feeling cornered, I agreed. My dad and I walked to the car, and once inside, he patted me on the back and said, "You're on your own. These people are Skid Row."

I met Maggie in the basement of a Catholic church the next night. "You should get a sponsor," she told me afterward. "A sponsor is someone who helps you stay sober. I can be your temporary sponsor if you want, but take your time and pick someone, a woman you connect with."

I didn't pick anyone. I went to one meeting a week and drank substantially less for the next two months. Things were working out, I thought, then one night, while I was filling my Styrofoam cup with coffee at a meeting, someone tapped me on the back and asked, "Do you have a sponsor yet?" It was Pam, an attractive woman with long brown hair and perfect teeth.

"No," I answered.

"I'll be your sponsor."

"Okay."

Pam was a stay-at-home mom. She was two years younger than me and her daughter was two years older than Max. They lived with Pam's parents. Pam and her mother got along like two tomcats in a duffle bag. I called Pam every day—because she insisted—and her mother usually answered the phone. "Pam!" she'd scream. "Pam! Pick up the phone!" She'd chuck the receiver, clunk, clunk, clunk, onto the kitchen table, and I'd hear footsteps, arguing, more footsteps, then Pam would answer. Pam's mother would continue talking to her in the background while Pam tried to talk to me until Pam would scream, "You know I'm on the damned phone! Shut it!"

Pam moved in with her parents after her husband died. The night Pam's husband, Vito, died, he'd been out drinking, pulled his car into the garage of their town home, shut the garage door with the remote control, and passed out with the car running. When Pam went to get her car out of the garage the next morning, she found Vito slumped over his steering wheel.

Pam and I began working out together. We went out to lunch. We took our kids to the park. And I quit drinking. But each meeting I went to confirmed my belief that everyone else's drinking was way worse than mine.

"My dad bought a Porsche," a twenty-year-old goombah with slicked-back hair and crotch-hugging jeans laughed. "I got drunk, took the keys, got it up to 110, 120, slowed down to take a corner, and BAM! This tree jumps out in front of me. I was in the hospital all fucked up for weeks."

A middle-aged biker with a potbelly leaned back in his chair and scratched his face. "You think that was bad? I totaled my Harley and was in a coma for a month. Got a plate in my head." He tapped his skull with his fingertips. "Don't know what the fuck happened I was so fucked up."

I cleared my throat when it was my turn. "About a week after I started coming to meetings, I wanted to drink," I began. "I didn't have any liquor in the house, but I had half a bottle of cooking sherry. It tasted like shit, but I drank it. How sad is that?"

"Shit," the guy sitting next to me said, adjusting the strap on his eye patch. "I loved cooking sherry. Drank it all the time at my sister's 'cause she'd hide the booze whenever I came over."

I started going to a women's meeting on Saturday mornings to see if I'd fit in better there. The meeting was more cerebral, and the women talked about their feelings a lot. I noticed a blonde named Kim who was well dressed and appeared to be normal. She was my age, a mom, and she seemed to have her head screwed on right. Then Kim told her story. She said she was divorced and that she and her ex-husband, a rich commodities broker, had been heavily into cocaine. Their wedding had been a coke fest, and their expensive apartment had become a flophouse for line-snorting friends. Then along came a baby.

"I can still see her toddling around the apartment, her diaper dangling between her knees because I was too busy snorting coke to change her," Kim said.

Piece of shit, I thought angrily. I did not want to get to know Kim.

Other women at the meeting started to irritate me, too, like The Crier. The Crier was a lesbian who'd purchased a two-flat with her girlfriend, then her girlfriend dumped her. The Crier lived on the second floor of the building and her ex lived on the first floor with her new girlfriend.

"I asked them," The Crier sobbed one morning, "very nicely . . . to turn down their music . . . but they wouldn't. It was late at night. I just laid in bed . . . and cried . . . all night."

The following week, The Crier blubbered about a fight she and her ex had had over landscaping. A week after that, the tears were streaming because her ex had snickered when she walked past.

Charlie and Max and I left for my mother-in-law's summer cottage the following weekend. As we pulled into the Michigan cottage on Friday night, Martha was drinking a vodka martini on her front porch. We brought our bags into the house and Charlie had a martini with Martha while I unpacked. We went out to dinner, and Charlie and Martha drank a bottle of wine while I had club soda. I put Max to bed and read him stories that night while Charlie and Martha had nightcaps on the front porch.

As usual, the cocktails came out at five the following night. Charlie took his tinkling beverage to the backyard and opened the grill. He grabbed a small bag of charcoal and dumped half of it onto the grate. I walked over as he doused the briquettes with lighter fluid.

"You know," I said. "I'm sick of not drinking."

Charlie looked at me with raised eyebrows and I began telling him one sad-sack drunkard's story after another.

"I'm not like those people," I said. "I developed a bad drinking pattern and I broke it."

Charlie lit the coals. Whoosh. "You want a drink?"

"Yes."

Charlie left and came back with a martini for me. It tasted fabulous.

• • •

I stopped going to meetings, and Pam didn't bother to call me. She'd gotten mad at me before I went to Michigan, and we hadn't spoken for several days. Pam had taken me to a recovery dinner where there had been a countdown. "Does anyone have twenty-five years of sobriety? Twenty-four years?" and so on. I stood up at the three-month marker and everyone clapped. They did that for everyone. When I sat down, Pam began to grouse about her pot-smoking sister.

"She really needs a recovery program," Pam said.

"Why?" I asked. "I smoke pot once in a while."

Pam looked at me shocked, then angry. "You just stood up and said you were three months sober!" she growled and stalked off. That was eight years ago.

• • •

My drinking was under control for a while. I had a glass of wine here, a martini there. Then I began having a bottle of wine one night a week, then two nights a week, then three. I began having martinis before my bottle of wine. Five years after I'd ditched the program, I got pregnant with Van and stopped drinking for the first seven months of my pregnancy. During the last two, I allowed myself two glasses of wine per week. Van nursed for six months and I kept to a ration of three or four glasses of wine per week. But when Van left the breast, I picked up drinking where I'd left off, which meant getting buzzed five or six nights out of the week.

By this time, we'd moved to a north shore suburb of Chicago for its great school district and charming historic downtown. I made friends with other stay-at-home moms and, to them, my life looked great. They didn't know that almost every morning, before I got out of bed, I asked myself, "What did we discuss at dinner? Who put Van to bed? What pajamas is he wearing?" to get myself up to speed before I fixed breakfast, drove Max to school, and hit the health club with my head pounding. Van would play in the Kid's Club while I lifted weights. Then I'd take Van to play dates, give Art Awareness presentations in Max's classroom, write newspaper articles, meet friends for lunch, all with my head slowly clearing. But by three o'clock the hangovers were gone, by four o'clock I was helping Max with his homework, and by five o'clock I was shaking a martini.

The first martini spread "Ahhhh," through my entire body. The second made me feel comfortably numb. I'd drink the first martini, sometimes the second, before Charlie got home so he wouldn't know how much I had. When he walked in, I'd shake up a martini for both of us, finish cooking dinner, and uncork a bottle of wine. We'd sit down to dinner, and Charlie and I would finish the bottle. I'd clean up and uncork a second bottle. The next morning, as I pulled milk and eggs out of the refrigerator, I'd check the second bottle's contents. Typically it was half to three-quarters gone. Then I'd tell myself, "I'm not going to drink today."

• • •

This morning, since I could barely lift my head off my pillow, Charlie realized he wasn't going to get lucky and got up and left me alone. I dozed for a while and woke up needing to go to the bathroom. I slowly pushed myself up to sitting. A sharp jabbing pain shot through my tailbone and I limped to the bathroom suffering more intense jabs. I foggily remembered falling while walking with Pat. Maybe I chipped my tailbone. I slowly descended the stairs—my tailbone radiating pain—and poured myself a glass of water in the kitchen before shuffling into the living room. I lowered my butt onto our antique couch, wincing, while Charlie continued to read the newspaper across the coffee table on our corduroy couch. Pieces of broken glass glinted on the floor at my feet. I leaned over and began picking up shards. My head felt like a split cantaloupe.

"Someone break a glass?" I asked.

"You," Charlie answered peevishly. "Don't you remember? Maybe not. You could barely stand up."

I threw out the glass shards and went back to bed.

About an hour later, Charlie walked into the bedroom. "You want something to eat?" he asked.

"Dry toast," I said. "And could you bring me the phone book?" Charlie raised his eyebrows. "I'm thinking I should try a recovery program again. You think I should?"

"I think it's time you did something."

I nibbled a piece of dry wheat toast, propped up by pillows. I stared at the unopened phone book on my bed. After twenty minutes, I opened it and dialed. This time I knew I'd be reaching an answering service, but the woman who answered was in recovery herself.

"I live near you," the woman on the line said. "There are lots of meetings in your town. Just . . ."

"I don't want to go to meetings in my town," I interrupted.

"There's one twenty minutes away this afternoon at six o'clock. I could meet you there."

"Uh, the thing is," I said, remembering the Wendts' dinner party, "I'm supposed to go to a dinner party at seven with my husband. I don't want to go. I'm so hung over. But this has been on my calendar for months."

"Why don't you cancel? Say you're sick. It's the truth."

"I can't," I said. I told her about my dinner party last night and the calls from Kelly and Liv. "They'd know I was just hung over."

"I think you should go to a meeting."

"I'll go tomorrow. What's going on tomorrow?"

The woman told me there was a meeting at ten the next morning.

I spent the rest of the day in bed vacillating between going to the dinner party or going to a meeting. Charlie was no help. "It's up to you," was all he said.

By five o'clock I felt vastly better. I decided to put on a good face, go to the dinner party, and drink for the last time. I'd hit a meeting tomorrow. I got in the shower and slowly pulled myself together.

Charlie and I arrived at the Wendts' at seven fifteen. The house was all lit up for Christmas. Tom took our coats and walked us back to the family room/kitchen. Liv, her husband, Reed, Kelly, and her husband, Joel, were already there. Wendy was shaking up hundred-proof Absolut chocolate martinis. Kelly elbowed me in the ribs.

"How ya feelin'?"

I shrugged. "Better than before."

Wendy walked over and handed me a martini.

"Bren here's feeling a little hung over," Kelly told her.

"Oh," Wendy said. "This'll make you feel better."

I sipped it gingerly. It tasted dangerously good. Wendy walked away to check on her standing rib roast. I scanned the countertops and tables for appetizers.

"Where's Wendy hiding the hors d'oeuvres?" I asked.

"There aren't any," Liv answered with a grimace. I raised my eyebrows. Liv laughed. "I know. And hundred-proof martinis. I'm switching after this."

"No shit."

I finished my martini quicker than I thought I would and poured myself a glass of wine. Wendy hovered near the oven and basted her roast. I'm not sure how much I consumed by the time we sat down to eat at ten o'clock, and I'm not sure how I got home, but I know at some point I told my girlfriends I was giving up drinking for a while after tonight. "I need to take a break," I told them.

[Sunday, December 8]

I spied the meeting address on a rundown office building downtown. I tried not to think about where I was going, which wasn't too hard since my alcohol-soaked brain was running slow. I parked the car and entered the building. I stood near a stairwell and listened for voices but didn't hear any. A man walked in behind me, and I followed him down to the basement and into a room packed with people. I took a seat in the back. Just like eight years ago, the meeting opened with literature reading and I kept thinking, *I can't believe I'm here, I can't believe I'm here*. Then a guy named Ted began telling his story.

"Hi, I'm Ted, drug addict/alcoholic. I'm fantasizing about killing my fucking wife, my soon-to-be ex-wife. That bitch is going to have to live with herself for trying to put a wedge between me and my kids. She took them away from me and put homophobic thoughts in their heads. I saw a really bad car crash. A semi hit a car and as I was driving by I hoped my fucking wife was in that car. Fucking bitch. That fucking bitch is living rent free in my head. I spend way too much time thinking about her. She's going to have to live with herself. But she's getting everything."

After twenty minutes of this tirade, the group split into two smaller groups. Half of the people left the room; the other half rearranged chairs into a cozy circle. I stayed in the room and joined the circle, wishing I could stay hidden in back. People began introducing themselves as they made comments in a clockwise fashion. Three-quarters of the way around the circle, it was my turn to speak. "Hi, I'm Brenda," I said. Then the tears came. I didn't even see it coming. I just sat there for what seemed like an eternity trying to compose myself, then I whispered, "I just can't believe I'm here again. I tried this eight years ago." I motioned for the next person to go.

Ted walked over to me at the end of the meeting and shook my hand. "Welcome back," he said. "I was a binge drinker. Didn't drink for weeks, then I'd go on a bender for days. The program has really helped me. I'm not even angry at my partner for giving me HIV. He didn't know he was positive when he infected me."

"Really," I said.

"Find some good women's meetings," he said. "Stick with the women. You're a good-looking woman and there are a lot of wolves in the program." He gave me a big hug. "Good luck."

• • •

Around dinnertime—martini time—I was feeling edgy. I didn't want to go to a meeting in town because I was afraid of running into someone I knew, but I was going to drink if I didn't get to a meeting, and I knew there was one in walking distance about to begin. I grabbed my purse and headed to my second meeting of the day. I entered an attractive building that housed recovery meetings and saw people gathered in a conference room. Two men, roughly ten years my senior, looked me up and down as I walked in. The meeting started and as the literature was being read, the guy chairing the meeting handed everyone a copy of a recovery book. He had us turn to the same page and he began reading one of the stories. After two paragraphs, he said, "Pass," and the person on his left began reading the next paragraph. So it went around the table until we'd read the whole story.

The story was about a writer. She loved gourmet food and wine. She threw a lot of dinner parties. And after her dinner parties, she drank her guests' leftover wine as she cleaned up.

As I listened to the story, I was reminded of when I hosted

book club last month and purchased a case of good chardonnay for it. Yummy appetizers filled my coffee table, and I kept my guests' wineglasses full as we discussed *The Lovely Bones*. Most of my book club friends left tanked. That didn't usually occur because most of my book club friends are light drinkers, and they don't top off wineglasses like I do. Afterward, I cleared dirty plates and glasses, and many of the wineglasses were a quarter to half full. The wine was too good to waste, so I downed the remnants while I cleaned. It was the first time I'd ever drunk leftover booze. I hesitated as I put the first used wineglass to my lips. It felt twisted and wrong, but I drank anyway.

This story about the writer hit me hard. The group split into smaller groups, and people began taking seats in discussion rooms. I joined one and sat on a couch. Across from me was a high school boy picking at his cargo pants and gym shoes. He started the discussion group off by talking about his mother and how hard it was to stay sober while she was drinking like a fish. "She tries to help my little brother with his homework at night and ends up screaming at him. Sometimes she throws his books on the floor."

It was like an arrow pierced my heart. I had scenes like that with Max.

I stopped at a literature rack on my way out and picked up a meeting directory. The vultures who'd been ogling me in the conference room swooped in.

"You have to go to ninety meetings the next ninety days," Vulture One said.

"You have to get a sponsor," Vulture Two said.

"I could take you to this great meeting," Vulture One said.

"I have a store the next town over where we could talk about what's going on with you," Vulture Two said.

"I'm married," I said.

"You're too young to be married," Vulture Two said.

"I'm thirty-eight."

"You're older than I thought," said Vulture Two.

[Monday, December 9]

I got the ninety-meetings-in-ninety-days advice from several people. The martini bell was going off in my head at five o'clock so I went to an evening meeting, but I had no intention of doing ninety meetings in ninety days. It just seemed like a good idea to hit meetings when I'd ordinarily be drinking. I walked into a church and saw a janitor vacuuming the vestibule. An organist was practicing Christmas carols. The janitor looked at me and turned off the vacuum cleaner.

"Can I help you?" he asked.

"Is there a meeting here?" I asked timidly.

"No," he said looking puzzled.

"There's supposed to be a meeting," I said, feeling sweat circles forming under my arms. I looked at the floor. "A recovery meeting."

"Oh, I bet that's in the rectory behind the church."

He gave me directions and I walked outside. A woman about my age with frizzy blond hair and two inches of dark brown roots was trying one of the church's side doors.

"Are you looking for a meeting?" I asked.

"Yeah."

"It's this way," I said, glad to have someone to walk in with.

We each took a chair in the packed room moments before the meeting began. The chairperson asked, "Is this anyone's first time at a meeting, or first time at this meeting?" The frizzy blonde and I both raised our hands. The chairwoman nodded at the frizzy blonde.

"Hi, I'm Jean, addict/alcoholic. This is my second meeting."

The chairwoman nodded at me.

"Hi, I'm Brenda." I swallowed. "I'm an alcoholic. I'm new and this is my first time here."

A woman sitting next to me asked, "Did anyone First Step you?" I had no idea what that meant so I shook my head no. The woman looked at Jean. Jean shook her head no. "We need a First Step meeting," the woman announced to the chairwoman.

"Who wants to go upstairs and do a First Step meeting?" the chairwoman asked the group.

Eight women and one guy got up and led Jean and me upstairs into what used to be a bedroom in a former pastor's house. We sat on folding chairs arranged in a circle and the regulars took turns telling their drinking and drugging stories. I remembered I'd had a First Step meeting eight years ago at that meeting with my dad. Tanya, like a woman in my first First Step meeting, had burned her house down. Todd was an asshole navy drunk. Deidre pointed her finger at Jean and me and shook it.

"Secretly, in the back of your head, even if you're unaware of it, you're planning your next drink," Deidre said. "And you have to squash that like a bug before it gets bigger." Crack! She smacked her hands together. "When you start to think about drinking, think about somebody else, what you can do for someone else. Get your mind off you."

A woman sitting next to Deidre said her name was Sophie. She said she was a high-functioning drunk and a good mother. "My children are grown, but I was very involved in their schooling," Sophie said. "I helped with Christmas pageants, was on the PTA, and didn't drink while I was pregnant. I actually considered getting pregnant to stop drinking."

I stared at Sophie. She had just described me. The room was silent, and I realized everyone was waiting for me to speak.

"I love my children with all my heart," I began. "I have never let my drinking interfere with being a good mother." My throat constricted and I couldn't talk. I waited and breathed deeply. "But I've known, in the back of my head, even though I've never admitted it to myself, that the reason I had my second child—part of the reason—is because I knew it would make me stop drinking." I tried to choke back tears. My chest heaved. I put my face in my hands and sobbed.

[Thursday, December 12]

I went to a meeting in a nearby town and a woman came up to me afterward and told me her husband was addicted to Internet porn. "He's a great guy otherwise," she said. "But I feel disgusted and cheated on. I don't think I can stay married to him."

I scanned the room hoping someone else would come over, but everyone seemed to be avoiding us like the plague.

[Friday, December 13]

I went to another meeting in town, this one in the basement of a church. There were a lot of people there, many of them strange. One guy was a thalidomide baby. On the end of his arms were a few pegs where hands and fingers should have been. He was dressed like a cowboy. Another guy was missing an eye. His sunken socket was made huge by magnifying eyeglasses. There was a woman named Dora who looked like a hooker. She was wearing skin-tight patchwork jeans with frayed stitching, a low-cut leopard-print halter top, and a black sport jacket. During the meeting she got up, lurched around the room dragging her high-heeled boot heels, and disappeared into the bathroom for fifteen minutes. She lurched back into the room, slammed her butt down on a metal folding chair, and sat spread eagle. Sitting across from me was a woman named Gwen. She identified herself as an addict and kept bending over, her boobs almost falling out of her scoop-neck spandex top.

Gwen walked up to me after the meeting and shook my hand. "I'm not an alcoholic, I'm a pothead," she said. "I came home one night when I first got sober and my husband had left this beautiful bud on the kitchen counter. I got panicky and called my boyfriend. I was having an affair at the time. I was like, 'I don't want to smoke it, what should I do?!' He screamed, 'Flush it down the toilet!' This is a great meeting. I hope you keep coming."

Holy mother of God, I don't want to hang out with these people.

[Saturday, December 14]

Charlie and I went to Wildfire for dinner with Reed and Liv. I felt very edgy before we left the house, but I was determined to be funnier and wittier than I was when I was drinking.

Wildfire was probably not the best restaurant for me to go to. Their martinis are excellent and they have martini flights: four flavored mini martinis served all at once, but martini flights were never a draw for me. Health nut that I am, I didn't want artificial colors, flavors, or sweeteners in my booze. Liv had made reservations two months in advance so we could get in on a Saturday night, and a table was ready for us when we arrived. Thank God we didn't have to sit in the bar. We all slid into a huge banquette and I ordered a club soda while everyone else ordered cocktails. I reminded Liv that I was giving up drinking for a little while.

"You're not drinking?" Reed said, sipping a manhattan. "How long are you going to keep that up?"

I shrugged. "As long as I feel like it. I'm bored with drinking. I need a change. When I get bored with being sober I'll start drinking again."

I scanned the tables to see what other people were drinking. A lot of people were having soda and iced tea. I was shocked.

During dinner I bantered, joked, told funny anecdotes—but it felt like work. I had to be on all night because I wasn't drinking and, damn it, I was going to be the best dinner companion ever. But I started feeling uncomfortable, like a dullard, when we all hopped into Reed's car after dinner. I was always the one to suggest going to a bar or back to my house for drinks and a joint, and we'd party until Charlie or Liv got sick of it. Tonight, however, Reed drove us home and pulled up in front of our house at ten thirty.

"I can't remember when I've gone home this early on a Saturday night," Reed said.

"Me too," I agreed, feeling lame.

"I'm glad," Liv said. "I won't waste the whole day tomorrow feeling horrible."

"Suits me just fine," Charlie said.

I washed up and crawled into bed. Charlie was waiting for me. We did it, him on top and me under a cloud of boozy breath.

[Tuesday, December 17]

I went to dinner at Bin 36 with my aunt Alina. Bad, bad restaurant for me. It's a new restaurant I suggested eating at over a month ago—which is how long this dinner date has been on my calendar. When I opened the menu, I was drawn to the extensive wine list on the right page. The less prominent left page listed the food, and all of it, appetizers to desserts, had wine suggestions.

Aunt Alina ordered a pinot noir flight and the waiter set a paper placemat in front of her with four circles on it. Each circle had a bin number written under it. The waiter then placed a half glass of wine on each circle and handed my aunt a card that described each of the wines. I couldn't have thought of a better way to torture myself.

"I'm on antibiotics for a sinus infection (true) and can't drink (never stopped me before)," I told my aunt.

"That's a shame," Aunt Alina said.

"Maybe a flight wouldn't hurt," I said, deciding to drink just like that.

"Oh, you can't do that," Aunt Alina said looking quite serious. "Not if you're taking antibiotics."

"You're right," I said.

Aunt Alina and I talked for four hours, and I watched her nurse her four glasses of wine the entire time. She'd take a tiny sip, set the glass back on her placemat, a while later take another tiny sip from another glass, place it back on her placemat, etc. It was killing me. My insides squirmed. When we finished dessert, there was still a little wine in each of the glasses. It brought back memories of the time I had dinner with my friend Emily.

Emily and I met for dinner at Wildfire this summer. Emily ordered a Cosmopolitan so I ordered one, too, even though I wanted a pure Kettle One martini free of high-fructose corn syrup and food coloring. However, I didn't want Emily thinking I was a lush who loved straight booze. I drank my Cosmopolitan slower than usual because I paced myself with Emily. When we both finally finished our last sips and I was about to suggest ordering another, Emily opened the wine list.

"That martini really hit me," she said.

"Yeah, me, too," I lied. "Should we order a bottle of wine?"

Emily looked at me with a raised eyebrow over her menu.

"Let's just order by the glass, huh?" I said. "I don't think we need a whole bottle."

"Definitely by the glass," Emily said.

We each ordered a glass of chardonnay. I drank mine slowly, again pacing myself with Emily. I wanted to scream.

[Saturday, December 21]

Tonight I felt like drinking. I'd gone to a women's meeting earlier and decided they were all losers. Whenever I think a woman looks interesting, she'll say something like, "I smoked crack while I was pregnant," or "I steal people's lunches at work and make myself get sick in the bathroom." I don't want any of these women for friends.

[Sunday, December 22]

I had tea downtown at the Drake with my old high school friends Hope and Audrey. Audrey is the friend I lived with when I quit working for my dad and went back to college. She is getting married one week from today. She was wearing a knock-your-socks-off beautiful engagement ring her fiancé had no business buying, she said, because he doesn't have any money. Plus he just bought himself a new Cadillac.

Audrey was my wildest, craziest friend in high school. She grew up in a secular Jewish household, sold quaaludes and pot, dabbled in the occult for a while with her first husband, then, after she divorced him, turned into an Orthodox Jew. Audrey's newfound Orthodox community fixed her up with Nehemiah, her fiancé. Audrey's first husband was a Pakistani named Peter. They had two gorgeous dark-skinned sons together, and Nehemiah, perhaps the only African American Orthodox Jew around, seemed like a good match for Audrey. Audrey and Nehemiah, who lives in Detroit, started a long-distance relationship eight months ago and Audrey decided to marry him, move to Detroit, and sell her house in Chicago to buy one in Michigan.

"You're buying a house in Detroit with the money you're getting for selling your house here?" Hope asked.

"The kids and I can't move into Nehemiah's dinky apartment," Audrey laughed.

"You're spending your money, none of his?" Hope asked.

"His money's sunk into his business," Audrey said. "He started it two years ago. I checked him out, don't worry. His rabbi said he's one of the biggest contributors to his shul. Everyone loves him."

"The house will be in your name, right?" I asked.

"Of course."

"How old is Nehemiah?" Hope asked.

Audrey blushed. "He's sixteen years older. He has a daughter from his first marriage who's slightly younger than me, but he and his daughter don't speak, so I guess I won't be meeting her," she laughed. "It's going to take some time for my boys to adjust to him. He keeps telling me how the boys aren't going to do this or that. But it's not like he's their father, you know?"

"Are you sure you want to go through with this?" I asked.

Audrey shrugged. "Are you ever sure of anything?"

"You don't have to do this," I said. "People change their minds all the time."

The waiter placed a three-tiered tray of finger sandwiches and scones on our table. "I'm sure these are kosher," Audrey said, reaching over a ham sandwich and grabbing an egg salad.

"Restaurants use Kraft mayonnaise and Kraft is kosher." Hope rolled her eyes.

We left the Drake, and Audrey said she wanted to go to Victoria's Secret. "I need something sexy for my wedding night."

"Aren't there rules against that sort of thing?" Hope asked.

Audrey ignored her and took a red corset into a dressing room.

I whispered to Hope, "I think there are rules against fucking your fiancé before you get married, too." Hope snickered. Hope and I'd caught a glimpse of Nehemiah lying in Audrey's bed through a cracked door that morning when we picked her up.

Audrey poked her head out of the dressing room door. "Come here and tell me what you think?"

"Sexy," I said. "It pushes up your boobs and cinches your waist just right. Buy it."

Audrey's cell phone rang. "I can't meet you at the jeweler's; I'm with my friends. Uh-huh, uh-huh, okay." She hung up and threw the phone in her purse. "I have to meet Nehemiah and take a final look at our wedding bands. It won't take long. I'll meet you guys in an hour. Sorry."

"Nehemiah's an ass," Hope whispered to me.

Audrey grabbed a matching garter belt, stockings, and robe and threw them on the counter with the corset. "I'll take these."

[Tuesday, December 24]

I drank tonight. I don't really know why, I just felt like it. I wasn't craving alcohol or anything. Having a martini just popped into my head and I went for it.

Charlie, the kids, and I went to church for the Christmas Eve service. We were right on time, which meant we were late and the sanctuary was already packed. People were being seated on folding chairs in the narthex and we quickly sat on four chairs before the narthex filled and people began sitting in the hallway. I tried to peek over the heads in front of me at the pageantry in the sanctuary, but I could see nothing through the window separating the narthex from the service. Max and Van began whining that they were bored and wanted to go. I visualized a martini glass in my hand, minuscule ice chips floating on the surface, and me sipping, the icy burn on my tongue.

As soon as we got home, I chucked my coat, checked the dinner I'd put in the oven before going to church, and grabbed my martini shaker. Charlie walked into the kitchen. "I'm having a martini," I said defiantly. "You want one?" Charlie laughed. "Yeah," he said. We each had two martinis and split half a bottle of wine. I checked the basement for more wine but there wasn't any.

[Wednesday, December 25]

I woke up without a hangover, which was nice. I took pictures of the kids opening their Christmas presents and decided that last night's little drinking episode was just a slip. Today I was back to no drinking. December 25 would be a good sobriety date. What a gift to Jesus.

We spent the afternoon at Charlie's brother's house and when we walked in, his brother, Chris, offered us eggnog. What the hell, it was Christmas. I finished the eggnog and had a glass of wine. What the hell, I'd already consumed alcohol. Charlie's sister, Liz, gave us a bottle of Veuve Clicquot. As soon as we got home I stuck it in the freezer, and when it was properly chilled, Charlie and I killed it. I'll give up drinking tomorrow.

[Thursday, December 26]

We celebrated a belated Christmas with my parents. Every year since Charlie and I began dating, we've had Christmas Eve with my family, Christmas Day with his family, and our little family gets lost in the shuffle. I wanted my family to have its own tradition this year. I wanted us to go to church on Christmas Eve (that didn't work out so well) and have a cozy dinner afterward. I mentioned this to my mother in early December and she suggested getting together tonight instead of Christmas Eve.

Charlie and I loaded up the car with food and presents and we hit the highway. As we neared my parents' exit, I started thinking about the oversized bottle of Woodbridge chardonnay my sister would probably bring. My father drank hard liquor and beer, so if my sister and I wanted wine, we had to bring it. My mother, a devout Seventh-Day Adventist, never drank. I figured since I'd been drinking over Christmas and, technically, we were still celebrating Christmas, I should get some wine. I told Charlie to stop at the liquor store as we exited the highway. I didn't want my last glass of wine to be Woodbridge. I walked into the store and bought two nice bottles of Oregon pinot noir. When I got in the car, I placed them at my feet. We drove off and a radio reporter announced that a woman had smashed up her car while driving her family home after a Christmas party yesterday. Her two children were dead. She and her husband were in the hospital. High levels of alcohol had been detected in both of their bloodstreams. I glanced at Charlie. He looked at me and winced. I turned and looked out the window.

My mother greeted us at the door. "I didn't like being alone on Christmas Eve at all," she blurted. "I never want to do this again."

My father appeared at the door with a manhattan in his hand. He gave me a hug and a kiss. "You want a martini?" he asked.

"Yeah," I said.

I drank a stiff martini, then had another. I probably drank more than one bottle of pinot noir before the night was over, too. On the way back home I stared out the window at the Christmas lights as Charlie drove. I thought about the woman who'd crashed her car. I pictured her lying in the hospital bed wishing her children were alive and she was dead.

[Friday, December 27]

I went to a meeting after having dinner with my family. I pulled into a church parking lot and two guys were standing by the door smoking.

"You here for the meeting?" I asked them.

"Yep," one of them answered.

"Could you tell me where it is?"

"Downstairs," the guy answered. He tossed his cigarette on the pavement and squashed it with his boot. "You can follow me."

We made our way down to a basement utility room where nine men were sitting around a table. I sat down and smiled. A man sitting at the head of the table, the chairman, asked if it was anyone's first time here. I raised my hand and introduced myself, feeling hugely uncomfortable. A guy nicknamed Red began speaking.

"I used to perceive being humble as being weak," Red began. "But now I see it as a strength. All the false bravado I had pushing my will on others, coercing them to do what I wanted, making people miserable until I got my way. I was a bully. I fooled myself into thinking I was powerful when it would have taken strength to stand back and not be a jerk. It takes guts to admit you don't have power over people."

Hmm.

[Sunday, December 29]

Audrey got married today. I wasn't sure how the not-drinking thing was going to go since weddings and booze go hand in hand, but being surrounded by Orthodox Jews made it a lot easier.

Charlie was not looking forward to Audrey's wedding at all. He knew we weren't going to be able to sit together during the ceremony or dinner. He knew I would be eating and dancing with the women, and he'd be eating and dancing with the men.

"You've got to be kidding," Charlie said when I told him how things were going to go. "I don't have to go, do I?"

"Hope and Paul will be there," I said. "You and Paul can dance together."

Charlie stared daggers at me.

"Oh come on, it'll be fun."

"No it won't."

Audrey had booked an expensive Orthodox musician who played blues and klezmer and had performed at Carnegie Hall.

"Why spend all that money on a band when you can't dance?" I'd asked her when she told me I couldn't eat or dance with Charlie.

"The men dance together and the women dance together," she said. "'Fiddler on the Roof' kind of stuff."

"Why can't husbands and wives dance together?"

"The men might get excited seeing women they're not married to swinging their hips."

"Oh."

"Make sure you wear a dress or a skirt that hits no higher than the knee," Audrey said. "And no spaghetti straps or low necklines. Wear something with long sleeves. And don't hug or kiss my dad or brothers. Women don't touch men they're not married to."

I wondered if Audrey and Nehemiah were supposed to have sex through a hole in the sheet tonight.

Charlie and I arrived at Audrey's shul and a young girl hung up our coats. We moved toward the appetizer tables and Charlie grabbed my arm. "Is that Audrey's husband-to-be?" he asked, twitching his head toward a large, overweight black man wearing a black hat and black suit. He was surrounded by a bunch of white guys wearing the same thing.

"Gotta be," I said. I hadn't gotten a good look at him through Audrey's cracked bedroom door. "He's the only black Jew here."

Charlie snickered. Out of the corner of my eye I saw Roger, Audrey's brother. He was planting his walker and swinging his hips and legs forward and moving in my direction. He pulled up next to me, sweating profusely. "Roger!" I said and gave him a big hug and kiss, ignoring Audrey's warning. I hadn't seen Roger since his motorcycle accident several months ago. Roger and I had gone to Sturgis, South Dakota, for bike week eleven years ago. We'd ridden out with the Chicago Hog Chapter, partied with thousands of bikers, saw ZZ Top, and had a blast. Earlier this year, Roger was riding along a canyon road in Arizona when he lost control of his bike, skidded toward the edge of a cliff, and a van ran him over, breaking three of his vertebrae.

"You look good," I told him.

"I been doin' a lot of physical therapy," Roger said. "They say there's a chance I could walk again."

"I bet you will," I said. "You already are."

"Hey you guys," Hope said, walking over with Paul. "Where's Audrey?"

"In a room back there," Roger said, motioning with his thumb over his shoulder.

Hope and I grabbed a few appetizers and headed in that direction. The room was packed with women. We looked around and caught sight of Audrey sitting on a throne-like chair surrounded by women.

"What's going on?" I asked.

"Everyone's giving Audrey their good wishes," Hope said.

We made our way through a sea of wigs—married Orthodox women have to hide their hair from men they're not married to—and reached Audrey. She beamed when she saw us and got up and hugged us.

"We're here to give you our good wishes," I said.

"Make 'em great," Audrey said. "I have God's ear now. He's listening."

"I wish you and your family good health, gobs of money, and lots and lots of happiness," I said. "You deserve it."

"Thanks," Audrey said, tears welling up in her eyes.

"You okay?" I asked.

"Yeah," she said, looking sick to her stomach but trying to appear happy.

"Well," I said, squeezing Audrey's hand. "A lot of women are lined up to see you." I gave her a peck on the cheek. "Love ya," I said and stepped aside so Hope could move in.

Hope and I left the room and returned to the virtually female-free hallway. We nibbled at appetizers, and a tall, beefy Orthodox guy lumbered over. "You two went to high school with Audrey," he said with a smirk. "What was she like?" The schmuck wanted dirt.

"Audrey was the kindest, most generous person I knew in high school," I said. "She still is. Nehemiah's lucky."

The schmuck's smile disappeared. Hope and I walked away and found Charlie and Paul. Minutes later, we were directed into the synagogue. Hope and I took seats on one side of the room; Paul and Charlie took seats on the other.

The wedding ceremony was beautiful. Audrey looked gorgeous. As we left the synagogue and headed for the banquet hall, I scanned the crowd for Charlie. He caught my eye, held up his wrist, and tapped his watch. I smiled and nodded. Hope and I found our table and sat down. I got chatty with a woman who had a house full of kids and an unemployed husband. A young girl set a couple of bottles of kosher wine on the table, and I scanned the unfamiliar labels wondering if they were any good.

"How's the wine?" I asked Hope.

"Good and sweet," she said. "Want some?"

"Nope," I said, glad it was probably syrupy swill. "I quit drinking."

Hope raised an eyebrow. She knew I'd tried to quit drinking eight years ago.

We finished dinner and the music began. The band was awesome. Before long, most of the women were dancing, and we could hear the men whooping it up behind the screen that separated us from them. Both men and women could see the band on stage. A curtained divider held up by metal poles in the middle of the floor began at the edge of the stage and ran the length of the room to the back doors.

"Look," Hope said. She and I were two links in a long chain of women holding hands and dancing around Audrey. Hope jutted her chin toward the top of the screen. Flames were shooting over the top of the divider. A few women were standing at the end of the screen near the stage and peeking around it and watching the men.

"Come on," Hope said yanking me loose from the chain and pulling me toward the end of the screen. Bands of circle-dancing men kicked their legs wildly as their black hats burned like torches.

"Oh my God, have you seen this before?" I asked.

"Never," said Hope.

"Won't their hair catch fire?"

"I would think so," she said.

Another man touched a cigarette lighter to his hat and, whoosh, flames shot up three feet.

"How do they do that?" I muttered.

Hope and I watched in amazement before giving up our spots so other women could see and rejoined the chain of women dancing around Audrey.

"I have to go to the bathroom," I told Hope.

Hope and I broke loose and walked out into the hallway. A large pile of black hats had been dumped against a wall. Some of the hats were upside down, their domes lined with aluminum foil. A mound of rubbing alcohol bottles was piled next to the hats. I elbowed Hope.

"I wonder if some Orthodox dude is going home tonight without a beard," I said. We giggled. On our way out of the bathroom, Charlie grabbed my arm.

"Let's go," he said. "I've had it."

[Tuesday, December 31]

Charlie and the kids and I went to Kelly and Joel's annual New Year's Eve party. It was the first time they hosted a kids' New Year's Eve. Usually it was just adults getting drunk. Kelly's son, Ryan, had invited Max to sleep over, so we arrived with Max's bags in tow and rang the doorbell. Kelly and Joel opened the door. At least twenty kids were running around and screaming in the background. I brought Van's portable crib with me so I could put Van to sleep and ring in the New Year before taking him home.

"Put the crib in our room," Kelly said and hugged me. "There's a cooler with LaCroix and pop." She walked away toward the kitchen. Joel bent down and gave me a kiss on the cheek. "I totally support you," he whispered in my ear.

"Thanks," I said and gave him a kiss. "That means a lot."

I took Van's crib upstairs to their bedroom and set it up while Charlie got a drink and took Van to the basement where other little kids were playing. I made my way to the kitchen and scanned it for the LaCroix cooler.

"It's outside, Brenda," Joel said as he shook martinis.

I grabbed a bottle of water and came back into the kitchen to get a wineglass. I'd taken up drinking Pellegrino with a slice of lemon in a wineglass at home because I liked my stemware almost as much as I liked my wine. Kelly was handing out the last wineglass to another guest. "I just found this chardonnay," Kelly was saying as she poured wine into the woman's glass. "You'll love it!" I turned away and walked downstairs to look for Max and Van.

Kelly had set up a craft table in the basement, and Max and a bunch of kids were standing around it decorating cigar boxes with glue, glitter, buttons, and seashells. Van was sitting on the floor playing with toy cars. Joan, one of Kelly's old high school friends, was standing off to the side watching her son and daughter glue feathers on their boxes. I sidled up next to her.

"You're not drinking," Joan said, nodding at my bottle.

"I'm taking a break," I said. "I was drinking every day."

A worried look crossed her face. "I drink every day," Joan

said. She leaned over and whispered, "I've been thinking about giving up pot. I don't want the kids to find out I smoke."

"I hear you," I said, giving her a knowing smile.

I went upstairs and immediately ran into Kelly's close friend, Nosey Rosy. "So, you're not drinking," she said loudly. "Why?"

Thanks Kelly, I thought to myself. I spied Candy, who is not a big drinker, excused myself, and walked away from Nosey Rosy. Candy looked at my LaCroix and said, "You're not having a martini with Bill?" Candy's husband, Bill, made a mean martini. I shrugged and excused myself to put Van to bed. I went back downstairs, got Van, and took him up to Kelly and Joel's bedroom. After I tucked him in, I went out to the deck where the nonalcoholic beverages were and lit up a cigarette. Joel was out there stoking a fire pit. He lit a cigarette, too, and we smoked together.

"I'm thinking about having a martini," I told him.

"Nah, don't," he said, shaking his head.

"Yeah, you're right," I said. We finished our cigarettes and reentered the house.

"Someone's kid is crying upstairs," a guy shouted.

I jogged upstairs and saw the door to Kelly and Joel's bedroom had been flung open. Van was standing up in his crib screaming. I lifted him out and hugged him. Van stopped crying. He rubbed his eyes with his fists and nestled his head into the crook of my neck. I held him for a long time. It felt so good. I kissed Van and tucked him back into his crib. I tiptoed out of the room and shut the door. A group of kids, Max included, was racing through the hallway, running into various bedrooms and slamming the doors shut. A bedroom door flew open and a pack of kids ran past me into another bedroom and slammed that door shut. I opened the door and scanned their faces. Most were ignoring me. "All of you stay out of

Kelly and Joel's bedroom," I announced. I zeroed in on Max. "Make sure," I told him, wagging my finger, "that these kids don't go into Kelly and Joel's room because Van's sleeping in there." Max nodded. I went downstairs. A few minutes later, Van was screaming again. I repeated the drill and put Van down for a third time. A short while later, Van was screaming again. I packed up his crib, thanked Kelly and Joel, and told Max we'd pick him up in the morning. Charlie and Van and I left. We got home and I put Van to bed and went to bed myself. Fuck New Year's Eve.

[Saturday, January 4]

Every winter my friend Emily (the one I had one Cosmo and a glass of wine with at Wildfire) and her sister, Anne, throw a retreat weekend at their parents' house in Door County, Wisconsin. The house, which could double as a modern art museum, has floor-to-ceiling windows that overlook Green Bay. Emily and Anne each invite three or four of their friends and the criteria for being invited is you cook well, appreciate good wine, and can enhance the weekend in some way.

Last year, we all read *The Intuitionist* before showing up and one of the women facilitated a book discussion. Another woman who sang like an opera singer led a sing-along. Another friend masterminded a literary game of charades. I led a yoga practice.

Emily emailed me and invited me to this year's retreat. It's January seventeenth through the twentieth. I emailed Emily that I'd be there, but I don't know. I don't think I can go and not drink. Maybe I'll take a little drink break and quit again after the retreat. When I asked Charlie what he thought of this idea, he said, "I'm not going to tell you what to do. That's your decision." But his downturned mouth was disapproving.

I decided to go to a meeting and see how I felt afterward. A young guy, maybe twenty, twenty-one, spoke after I mentioned I was thinking about going to the retreat and taking a sobriety break. He had just been to Cancun with a bunch of his friends.

"Everyone told me I shouldn't go," he said glumly, looking down at the table. "I had more than a month of sobriety. But I went. I drank a ton. I had a lot of fun, but now I'm starting all over again—making another stab at it."

A handsome, professional, together-looking man in his fifties grabbed my arm after the meeting.

"I think you know it would be a bad idea to go," Brent said.

"Yeah," I nodded. "I know."

"Door County will be there next year," he said. "Then you can go and drinking won't bother you." He waved at a woman who was about to leave and motioned her over. "Hey, do you know Kat?" Kat walked over and gave Brent a hug. "You ever been to Marytown before?" Brent asked me.

"No."

"Oh, it's wonderful," Kat said. "It's a beautiful Catholic church that's open twenty-four/seven. There's a continuous prayer chain. You can walk in anytime and someone will be praying."

"I feel a real spiritual connection there," Brent said. "You guys doing anything? You want to go?"

Kat looked at her watch. It was almost ten o'clock. "Yeah, I can go," she said.

"Yeah, okay," I said.

We drove there separately and walked into the church together. About twenty or thirty people were there praying in the pews. Kat noticed a guy from the program standing by a side door and led us over to him. She introduced us to Sam, who is new to recovery. A scowling priest swept over and whisked us down a hallway.

"You can continue your conversation here," he said and left.

Brent led us to a meeting room down the hallway. We sat down and Sam told us he is a flight attendant and he'd gone to work drunk, gotten into an argument with another flight attendant, threatened to beat him up, and gotten into a heaping mess of trouble. The airline sent him to treatment and he was now going to meetings to save his job.

"I go home after work and have Perrier in a wineglass," he said. "It makes me not miss my wine so much."

"Oh, you shouldn't do that," Kat said. "That's a huge trigger. That wineglass will get you drinking again."

I was glad I hadn't commiserated with Sam. I was about to share that that is exactly what I do.

"Brenda was thinking about going on a retreat," Brent said, changing the subject. He told Kat and Sam what I'd said during our discussion group. "There was a guy there who went to Cancun after one month of sobriety and blew it," he added. "He was pretty down-and-out, wasn't he Brenda?"

"Yeah," I said. "But he also said he had a lot of fun."

[Sunday, January 5]

I keep hearing Brent say, "Door County will be there next year." The retreat is scheduled over Martin Luther King Jr.'s birthday, and Max will be off school. Maybe I should do a ski trip with him instead. It would be a good opportunity for Max and me to hang out like we used to before Van was born. I told

Charlie I was thinking about going skiing with Max in lieu of the retreat. He was all for it. I emailed Emily that I'd forgotten I'd promised to take Max skiing and canceled.

[Tuesday, January 7]

I went to a meeting that totally pissed me off. Everybody sat at a conference table with a recovery book and a middle-aged guy sitting at the head of the table, the guy who was about to chair the meeting, was talking to a woman who mentioned her sister's birthday was yesterday.

"Did you spank her?" the chairman asked.

"No," the woman replied and giggled.

"Did her husband? Did you take pictures?"

Finally the guy noticed it was time to start the meeting.

"We'll be taking turns reading Step Four of the Twelve Steps: 'Made a searching and fearless moral inventory of ourselves.' In this meeting you can interrupt at any time by saying, 'stop,' and say what's on your mind."

The woman sitting across the table from me started reading. When she finished the first paragraph she passed and the man sitting next to her began to read the second paragraph. When he finished reading a part that said, "Our desires for sex, for material and emotional security, and for an important place in society often tyrannize us," the chairman yelled, "Stop."

"Yeah," the chairman said. "Your life can be screwed up if you obsess about anything, like sex. If all you think about is sex, and that's all you want to do all the time, other parts of your life will suffer."

The man finished reading the second paragraph and the guy sitting next to him started reading the third. "We want to find exactly how, when, and where our natural desires have warped us," he read. "We wish to look squarely at the unhappiness this has caused others and ourselves."

"Stop," shouted the chairman. "I know a sex addict. Yeah. All he wants is sex. Can't get enough of it. As soon as he finishes having sex he's thinking about how he can get it again. He's zipping up his pants and planning for the next time. His wife is like, 'Isn't three times a day enough? We just did it.' Yeah. There are people out there like that who're totally obsessed with sex."

I felt like slamming my book down and leaving, but didn't. I'd heard people in meetings say they treat other people in meetings who try their patience as an exercise in developing tolerance and patience. Since I desperately need to develop tolerance and patience, I decided to stick it out. The reading continued and we got to a part that read, "Our present anxieties and troubles, we cry, are caused by the behavior of other people—people who *really* need a moral inventory," and the chairman yelled, "Stop!" again.

"Have you ever thought, *Yeah, I'm going to that meeting because so-and-so will be there*?" he asked. "And you make comments to impress her. And you offer to drive her to meetings because she lost her driver's license and she takes you up on it. And you drive her here and there, and you go out with her and the group for coffee afterward, and she talks to everyone but you, and you're thinking, *The bitch is just using me for rides!?*"

I wanted a martini, bad.

[Wednesday, January 8]

I went to a meditation meeting that was weird. About sixteen of us met in a conference room and broke up into smaller groups that met in little sitting rooms. My group consisted of me and three guys. We sat on a couch and some chairs. One of the guys dimmed the lights. The woman running the meeting started playing an audiotape that got piped into each of the rooms. The tapes reminded me of the old *Saturday Night Live* skit "Daily Affirmations with Stuart Smalley." "I'm good enough, I'm smart enough, and gosh darn it, people like me." Two fifteen-minute tapes were played. Both were soothing and disturbingly pleasant.

When the tapes finished, our group took turns commenting on what we got out of them. Turns out I was the only one who'd been to more than two meetings.

"How do we end this meeting?" a middle-aged guy asked. "Do we just leave?"

"Every meeting I've been to so far has closed with the Lord's Prayer," I said. "We stand in a circle, hold hands, and recite it."

Our group stood in a circle, held hands, and recited the Lord's Prayer.

"Then what usually happens is everyone says, 'Keep coming back; it works if you work it sober,'" I said. "Then it's done."

A crusty old guy who looked like Allen Ginsberg fidgeted and cleared his throat. "I don't like that gung-ho, rah-rah stuff. I don't go in for that sort of group cheerleading kind of thing." He glanced at us through thick horn-rimmed glasses. His eyes were focused in different directions.

"Well, that's just what they do," I said.

"Yeah, well I don't go for that stuff," he said gruffly.

A young guy said, "Oh, well, if that's what they do, it's kind of nice."

"Yeah, well, I don't go in for that," Ginsberg growled.

I looked at the young guy and shrugged. He looked at me and shrugged. The four of us looked at each other for a moment and we left.

[Sunday, January 12]

I'm being excluded now that I don't drink, and I'm hurt and angry. My family went out to lunch with Liv and Reed and Kelly and Joel yesterday after our kids' soccer game. Max plays on the same team as Kelly and Joel's son, Ryan, and Liv and Reed's son, Seth. Max and Ryan have been friends since preschool, that's how Kelly and I connected, and Max and Seth attend the same grade school, which is how Liv and I got to be friends. I threw the first bacchanal dinner party and introduced Kelly, Liv, Wendy, and Viola; they and their spouses liked each other. So yesterday, after lunch, Seth came over to play with Max and pretty soon the two were asking if Seth could sleep over. Reed answered the phone when I called. He began hemming and hawing when I offered to have Seth sleep over.

"Uh, Liv and I are going out to dinner tonight and we don't want Pete (Seth's older brother) to be alone," he said. "So I'll pick up Seth."

This morning, when I took Max to soccer practice, Joel was sitting in the stands hunched over with one elbow on his knee propping up his head with his hand. I sat down next to him.

"You look like you're hurting," I said.

"I'm hung over," Joel said. "Kelly and I went to Gabriel's last night and drank way too much."

"Just the two of you tied one on?"

Joel opened his mouth and shut it. After a pregnant pause he said, "Uh, no. We went out with Liv and Reed. Can you believe they'd never been there?"

"Oh," I said, feeling like I'd been punched. Joel had probably taken Ryan to Liv and Reed's last night and Pete probably babysat. More than likely, Ryan slept at Liv and Reed's and

Joel had picked the boys up and brought them to soccer this morning.

I thought back to soccer practice last week when Reed and I were sitting together and Reed asked me how the not drinking thing was going. I told him fine and he said, "You know, some people wouldn't want to go out with a person who doesn't drink."

"Fuck 'em," I said.

[Monday, January 20]

Max and I got home after skiing Granite Peak in Wausau, Wisconsin, this weekend, which was the weekend Emily had her retreat. Max and I drove to Wausau on Friday, and I rented skis for Max. We wanted to be ready to hit the slopes first thing Saturday morning. As we were pulling on our long johns Saturday morning, it became apparent I'd forgotten to pack Max's ski pants, so we killed half the morning shopping for a pair. It was a blessing in disguise. By the time we hit the chairlift, the temperature had warmed to a balmy fifteen degrees. It was frigid, but it was sunny and windless, and Max and I had the place to ourselves. We got in a lot of runs in a short period of time and hit the hot tub at the hotel before going to dinner. All in all, we had a great day. Sunday, however, was overcast, windy, and hit a high of ten degrees. Max and I got on the chairlift and cryonic winds blasted through our ski wear. We skied two or three runs, hit the lodge, repeated this three more times, and left. We bought sub sandwiches, brought them back to our hotel room, and watched movies. I'm glad I spent the weekend with Max and bailed on the retreat, but I can't say drinking didn't cross my mind.

My mother grew up in Wausau. She was number eleven in a family of twelve children who grew up on a dairy farm. My family spent a lot of time in Wausau when I was a kid. We'd get in the car, drive the four-and-a-half, five hours it took to get there, check into the Holiday Inn, and go to my Aunt Theresa's house. Five minutes later, my cousin Tami, who lived down the road from my aunt, would walk in. Tami and I would ditch my sister Paula, and Tami's little brother Scott, and hide in her grandmother's barn or hike in the woods to smoke Kool cigarettes. Once in a while we'd drink warm beer we'd pinch from her dad's case of Old Style.

As we got older, Tami and I always seemed to pick up where we left off, even though years passed between visits. My family drove up for a family reunion when Tami and I were in our mid-twenties, and she and I went to some hole-in-the-wall tavern and pounded shots of Jägermeister and beer. A jar of homemade pickled eggs sat on the bar and I ordered one.

"You're going to eat that?" Tami asked making a face.

I took a bite. "It's actually pretty good," I said and popped the rest into my mouth. I thought of Pickled Pete, a cadaver from an anatomy/physiology class I took in college.

"I want to be cremated when I die," I said. "I can't stand the way our family stuffs our dead relatives and displays them, takes pictures of them. My mom's got lots of dead snapshots in her photo album. How sick is that?"

Tami nodded and said she wanted to be cremated, too.

"Look at my lifeline," I said, showing Tami my palm. I'd recently been to a palmist. "It's pretty short, but if you look closely, there's a crease that kind of connects it with this one running down my palm. A friend of mine told me it doesn't count, but I say it does. Let's see yours." I took Tami's left hand in mine and stared at it. "Shit. Yours is way shorter than mine!"

The next time I went to Wausau was for Tami's funeral. She and I were both thirty. Tami had been killed in a car accident.

Her neck had snapped. I walked into her wake and saw Tami lying in a coffin against a far wall. Her face was caked with makeup. Her hair was teased like an old lady's. Someone was snapping pictures.

On the trip home with Max, we drove past the church where Tami's funeral service had been held. We stayed at a hotel near the old Holiday Inn where Tami and I had done cannonballs and held each other's heads under water. I wanted to drink.

[Thursday, January 23]

It was Tina's turn to host book club tonight. Everyone was drinking wine but me and I felt like the high school goody-goody steering clear of the party keg. No one but me gave a rat's ass that I wasn't drinking, but once again I felt I had to go out of my way to be more engaging than my drinking self. We'd all read the book *Rapture,* which is one long description of a blowjob, and I shared my grocery store story.

"I ran out to pick up chocolate pudding and whipped cream for dessert after dinner one night and as I was leaving the house, Charlie asked me to pick up condoms. I put the whipped cream, chocolate pudding, and condoms on the conveyor belt and as they moved toward the cashier, I realized what it looked like. The cashier, this huge black dude, stared at my items, looked at me, and started laughing. He rang me up, laughing his ass off the entire time. I see him every time I shop, and he sees me and laughs."

My friends knew exactly which cashier I was talking about and thought it was hysterical.

"I'm trying to get Liv to join my ballet class," Kelly announced.

"I went to one class and I wasn't very good," Liv laughed. "I won't be going to another."

"I'm trying to get her to join my new health club, too," Kelly said. She looked at Liv slyly and smiled.

"I don't know," Liv laughed.

Months ago, Kelly acted aloof toward Liv when I invited Liv into book club. It seemed to bother Kelly that Liv and I were friends. But now that I'm not drinking, it appears that Kelly is out to make Liv her new best friend.

[Tuesday, January 28]

I was lying in bed this morning thinking about how I thought I didn't give a shit about what people thought of me. I was a what-you-see-is-what-you-get kind of girl. But I care what people think of me more than I want to admit. Drinking swanky martinis and expensive wine was part of a party diva image I tried to manufacture for myself. I liked people who stood out and spoke their minds, and I tried to model myself after them. As I lay in bed, I wondered if I was becoming a dullard.

It's irritating how much I worry about what others think. Last Friday, Charlie and the kids and I went out to dinner, and I scanned the tables to see what everyone else was drinking. I expected to see a lot of wine drinkers, but many of the people were drinking sparkling water, pop, and iced tea. I felt more comfortable ordering my San Pellegrino. Then I became agitated because I was comparing myself to other people. Who cares what other people do? What the hell is wrong with me?

I was shopping in one of the wealthier suburbs in Illinois, and got out of my Jeep Grand Cherokee in a parking lot full of

Mercedes, BMWs, and Land Rovers. I began feeling self-conscious, like I was less than. Pathetic. When I'm around people who have less than me, I worry about having too much. Does that old hippie think I'm bourgeoisie? It's sickening.

The chairperson at the women's recovery meeting I went to tonight asked if anyone was celebrating an anniversary. I raised my hand and said I had a month of sobriety yesterday. Everyone clapped. The chair said people celebrating anniversaries at the meeting were given the opportunity to give their story or the lead topic.

"I don't know, I'm kind of drawing a blank," I said.

Deidre, the woman who had pointed her finger at me at my First Step meeting and had told me I was planning to drink, fished an inspirational book out of her coat pocket and handed it to me. "Maybe this will help," she said.

The book flopped open to a reading on fear. "Okay," I said, and read the passage out loud. The author of the book told a story about how her daughter's Brownie troop was rewarded for trying new things, like eating "ants" made out of celery, peanut butter, and pretzels. A lot of the girls didn't like the ingredients but enjoyed biting into the ants. The author made the leap from celery ants to skydiving. If you're afraid of heights, go skydiving, she said. If you're afraid of success, try your best. You'll be rewarded for just trying. I told the group I was afraid that my drinking friends were starting to think I was boring, but maybe being a sober rebel was the most un-boring thing I could do.

Tracy, the chairperson, said she shares a birthday with Mother Teresa. Madonna's birthday is a day away. "I used to wish my birthday was on Madonna's birthday instead of Mother Teresa's," she said. "Now I'm happy it's on Mother Teresa's. When I was drinking I didn't know who I was, I just knew who I wanted to be. Today I know who I am."

I want to know who I am.

[Sunday, February 2]

It's Charlie's birthday tomorrow. We went out for pizza with Liv and Reed and Kelly and Joel after our kids' soccer game for a pre-birthday celebration. The waiter set the pitcher of beer we'd ordered on the table, and he and I recognized each other from meetings. The waiter skittered around the table, avoiding making eye contact with me.

Besides Charlie, Max is the only person who knows I'm going to meetings, and Max doesn't *really* know what they're for. I've been leaving the house most nights to go to meetings when I would otherwise be drinking, and Charlie says it's bothering Max. I told Max I'm going to the No Alcohol Club where people like me who've decided not to drink discuss the alcohol problem.

Before I quit drinking, I was uncomfortable drinking around Max because his school delivers a big antidrug message. Whenever I'd have a cocktail he'd say, "Is that alcohol? It's not good to drink alcohol. It ruins your brain."

"A little glass of wine here and there doesn't hurt," I'd answer, knowing I was a rotten example.

When Max asks me if I'm going to the No Alcohol Club, I see his face fall when I say yes. It tears me up. But if I don't go to meetings, I know I'll end up sucking down martinis. I told Max, "I don't want a lot of people knowing I go to the No Alcohol Club," and asked him not to discuss it with his friends. I wonder what he thinks.

At a meeting a few nights ago, I said I hadn't told anyone I was going to meetings and wasn't planning to.

"The last thing I need," I said, "is everyone at Max's school knowing his mother's an alcoholic."

The woman sitting next to me said, "I'm worried you're not telling people so you can go out and drink again."

I felt like slapping her.

The woman who spoke next said, "Before you tell anyone you're going to meetings, you should consider your motives. Are you telling someone you're working a program so you can feel superior, self-righteous?"

I looked at the woman sitting next to me and she looked stung by those words. Good. But there was some truth in what she said to me.

The first time I tried a recovery program I told everyone I quit drinking. Then I started drinking again. If I decide to drink again, and I'm not ruling it out, I don't need people whispering about my alcoholism.

[Monday, February 3]

Today is Charlie's fortieth birthday. I threw a big surprise bash for him on his thirtieth, but I couldn't bring myself to throw a big drink fest for him this time around. Instead, I made reservations for us at the Sybaris, an upscale romantic resort. I booked a cottage for the afternoon with a private swimming pool, waterfall, hot tub, steam room, and enormous bed with a swing over it. I told Charlie to come home from work at lunchtime and take the rest of the day off. I packed food into a picnic basket and grabbed the bag of sex toys I'd bought. When Charlie arrived home, I told him to get in the car.

"Where are we going?" he asked.

"You'll see," I shrugged.

I pulled into the Sybaris and Charlie got a big shit-eating grin on his face. We pulled up to the cottage and I unloaded the picnic basket and toy bag from the back. I set up lunch in a little dining area and we sat down. Charlie hardly touched his food, which is strange for a guy who normally inhales it. Charlie took a couple bites, looked at me nervously, and said, "Well?"

Suffice it to say we had a fun four hours. But sex isn't the same sober. It's not as uninhibited and naughty. It's good, but it's not wicked fun. We took a Jacuzzi bath together before we left and laughed about how we used to rip on Sybaris commercials.

"How sad to need a tacky joint to get a good fuck," I'd said.

"Sometimes you need to throw good taste out the window to have a little fun," Charlie laughed. He sipped sparkling wine that the Sybaris provided and I felt a twinge of longing for a glass, but I pushed that thought out of my head and we got dressed for dinner.

[Tuesday, February 4]

Tonight was Max's first band concert. I'd forced Max to take piano lessons for two years, but it had gotten ugly and I let him drop piano and take up the trumpet in the fourth grade. Trumpet was working out better. I couldn't play the trumpet, so I couldn't be the trumpet Nazi.

"That sounded sloppy!" I'd shout from wherever I was in the house while Max practiced piano.

"That's the way it's supposed to sound," he'd shout back.

"Bull!" I'd yell, stalking into the room and making Max slide over on the bench. Then I'd play the piece. "That's how it's supposed to sound. Now keep practicing until it sounds like that." I'd return to what I was doing and scream, "That's not right," as Max continued to slop through the tune.

"That's the way Miss Olga played it!" Max would insist.

I'd stalk back into the room, play the piece again, and yell some more. This would go on and on until Max's practice half hour was up. Life got easier when Max began playing the trumpet.

"Sounds good," I'd yell as he practiced. I didn't know what the piece was supposed to sound like, and it was better that way.

My expectations were pretty low for the band concert tonight. We dropped Max and his trumpet off in the band room and Charlie, Van, and I found chairs in the already-packed gymnasium. Soon after, the band filed in. They began playing. They were good. They were tight. There was no disjointed noise. I looked down at the floor to check on Van, who'd been playing with Play-Doh on the seat next to me. He'd been rifling through my purse and my bright orange Twelve Step directory was lying on the floor in front of the woman sitting on Van's right. I felt the blood drain from my face. I bent down and swiped the directory off the floor. As I straightened up, I locked eyes with the woman. She gave me a pinch-lipped smile and turned her attention to the band.

[Thursday, February 6]

I had dinner with Kelly, Kelly's friend Lexi, and my sister-in-law Bonnie at Café Francesca's. Bonnie went to high school with Kelly and Lexi, and Lexi and I have become friends after repeatedly seeing each other at Kelly's shindigs. I picked up Kelly and we drove to the restaurant, put our names on the waiting list, and sat at the bar. Kelly ordered a glass of wine and I ordered a club soda with lime. The bartender looked at Kelly, raised his eyebrows, and said, "Club soda? We're gonna have to do something about that." Kelly laughed and nodded. I thought about saying, "Hey asshole, I'm an alcoholic."

Lexi and Bonnie arrived a little while later and the hostess seated us. Lexi, a light drinker, was pregnant and she and I split a bottle of San Pellegrino. Bonnie ordered a glass of wine. "Good," Kelly sighed. "I have one person to drink with."

Kelly was one of the few people who could match me drink for drink. Every time we went out for dinner, we'd plow through a bottle of wine, order a few more glasses, and as we waited for the check I'd ask, "Should we go somewhere else for a drink?"

Kelly would smile impishly. "Should we?"

We always did.

Three months earlier, Kelly and I would have been half in the bag by now, but tonight Kelly was pacing her drinking with Bonnie's, and Bonnie is an extremely light drinker who nursed one glass of wine all night. It reminded me of my dinners with Emily and Aunt Alina, and I felt sorry for Kelly.

On the way home, our drive was not filled with the usual laugh-filled banter. We were pretty subdued. I miss getting messed up with Kelly.

[Saturday, February 8]

Today is my thirty-ninth birthday. Charlie and I went out for seafood with Sean and Marcy, and Tim and Clio, two high school friends of Charlie's and their wives. I ordered a San Pellegrino with lime and got miffed when the waiter brought me a tumbler instead of a wineglass with the big green bottle. I handed the waiter the tumbler and told him I wanted a wineglass. Sean looked at me. "Are you not drinking again?" he asked.

Sean is the friend of Charlie's who went to rehab and met a rock star there years ago. I'd called him when I decided to get sober the first time. Sean has been on and off the wagon since. The last time I saw Sean, he'd been sober six months, ran every day, and looked great. However, he was drinking tonight.

"Yeah," I said and told Sean about the Mary and Pat bacchanal weekend that "pushed me over the edge."

Marcy, who'd been listening, said, "I've heard lots of stories about Mary and Pat showing up for dinner parties with their baby and drinking into the wee hours. I hope nothing bad happens to them."

"Keeping up with them got me to quit," I said, feeling guilty for blaming them.

"There was more leading up to it than that, right?" Sean asked.

My face felt hot. "Yeah," I said, completely ashamed.

"Well I'm proud of you," Sean said. "I need to get back in a recovery program. I'm gonna do it soon."

[Friday, February 14]

Charlie and I went to Café Pyrenees for dinner with Liv and Reed. There is an extensive wine list there, and I was trying hard to ignore it and be the best company ever. I'm sick of all this effort.

Charlie and I went home and had sex afterward. I told Charlie it was the last time he was getting sex when he was drunk. It sucks having some drunk ass pounding away on top of you.

[Saturday, February 15]

I took Van to see *Blue's Clues Live* at the Rosemont Theater with my sister and her two boys, Zach and Riley. *Blue's Clues* is Van's favorite show. I expected Van to jump and dance excitedly with his cousins, but when the curtain opened, he sat like a statue, mesmerized, never taking his eyes off the show. It was the cutest thing. We all went to lunch afterward and Van talked about the show incessantly. It was the best eighty dollars I'd spent in a long time.

[Monday, February 17]

I play scenes over and over in my head of things I'd like to say to my mother but know I never will. I have these fantasy conversations while I'm in the shower, driving, working around the house. No matter how they start out, I inevitably get on my high horse and deflate her rigid religious beliefs. I point out how her ignorant piety damaged me and prove myself to be more enlightened spiritually than she is. What a head case I am.

This morning, however, I was having a fantasy conversation in my head with my friend Fay. Fay recently made a crack about a cokehead mom who lives in a dilapidated two-flat at the end of her street—a building everyone in our neighborhood wants razed. The woman has a little boy who runs around the neighborhood, and the principal of our elementary school often picks him up and takes him to school.

"Just look where she lives," Fay commented. "If you can't get it together and have a house by the time you're our age . . . blah, blah, blah."

What the hell does having a house have to do with anything? What would Fay have if she were on her own supporting her kids? What if she had a deadbeat husband? What if her parents were poor? What if she grew up without a good education and positive role models?

Fay rambled on and on about this poor sad sack of a woman at book club. Then the conversation segued into everyone's home improvements.

Kelly was turning her basement into a plush rec room, just like her neighbor's. She'd recently ripped out her deck to install a different shaped one. She'd also just remodeled her kitchen.

"I just couldn't live with that dark cabinetry," she lamented.

Tina mentioned that another book club friend of ours was moving back to town. Shelly's husband's temporary transfer was up and Tina had been talking to her about buying a new McMansion.

"Ted and I have been looking for a new house," Tina said. "Wouldn't it be fun if Shelly and I were neighbors?"

I thought back to a conversation I recently had with Max about buying a new car. Our Jeep has been having transmission trouble and I told Max we'd probably be trading it in.

"Make sure you buy a nice car because I don't want my friends thinking we have a crappy one," Max said.

This town is sickening.

[saturday, February 22]

I've got to dump my sponsor, Lida. Lida is the last person I would have picked for a sponsor (which is probably why I haven't mentioned her until now). Lida was at the first meeting I went to on December 8, and she attached herself to me. During that meeting I was feeling sorry for myself, sniffling, and half listening to the people speaking. But Lida's comments knocked me out of my self-absorption.

"Feelings, yeah," Lida said. "Yeah, they're important, yeah. You know? Um, I've got to talk about my feelings. That's what you're supposed to do at meetings. Yeah, talk about your feelings. Yeah, uh, a lot of meetings you can't do that. Um, so I go to meetings where I can, uh, talk about my feelings."

This went on for five stupefying minutes. When the meeting ended, Lida cornered me.

"Do you have a sponsor?" she asked.

"No. This is my first meeting."

"You need a sponsor. I'll be your sponsor. Here," she said, handing me a piece of paper with her phone number on it. "What's your number?"

Lida called me a couple days later. I was her only sponsee—go figure. I learned that she is a suicidal head case, spends a lot of time on her therapist's couch, doesn't believe in meds, and in her mind is qualified to psychoanalyze me.

A couple of days after that, Lida called me again. I happened to be angry with Charlie and started bitching about him. "He takes his boots off and leaves them in the middle of the stairs for the kids and me to trip over. I whip his shoes down the basement stairs and you'd think he'd get the hint, but he keeps doing it. I just threw his boots into the basement again. This morning he shoveled the sidewalk because I asked him to. He'd never have done it otherwise. He barely shoveled a shovel's-width snaking path full of clumps. Now the shovel is lying in a mound of snow in the backyard. I'm looking at it from the window right now."

"Why do you think you're so angry?" Lida asked.

"Why?" I asked, totally irritated. "Because I expect Charlie to be a partner, not behave like one of the kids. I expect to nag my ten-year-old into a crap job, not my husband."

"I think there's more to it than that," Lida said. "We need to look at this and examine it more closely."

Another time Lida told me I was in denial about my alcoholism.

"Alcohol wasn't my favorite drug in high school or college," I had told her. "But it was my downfall because it's legal.

It became my drug of choice after I became a parent. I think anyone can become addicted to drugs or alcohol if they keep doing them, regardless of genetics."

"No," Lida said. "Your alcoholism kicked in the day you took your first drink. That first drink affects alcoholics differently than nonalcoholics. It's a disease we're born with."

"I didn't like my first drink," I told Lida. "I drank nonalcoholically for a long time before I developed a problem."

"You're intellectualizing this," Lida said testily. "And you're in danger of drinking again. You could die!"

I don't believe I'll die if I drink again. I suppose anything could happen, but I don't see myself picking up a drink, guzzling the bottle, and killing myself in the process. I didn't share this with Lida, however, for obvious reasons.

A couple of weeks ago, Lida called me at dinnertime. While I was talking to her, Van showed me some of his drawings in his *Blue's Clues Handy Dandy Notebook,* Max asked me a homework question, and Charlie motioned me toward the dining room for dinner.

"Hey, I need to sit down with my family and eat," I told her.

"Yeah, I think that's a good idea," Lida snapped. "I'm tired of being interrupted!"

"Look," I said. "I have two children who need my attention. You called during the most hectic part of my day. It upsets my ten-year-old that I've been disappearing in the evenings to go to meetings, and I'm not about to push my kids off when I'm around. You don't have children. You go to work, to meetings, and you're in bed by nine. Our lives are very different."

Two days later, Lida called again. "I just want to say that if I'm going to continue to be your sponsor, you're going to have to call me every other day and we're going to have to meet at a meeting at least once a week," she said.

Lida had been bugging me to attend a meeting with her

once a week that was an hour away from my house. I'd suggested meeting her halfway, but she said, "I only go to meetings where people talk about their feelings. We need to go to this one because people really talk about their feelings there." There was no way I was going to that meeting, and there was no way I was going to call her.

"Thanks for being my sponsor, I really appreciate it, but I need to find a sponsor who lives closer," I told Lida.

"Oh," said Lida. "Well, uh, I'll continue to be your sponsor until you find a new one."

"Uh, okay," I said, irritated with myself for not saying, "No."

So today Lida called and said, "I still want to be your sponsor."

"I asked someone else to be my sponsor today," I told her. "She lives close by, I see her at meetings, and I think she'll be a good sponsor."

I'd thought about replacing Lida with Sara weeks ago. Sara's smart, says insightful things, and has been sober for ten years, but I changed my mind during a meeting when Sara mentioned her son had been taken away from her when she was drinking and she'd spent time in a loony bin. Sara got her kid back years ago and works as a psychotherapist now, so hopefully I made a good choice.

"You know, a lot of people have two sponsors," Lida said.

"Oh, really?"

"Yeah, so I'll continue to be your sponsor," she said.

"Uh, okay," I said, hating myself for being gutless.

[Monday, February 24]

I called Lida at home when I knew she'd be at work. It's cowardly, but I didn't want to deal with her. I left a message on her answering machine thanking her for her help and telling her, "I only want one sponsor." I hope Lida doesn't call back. I don't want to hear anymore about how I should get rid of my mouthwash and Grey Poupon because they contain alcohol.

"They could trigger you," Lida insisted. "Did you get rid of them like I told you to? If you drink again you'll die!"

[Saturday, March 1]

I went downtown for a makeover at Nordstrom. Sue Devitt, the Aussie cosmetics diva herself, selected colors for me out of her new cosmetics line and a makeup artist did my face. I dropped a bundle and went to the Art Institute. It felt great!

[Sunday, March 9]

Audrey is moving to Detroit and Hope threw a good-bye brunch for her today. I made a blintz soufflé, and Hope bought lox and bagels. I don't know what Audrey sees in Nehemiah. He's fat, sixteen years older than she is, and doesn't have two nickels to rub together. I'm really going to miss her, but I have a feeling she'll be back.

[Tuesday, March 11]

I want to drink again. Maybe I can do it. It's hard to relate to the homeless stories, whoring stories, my-children-were-taken-away-from-me stories. I've been trying to work the Steps, but I've been having a hard time.

Step One: "We admitted we were powerless over (enter substance or behavior)—that our lives had become unmanageable." I go back and forth with this one but, yeah, I know I'm powerless over alcohol, especially when I remind myself that part of the reason I had Van was to sober up.

Step Two: "Came to believe that a Power greater than ourselves could restore us to sanity." I never thought I was insane. I was a pothead-turned-drinker who let alcohol spin out of control.

• • •

I started smoking pot my junior year of high school. I liked it. It made me feel uninhibited and comfortable in my own skin. My usual negative thoughts—I'm not pretty enough, I'm too skinny, I'm a Seventh-Day Adventist freak—evaporated when I got high.

I had attended a parochial Seventh-Day Adventist school from first grade through ninth grade. My mother was devout and she, my sister, and I kept the Sabbath from Friday night sundown to Saturday night sundown and went to church on Saturday. My sister and I were taught that drinking was bad, gambling was bad, dancing was bad, wearing jewelry was bad, reading novels was bad, going to movies was bad. My father, however, had immunity. He spent Friday nights at the Moose Lodge playing poker and getting sloshed and never went to church.

Paula and I were allowed to watch *The Brady Bunch, Little House on the Prairie, Happy Days,* and *The Waltons*. We wished we could be like the normal kids on TV who went to parties and danced.

My sophomore year of high school, I began attending public school. The Adventist school I'd gone to for nine years, North Shore, ended after ninth grade. The plan had always been for me to attend an Adventist boarding school, but I decided I wanted to mainstream and go to public high school. One evening, while my mother was filling out the paperwork to send me away, I told her I wanted to go to the public school. My mother told me I was going to Broadview Academy. I told her I wasn't. She told me I was.

"If you force me to go to Broadview, I'll get kicked out," I threatened. "You'll have to pack me up because I won't pack. When we get there, I'll sit in the lobby of the girls' dorm and chain smoke and swear at everybody. We'll be out of there in ten minutes."

My mother glared at me and said, "If you go to public school, your sister won't have to go to North Shore for her freshman year. I'll send her to Broadview this year instead of you."

I had begged my mother to send me to Broadview a year ago. North Shore was the last place I wanted to spend my first year of high school. I resented having to attend a school where first and second grades share a classroom, third and fourth grades share a classroom, fifth and sixth grades share a classroom, and seventh and eighth grades share a classroom. Paula was a year behind me so every other year we were in the same room. Ninth grade, high school, got its own classroom. What a privilege.

"Go ahead," I told my mother. "Put Paula's name on the paperwork."

This was working out better than I expected. I was going to public school and getting rid of my sister in one fell swoop.

A hateful look crossed my mother's face. "You're going to be miserable in public school," she growled. "You won't be able to participate in anything. All extracurricular activities are on the Sabbath. You'll go to school and do nothing else."

I knew from watching TV that the popular girls were cheerleaders, and I desperately wanted to be one. Football and basketball games were on Friday nights or Saturdays, however, so I didn't bother trying out. Instead, I auditioned for the school musical. I was cast in fifty percent of the show, but one of the performances was on Friday night. After going to two rehearsals, I got up the courage to tell the student directors, two upper-classmen, that I couldn't perform on Friday night.

"We can't recast all your parts for one night," Ellie said. "Why don't we talk to your mother and see if she'll change her mind."

I shook my head and started to cry. "You don't know her," I said. "She's not going to let me do it."

Norman, Ellie's codirector, drove me home. My mother was in the kitchen, and I sat down at the kitchen table and sobbed. My mother sat down next to me. When I lifted my head, I saw that she was smirking. "I told you this would happen," she said.

Next year, I discovered the joys of marijuana and alcohol. I started questioning authority, who I was, the existence of God. The first two questions persist today. As for the third, once I had Max, I started thinking it might be a good idea for him to believe in God. Believing in God would give Max a moral compass, and why not hedge Max's bets? If there were a heaven and hell, believing in God would be Max's ticket to the good life. But I couldn't teach Max something I didn't believe.

One evening, while I was flipping through TV stations, I landed on a cartoon where a rabbi and a priest were explaining God to children. The cartoon rabbi pointed to objects in a room. He explained that everything in the room had to be designed before it was made. Before the world existed, the rabbi said, it had to be designed, too. You can think of God as the master designer, he explained. That made sense to me.

So back to Step Two: "Came to believe that a Power greater than ourselves could restore us to sanity." I do believe in a Power greater than myself. And recently, I came to believe my behavior—throwing mass quantities of booze down my throat and repeatedly promising myself I wouldn't drink like that again—was, yes, insane.

So I guess I'm on the Third Step: "Made a decision to turn our will and our lives over to the care of God *as we understood Him.*"

I don't know about this. What if God's will doesn't jibe with mine? What if God's will is going to be unpleasant and painful, as most character building stuff is? How am I supposed to figure out His will anyway?

Last night I went to a meeting and the woman who gave the lead talked about Step Three. She said she used to have grandiose ideas of making a mark on the world, becoming a historical figure. "But now," she said, "I'm looking for something right-sized, not so big, so grand. I just want to do the next right thing, not focus on winning prestige and honor."

How uncomplicated and pure. But what's wrong with wanting to make a mark on the world? Furthermore, it's not always clear what the next right thing to do is.

When Charlie and I went to dinner with Reed and Liv on Valentine's Day, Reed said he was reading a book about the fifteen rules of success. The most important rule, Reed said, was to avoid the unhappy and unlucky at all costs. Last night, when I looked around the room at the people in the meeting, I thought, *Here are the unhappy and unlucky.*

[Saturday, March 15]

Tonight was Kelly's turn to host the Bacchanal Dinner Club. She had a fondue party—again. The last time Kelly served fondue, Charlie had to sling me over his shoulder and carry me out of her house after I lost my balance and fell into her recycling bin while smoking a cigarette in her garage.

I believe Kelly wants to get her guests as plastered as possible. Fondue requires heating oil to the right temperature in little pots, placing bowls of dipping sauces all over the table, and diners cooking each bite-size morsel of food before eating it. Kelly's first fondue was served just before midnight. I don't even remember eating. Tonight, it was served just after nine and everyone was sloshed, except me.

Before dinner Liv started tap dancing and unsuccessfully attempted the pepper grinder. The pepper grinder is when the dancer squats and swings her legs around like the top of a pepper grinder. Liv gave it a try, flopped on the floor, picked herself up, and yanked Wendy into the family room and begged Wendy to dance with her. Wendy humored Liv for a couple of minutes and when the song ended, backed away saying, "Enough." Liv grabbed Joel and danced him into the couch. She fell onto the couch, yanking Joel on top of her. Kelly watched her husband and Liv struggle to get up with an unpleasant look on her face. She turned and set out a pot of bubbling cheese fondue. I grabbed a bowl of bread cubes and placed them next to the molten cheese.

"I'm determined to get you drunk," Kelly said. "Eat a lot of this cheese. There's a shitload of alcohol in it."

"Cooking burns off the alcohol," I laughed and popped a cheese-drenched chunk of bread into my mouth.

Kelly made a face. "I could never quit drinking."

"You could if you wanted to."

"I don't want to."

"Then don't."

Kelly frowned.

Feeling compelled to make Kelly feel better, I said, "I can't have one or two glasses of wine. I want a bottle or two."

"Well I drink a bottle or more."

"Yeah, but I drank like that almost every night."

"Hmm."

Wendy walked over. She patted my head like a puppy and

hugged me. “I’m so proud of you,” she said. “You’re so strong. You just decide not to drink and you stop. What willpower! I don’t think I could do that. I know I couldn’t.”

“I got bored with drinking,” I said. “It was old. Being sober is different and interesting.”

“That’s what my brother said,” Wendy said. “He quit drinking for thirteen years. He just started up again. He got bored with not drinking.”

“How’s that going for him?” I asked, feeling giddy at the thought of drinking again.

“Okay, I guess.”

“I’ll probably get bored with not drinking, too,” I said.

“Wanna smoke?” Wendy asked.

“Yeah.”

We walked out the sliding glass doors that led from the kitchen to the back deck. Kelly followed us out. “What do you think about the book club book?” Kelly asked me with a smile.

“I don’t think there’s much to discuss,” I said. “The characters are cardboard cutouts. It’s a cheap romance novel, for God’s sake.”

Kelly’s face fell.

“But I’m enjoying it,” I added quickly. “It’s a page-turner.”

Kelly looked crestfallen. I wished I’d kept my mouth shut. She hadn’t picked the book, but she apparently loved it. We left the deck and returned to the kitchen.

“You left me out!” Liv bleated, staggering over. “You didn’t come get me before you went out! You didn’t want me around!”

“We need a group hug!” Wendy said. We group hugged and almost fell over.

“Let’s have dinner,” Kelly said.

Everyone sat down to dinner, skewered chunks of meat and vegetables, stuck their skewers into pots of bubbling oil, and waited for their food to cook. Wendy's husband, Tom, leaned over the table. "So what's it like not drinking?" he asked. "Does everyone seem stupid?"

"Yes," I said.

Tom blanched. "Really?"

"Oh, you know, it's funny," I laughed. I couldn't wait to get the hell out of there.

[Sunday, March 16]

I called Kelly and thanked her for a lovely party.

"I hope you had a good time," she said.

"Charlie and I had a great time," I said.

"Charlie looked bummed when you said you had to leave," she said. "He looked like a sad puppy."

"Really? He was the one who tapped my watch and pointed out we had to relieve the babysitter."

"Did he have a good time?" Kelly asked, sounding worried.

"Yeah. Did everyone else stay late?"

"Liv and Reed stayed until two," she said. "I had so much fun with them. I just love Liv. I'm so glad she's my friend."

I pictured Liv and Kelly hugging and telling each other how much they loved each other. It turned my stomach.

When I got off the phone, I called my new sponsor, Sara, and told her about the party.

"What was interesting," I said, "was that I had no problem not drinking. I wasn't tempted at all."

"Look out for that," she said. "Thinking you have no problem not drinking can get you into trouble. It can sneak up on you at unexpected moments in unexpected ways."

[Monday, March 17]

Charlie and I flew to Savannah, Georgia, today. Charlie's here for a conference and will be working most of the five days we're here. I'll sightsee on my own, which is what I like to do anyway, and save the best stuff for when Charlie can join me.

I took Van to my parents' house last night, dropped off Max at school this morning, and pulled into Liv's driveway. Liv is watching Max for us while we're gone. I gave Liv a hug and a kiss, thanked her profusely, handed her Max's suitcase, and took a limo to the airport.

Since tagging along with Charlie was a last-minute decision, he and I were flying separately. I got to O'Hare, presented the agent with my ticket, and he told me my flight to Savannah had been cancelled and there wasn't another. After messing around on the computer for a while, he booked me on a flight to Charleston. I killed several hours in the airport, flew to Charleston, rented a car, and drove to Savannah. The drive was supposed to be lovely, but it was pitch black by the time I hit the road and the only thing I saw were bright cigarette depot signs. Halfway to Savannah, it started to rain. I flicked on my windshield wipers, and they made one swipe and stopped. I tested the settings. I couldn't get them to work. I flicked the wipers on and off manually all the way to the damned hotel. Charlie was asleep when I got there. I wanted a drink, bad.

[Wednesday, March 19]

Charlie had a couple of hours free this morning, so we went to Shavers Book Store and gawked at Jim Williams's infamous Mercer House immortalized in John Berendt's *Midnight in the Garden of Good and Evil.* Charlie left for his conference and I drove to Bonaventure Cemetery. Berendt had written about an eccentric old woman he'd met there who was sitting on a bench shaking up martinis for herself and a dead guy. The thought of drinking a cold vodka martini as I strolled through the cemetery was enticing, but I kicked the thought out of my head.

I drove back to the hotel, got ready for dinner, and Charlie and I went to a restaurant with two of his co-workers and a client. Charlie's boss, Neil, apparently likes to play wine aficionado and made a big to-do over ordering two bottles of cabernet. The waiter began pouring and I shifted in my chair. I held my hand over my empty wineglass as he tipped the bottle toward me.

"No thank you," I said.

Neil looked at me like I had scurvy. As we ate, I reflexively reached for my wineglass several times and stopped myself. I really wanted a glass of that wine. It sucked.

[Thursday, March 20]

Stories of pirates, slaves, yellow fever, and ghosts haunt Savannah. I wandered through town with my guidebook, part of me feeling guilty that Charlie was working, part of me happy I wasn't. I made my way to historic sites, trolled antique shops, and bought a politically incorrect salt and pepper shaker set to add to my lot of African American collectibles. I hit the Savannah College of Art and Design (SCAD) Gallery and toured the home of Girl Scout founder Juliette Gordon Low, who married a philandering gold digger who gave her VD.

During dinner I told Charlie I saw a $2,000 collage at the SCAD gallery I wanted to buy.

"No fucking way," he told me.

“We’re booked on a haunted walking tour tonight,” I said.

“You’re kidding, right?”

“Nope.”

“Well, I guess there’s nothing I can do about that,” he said.

We walked past Savannah’s haunted houses, restaurants, and hotels. No glowing orbs bobbed in trees where people were hanged. No vicious apparitions leered at us from attic windows. Our guide told us even though we weren’t seeing supernatural beings, some might appear on the pictures I was snapping. We’ll see. We’re flying home tomorrow.

[Saturday, March 22]

Tonight, I missed a boxing match I purchased tickets to. The boxing match was a fundraiser for a little girl with cystic fibrosis, and Charlie and I were supposed to go with Liv and Reed, Kelly and Joel, and a few other couples. We were supposed to meet at Kelly’s beforehand for cocktails, but Van is sick.

Van came down with an upper respiratory thing that mimics asthma, which is freaking me out. I’ve prayed for Van to be free of allergies and asthma ever since I found out I was pregnant with him. Max was diagnosed with asthma when he was two and it was a hell ride for years. Now I’m watching the skin between Van’s throat and chest suck in every time he breathes.

I called Van’s doctor and he told me to drag out Max’s old nebulizer and give Van breathing treatments. The doctor said this upper respiratory thing was hitting a lot of kids hard and that Van would probably be fine in a few days.

Pete, Liv’s oldest son, was supposed to babysit for Van, Max, and Seth at our house. I called Liv and told her Van was sick.

"What am I going to do with Pete and Seth?" she asked, sounding panicky. "They try to kill each other when they're alone."

"Bring them here," I said. "We'll rent some movies."

I called Kelly and told her Charlie would be coming to her cocktail party minus me.

"Oh," she said, sounding irritated. "Don't you think Van will be fine? You can give him a treatment, put him to bed, and come. Everyone's got that upper respiratory thing."

"He's two, Kelly. I'm not leaving him with Pete."

"Okay," she sighed, her tone implying I was making lame excuses.

[Monday, March 24]

I went to a meeting this morning and the topic was loving your enemies.

"My mother picked up and moved away without saying anything to anyone," Krissy said. "Now she's back—and I don't want to see her." Krissy leaned back on the couch and rubbed her eyes. "My mother was psychologically and physically abused by her husband. I don't know. Somewhere I feel guilty for not looking in on her more. But when you feel hate and anger in your core, you know it's taken you over and you have to forgive and let it go, but it's easier said than done."

All of a sudden I was furious at my father.

My mother had offered to pick up Max from Liv's last Friday when Charlie and I were flying back from Savannah. She was going to hang out with the boys at our house until we got home. When Charlie and I walked through our back door, Max ran up to me and gave me a bear hug. My father swept up behind him.

"Where the hell have you been?" my dad shouted. "Did you stop off for dinner? Here I am and you've got nothing in your fucking house! You don't have any food or anything to drink." He stalked over to the pantry and yanked out a half-gallon bottle of vodka. "I had to go out and buy my own fucking booze. And it's dinner time and I'm looking around in your refrigerator and there's nothing in there except some old turkey. I hope to hell I don't get sick now because I ate some."

"I'm supposed to stock my refrigerator before I go out of town?" I screamed at him. "Who the fuck does that?"

Charlie touched my arm. "Brenda, come on now," he said.

"So? Did you stop somewhere for dinner?" my father yelled. "You called Max from the airport and said you'd be home in half an hour, forty-five minutes."

"I was wrong. It took longer than I thought. And no, we didn't have dinner."

"Yeah, well, I put up your ceiling fan and it was a mess," my dad shouted, thrusting his arm at the ceiling. "That's a hundred dollars worth of work. You have someone put that up for you that's a hundred dollars. And you got no fucking food or booze in the house."

I blurted out this story this morning and started crying. I didn't even know I was bothered. I'm used to this behavior from my dad.

"It's typical," I said, swiping at tears. "And I have to suck it up because somewhere he's done me a favor. Max told me, 'Papa wanted to leave, he was so mad. Van was in bed and he said I was old enough to stay by myself.' What a bastard." I sat back and sighed. "That's all I've got. Pass."

When I was a kid, my dad would ask me for a bite of my sandwich, intending to devour half of it in one bite, and get angry when I refused to hand him my lunch.

"After all the nice things I do for you and you won't give me a bite of your sandwich?" he'd growl.

I'd feel guilty and offer it to him.

"No, no," he'd say. "Keep your damned sandwich. You can stick it up your ass. I just wanted to see if you'd give me a bite."

He'd use the horse he promised but never bought against me.

"I was going to get you a horse until you did (fill in the blank). But you're not getting one now."

Christmas Eves sucked at our house, too. Instead of opening presents Christmas morning, my family opened presents Christmas Eve because my mother didn't want my sister and me believing in Santa Claus as it would take away from Jesus and cause her to break the "Thou shall not lie" commandment. My father would often show up late and drunk, having shared some holiday cheer with coworkers. My parents would fight, and my mother would cry. One Christmas Eve, my dad punched a hole in the living room wall while my sister and I sat silently waiting to open presents.

My father can go to hell.

[Tuesday, March 25]

Kelly is getting together a group of us to stay at a hotel for a sleepover/swim party during spring break, and I told her the kids and I would go.

"I'm going to invite Liv and Wendy, too," Kelly said. "We'll get Wendy out by the pool and watch her stumble around, ha, ha, ha."

Sometimes I hate Kelly. I was probably Kelly's cheap entertainment when I was drinking. I was the wacky broad who would sing, drink from everyone's wineglass, demonstrate yoga poses and fall down, break something. Kelly's a bitch.

[Wednesday, March 26]

I went to a meeting this morning and the topic was slips, relapses, how you set yourself up to use before you actually do. Drinking definitely lurks in the back of my mind.

Lately, I've been treating myself like a science experiment: dissecting myself to see what's in there. It's been interesting, but I anticipate getting bored with being sober. I get random urges to be bad, get hammered, let the good times roll.

At the meeting this morning, a guy named Tom said he had intrusive thoughts, thoughts like throw the baby up in the air, put your hand on the hot stove, ride your bike in front of a semi. He said his shrink told him that as long as he doesn't act on them, he's okay.

I have intrusive thoughts. I just never knew they had a label. I'll be at the shopping mall and have the urge to throw myself over the second-floor railing. I'll be standing on a train platform and think about pushing someone on the tracks. Don't most people have random twisted thoughts? Maybe not. Maybe I'm a freak.

I had a dream last night that I was on the second floor of an unfamiliar house. I was bending over a railing looking at the living room below. I climbed onto the railing and stood on it, teetering, about to jump. Then I thought, *What am I doing?* and got down.

Tom works at a cemetery. I think he's a grave digger. When he finished talking about intrusive thoughts, he said, "A woman at a meeting last night was clucking her tongue at me. She was shaking her head at me while I was speaking.

I leaned over and told her, 'When people do that it gets me excited. There's some action going on in my pants. You keep it up we'll be walking down the aisle.'

"I love to drink, just love to drink," Tom continued. "I just hate the consequences. If I had a pill that would allow me to drink and not have any consequences—the vomiting, the nut house, jail—I'd have a garage full of those pills and I'd be drinking. To have that drink and feel that ah in the brain . . ."

I'm on the same page with a crazy grave digger.

[Thursday, March 27]

It's my three-month anniversary of being sober. I went to a meeting, and when the chair asked if anyone was celebrating an anniversary, I raised my hand. Everyone clapped and some guy handed me a three-month coin. It was embarrassing but cool at the same time. A young kid, maybe sixteen or seventeen, gave the lead. He was very cocky, thought he was cute, but he described some painful loneliness that he attempted to numb with drugs.

When I became a stay-at-home-mom and housebound freelance writer, I started hitting the wine and vodka pretty hard. Charlie got to leave the house, go out for drinks after work, travel, play tennis. I was at home and angry about the mind-numbing tasks that filled my day. Much of my day was spent standing in the kitchen making food, feeding people, and cleaning up the food. I would stew and tell myself I was meant for greater things.

During the meeting I said that while I was sucking down vodka by myself, I knew I was on a bad path but didn't care. It had crossed my mind I'd probably wind up in a recovery program, but I thought, *At least I'd get out of the house.* People nodded their heads and laughed.

[Tuesday, April 1]

Tonight's the swim fest/sleepover Kelly organized for spring break. It had been seventy degrees today, and I'd taken the kids to a playground with a massive jungle gym castle before doing mountains of laundry, packing, and leaving. On the way to the hotel, Max opened the glove compartment.

"What's this?" he asked accusingly, waving a pack of cigarettes and a book of matches.

"What does it look like?" I retorted.

"Is your head up your you-know-what or something?" Max asked.

"Actually, I'm kind of in the mood for one of those," I said, snatching the pack from him.

The temperature had plunged from seventy to forty-something during our drive. April fool! I lit a cigarette and rolled down my window. I held my cigarette at the edge of the window and tried to blow the smoke outside without success. Van was in the back seat getting blasted by cold air and smoke. The poor kid had just recovered from his upper respiratory virus. Max was in the front seat holding his T-shirt over his nose and staring at me in shock. I threw the cigarette out the window after three puffs and rolled up the windows. Max pulled his shirt down from his nose.

"You know, that really makes me feel bad," he said, almost crying.

"I'm sorry," I said. "That was really stupid. Smoking is stupid." I crunched the cigarette pack in my fist. "But don't you ever talk to me in that snotty way again."

"I won't."

I felt like a big baby acting out. We arrived at the hotel and were told we had no reservation and none of our friends were there. I was fuming as we drove back home. I had the kids put on warmer clothes and called Kelly.

"Where are you?" I asked testily.

Kelly insisted she'd told me we were staying at another hotel. She probably had, but it didn't stop me from toying with the idea that she'd purposely misinformed me just to screw with me.

The boys and I checked in at the correct hotel and found our room, which had a sliding glass door that opened to the indoor swimming pool. The room smelled like chlorine, mildew, and cigarette butts. We put on our swimsuits and jumped in the pool. I waved briefly to Kelly, Nosey Rosy, and Liv. They were sitting at a table on an elevated platform overlooking the pool with Joel, Reed, and Joel's friend Trip. Charlie was swamped with work and chipping away at it at home. Liv and Reed weren't staying. They'd just stopped by for a couple of drinks. Seth was going to sleep at the hotel with the boys and me.

When Van tired of swimming, I wrapped him in a towel, carried him over to the table where the adults were sitting, gave him a snack, and popped open a can of LaCroix. Trip was chain smoking. Hotel guests at other tables were chain smoking. The smoke hung in the humid, stagnant air like a mushroom cloud. I like to have an occasional cigarette, but this was gross. I watched our kids running back and forth between the pool and the hot tub, squirting each other with the squirt guns I'd brought. Van periodically darted from the table we were sitting at, ran for the pool, and I ran after him. Kelly uncorked wine bottle after wine bottle. Eventually, Liv and Reed left and I put Van to bed. When I returned to the table, Kelly and Nosey Rosy were playing ping-pong and Joel and Trip were watching them. Nosey Rosy beat Kelly three games in a row and Kelly was unhappy. Kelly huffed back to the table while Nosey Rosy checked on her kids in the pool.

"She's so competitive," Kelly grumbled. "And she's a cheater."

I checked my watch. It was ten thirty. My sinuses and eyes were burning.

"I'm going to bed," I said, waving my hand in the cloud of smoke surrounding my head. "I can't breathe anymore."

I got up to round up Max and Seth and Kelly put her arm around my shoulders and slurred, "You're not there with us, and you wish you were."

I looked at her and smirked. "Yeah, that's it," I said.

[Wednesday, April 2]

I took Seth, Max, and Van out to breakfast. I checked the pool and hallway before we left and no one else was up. When we returned, Nosey Rosy, Kelly, and the kids were by the pool. Nosey Rosy was in the hot tub and Kelly was sitting at a patio table in front of her room looking like shit. Max and Seth jumped into the pool with the other kids, and Van and I got into the hot tub.

"Kelly's hurting bad," Nosey Rosy said.

"Looks like it."

"How do you feel about going to those heavy drinking parties now that you're not drinking?" she asked.

"I like seeing everyone at the beginning and having a nice dinner," I said, knowing full well my words would get repeated to Kelly. "But when everyone's gone from slightly buzzed to stupid it's a drag. I'm the first one to leave."

But now it's my turn to host and I don't know what I'm going to do.

[Friday, April 4]

We had Liv, Reed, and their kids over for dinner as a thank-you for watching Max while we were in Savannah. I made cheese biscuits, collard greens, and cassoulet. Charlie picked up Maker's Mark, Absolut, and wine.

Liv had one martini. I was pretty sure she was holding back because of me. Things felt a bit strained between us. I don't know. We're maneuvering new ground with me being sober and it's weird. Reed didn't slow his drinking up one bit, however, which felt more normal. He walked through our front door swigging bourbon and Coke out of an enormous disposable plastic cup and immediately started bitching about the nasty traffic he'd just been stuck in. He's so much like my dad.

I put the finishing touches on the collard greens and noticed Max crawling on top of the kitchen counter and grabbing something out of the cupboard. On his way out of the kitchen, a shot glass fell out of his pocket and smashed on the floor.

Whenever Pete babysits for Max, Seth, and Van—when Liv, Reed, Charlie, and I are going out—there is an array of fancy drink glasses littering Max's bedroom the following morning: beer mugs, brandy snifters, champagne glasses sticky with soda. It's disturbing. What a great example I've been.

[Sunday, April 6]

I went to a meeting and ran into my neighbor, Henry, who lives down the street with his wife and kids. It was awkward but at the same time nice. Henry seemed genuinely happy to see me. He told me my old next-door neighbor had attended this meeting for years before he moved. Bummer he wasn't still around.

We took turns reading out of a book that describes the

addict's effect on his or her family. I didn't have the gnarly stories the others did. I got sober before my life went to shit. But that's caused me trouble believing I have a problem. I don't believe my life would have gone down the toilet like other people's lives did.

When I got home, I told Charlie I was blowing off hosting the Bacchanal Dinner Club. If someone else wanted to do it, fine, but I wasn't hosting a let's-get-shit-faced party. Charlie got this sappy look on his face like I was spoiling his fun. I suppose I am. Charlie doesn't socialize unless I arrange it.

Most people trying to recover don't hang out with their drinking or using buddies. The ones who do usually start getting messed up again. I've been telling people at meetings who question my socializing that I'm doing it for Charlie. "Why should his life have to change, why should he stop having fun just because I stopped drinking?" However, I'm hanging out with the old crowd as much for me as Charlie because I don't want to get rid of my friends. I don't want to feel like a sicko who has to isolate and only hang out with sober people. A lot of people in recovery shield themselves from drinking situations, hide out at meetings, talk incessantly about how messed up they were. I don't want to be like them. I just want to be normal.

[Tuesday, April 8]

I met my sponsor, Sara, at Starbucks. I told her I thought I was on the Fourth Step: "Made a searching and fearless moral inventory of ourselves," and she told me not to do it yet. "Start from scratch and reread Step One every day for a week," she said.

Give me a break. I'll read it, but not every day for a week.

Going back to Step One is probably a good idea since I glossed over the first three Steps. I accepted the first two

Steps—admitted we were powerless over (enter substance or behavior), and came to believe that a Power greater than ourselves could restore us to sanity—but in the back of my head, if I'm completely honest, I'm planning to drink in the future. As for the Third Step, "Made a decision to turn our will and our lives over to the care of God *as we understood Him,*" I checked this one off because everyone working the Steps has to work it for the rest of their lives. It's not like you align your will with God's and it sticks forever. Anyway, I'm glad to be blowing off my Fourth Step, my searching and fearless moral inventory, for now.

I don't know why I want to drink in the future. I don't want to get back on that hamster wheel of drunkenness, hangover, drunkenness, hangover. And I don't like controlled drinking. I can control my drinking for a while, but it sucks. I want to drink until I'm messed up. Why drink if you're not going to go for the buzz?

"I've been on an emotional roller coaster lately," I told Sara. "I can be fine one minute and crying the next. I'm singing in the car, then I'm sobbing."

"Our brains made a lot of alcohol-soaked connections," Sara said. "Your brain is making sober ones now. You'll probably feel edgy and moody for the next six months. You've been numbing your feelings with alcohol for years, and now you're experiencing them."

What a trip.

[Thursday, April 10]

I went to a meeting tonight with plans to go out afterward with three women I've met in recovery: Darcy, Eve, and Kat. Kat bailed and went home halfway through the meeting because, like Max, her daughter is having problems with her going to meetings all the time and called Kat twice on her cell phone.

Darcy and Eve and I decided to go out for pie. Eve is a cute fifty-something redhead who owns a housecleaning service. She married a rich guy, lived in a big house on a golf course, and used to play tennis and get sloshed every day. "I signed a prenup and got screwed in my divorce," she complained as she rifled through her battered old Coach bag and extracted a pack of cigarettes at the restaurant. "I got enough money to start my company, though," she said, lighting up. "God, the parties I used to go to, the parties in limos."

I'd considered asking Eve to be my sponsor some time ago but was warned not to. I'd gone out for coffee with two guys after a meeting who had alcoholic wives, and they wanted to know why I got sober in hopes I'd share something they could use on their spouses. I told them I was considering asking Eve to be my sponsor, and they looked at each other with raised eyebrows and frowns. "Uh, I think she's having some problems and I wouldn't recommend it," one of them said. The other nodded vigorously.

Darcy is forty-three, divorced, childless, and recently lost her job due to corporate downsizing. She was quick with a joke and a laugh, however.

It felt good to socialize with a couple of smart sober women, but I hope in time we'll have conversations that don't constantly revolve around drugs and alcohol. When I talk to people in recovery, the subject always comes back to what they're recovering from, and it gets tedious.

[Friday, April 11]

I went to a bunco party tonight. Bunco's a mindless dice game that seems to be all the rage among the suburban-mom set. I was invited to join two bunco clubs since getting sober but passed because they're mainly an excuse to drink wine. Liv, however, was hosting her bunco club and asked me to play.

"I'm setting up an extra table for my friends," she said. "Come. It'll be fun. You could get on our sub list if you like it. I asked Kelly and Wendy, and they're coming."

I arrived early. Liv had asked Wendy, Kelly, and me to come before everyone else, and we stood in the kitchen eating appetizers, watching the regulars file in.

"That's Nutty Nancy," Wendy whispered out the side of her mouth. "She's the most offensive woman in town. Talk to her for more than a minute and she'll piss you off. She can't help herself. She tried to get into my bunco group but was blackballed."

Liv's bunco club was formed by Nutty Nancy after she failed to get into everybody else's.

Someone ding-ding-dinged a teacher's desk bell, and Nutty Nancy and Androgynous Jaime ordered everyone to sit down. Wendy and I sat at a card table with two other women, and we took turns shaking a cup full of dice trying to roll ones, then twos, then threes, and so on, making tally marks for every die that came up right. When the bell rang again, we tallied our marks. Based on our scores, we rotated to new seats and new tables.

It was a lot more fun than I thought it would be. If I were still drinking, I'd join the next bunco club that wanted me. But I'm in no position to host a house full of drunk bunco broads.

[Saturday, April 12]

I went to a meeting tonight and the guy who spoke really struck a chord with me. He talked about the Fourth Step, "Made a searching and fearless moral inventory of ourselves," which entails listing the people we resent, our bad behavior toward them, and our fears that lurk under our resentments. Usually our fears have something to do with not getting what we want or losing something we have. The speaker said he resented his parents for not recognizing and nurturing his brilliant potential. He said he resented his repressive parochial school and church. He said doing the Fourth Step had allowed him to take ownership of his behavior and forgive the people he resented; however, he hadn't found a soft spot for his school or church.

Sybil, the infamous split personality, was raised by a Seventh-Day Adventist mother. David Koresh, the Waco Whacko, built his cult off whacked-out Adventist beliefs. I, too, was raised an Adventist, a faith that focuses on a judgmental doomsday.

My mother, teachers, and preachers drilled into my head that the end of time, "The Time of Trouble," was right around the corner, and I, as an Adventist, was going to be persecuted, jailed, tortured, and perhaps killed for going to church on Saturday. Sunday laws would require businesses to close and people to attend church on Sunday. Anyone worshipping on Saturday was going to experience a new holocaust. And staying true to the Sabbath was God's lynchpin in figuring out who was going to heaven and who was going to hell. The preachers in my church would sweep their arms and shout, "Who among you will be saved? The road is narrow. Most of you will fall by the wayside. Who among you will stand firm and be saved?" Congregants' heads would swivel, like mine, eyes scanning the pews, making mental lists of who was going to hell.

A pastor would come to my school once a week and tell us, "You're different from the children of the world. You must be a shining example and show them what it's like to be a child of God."

I didn't want to be a shining example. When anyone asked what religion I was, I got embarrassed and said, "Christian." This question occasionally came up because I couldn't play softball, go swimming, or roller skate with the neighborhood kids from Friday night sundown to Saturday night sundown, the Sabbath, and the neighbors wanted to know why. Basically, I sat in the house during that twenty-four-hour period and waited for the Sabbath to end.

During the other six days of the week I couldn't dance, go to movie theaters, or read novels because Adventists didn't do those things either. I also didn't eat meat, which a lot of Adventists don't do, and the Adventists who do eat meat don't eat pork or shellfish because the Old Testament says they're unclean.

"Say it's The Time of Trouble," my dad, who ate and did whatever the hell he wanted, would say to my mother as we ate breakfast. "Say they arrest me and are going to kill me unless you eat a piece of bacon." He'd hold up his bacon. "Would you eat the bacon?"

Stone-faced and rigid, my mother would say, "No."

"You wouldn't eat a piece of bacon to save my life?"

"No."

"What about the girls? Would you eat a piece of bacon to save them?"

Paula and I would look at each other anxiously, hoping our mother would eat bacon to save us.

"That's a stupid question," my mother would say.

"Answer it. Would you eat the bacon to save them?"

"No," my mother would say.

"You would let us all die?" my father would yell. "Unbelievable. You're sick. Sick." He'd wave his hands disgustedly and stomp out of the room swearing.

Periodically, my father would pose this question in various

forms. Would you eat a lobster? Would you tell a lie? The answer was always no. I wanted my mother to lie. I wanted her to eat clams. But she said she never would.

Weirdly enough, my parents met in church. My dad was raised an Adventist and, like me, turned his back on his religion. When my parents met, my father was paying his mother back for bailing him out of jail. He'd been hunting deer without a license and tried to outrun the cops with a dead deer tied to the roof of his car.

[Sunday, April 13]

A guy named George made a good point at tonight's meeting. He said, "Resentments are like swallowing poison and waiting for the other person to die."

[Tuesday, April 15]

I joined a second, more serious book club that Kelly's friends, Lexi and Candy, started. Candy picked me up and we drove to some woman's house. The book club women seemed nice, with the exception of Sherry, who resembled an Italian Greyhound. Sherry looked like she wanted to nip me. Her porcelain skin showed blue veins; her body visibly trembled; she eyed me up and down. Without a "hello" or "it's nice to meet you," she launched our discussion of *A Heart of Stone,* a book about a mother's homicidal insanity. We spent a lot of time dissecting the milquetoast father who allowed his wife to whack their family, and Sherry segued from the wimpy father to a guy she works with.

"He injured his knee and kept whining about it," she hissed, straining like an angry dog on a leash. I told him, 'You don't know what pain is until you've been through childbirth. What you're dealing with is nothing.'" She railed about what a lousy salesman the guy was, then said, "I have little tolerance for stupid people."

After Sherry got through with her tirade, other members began suggesting a new book to read for the next book club. Sherry nixed everything that was suggested, then recommended *Naked* by David Sedaris, which is one of my favorite books.

"David Sedaris is a funny, witty, neurotic Jew," Sherry said.

"He's not Jewish, he's Greek," I said, sounding intentionally snotty.

Sherry's blue neck veins rose closer to the surface, nicely complementing the icy blue stare she was giving me. "I'm quite sure he's Jewish," she sniffed.

"He's not," I said and smiled.

I'm going to have fun with Sherry.

[Wednesday, April 16]

I worked at a homeless shelter from eleven at night to three in the morning babysitting thirty-one homeless men. I'd volunteered at church, planning to take Max to the shelter to serve dinner, but the dinner slots were already taken by other like-minded parents and their children and I got talked into the homeless-sitting shift. An old guy named Bill who looked like Santa Claus was sitting next to me behind a blockade of three school lunchroom tables that separated us from the guys sleeping on the floor and those roaming the room muttering to themselves.

During the four hours we spent together, Bill told me he had non-Hodgkin's lymphoma and prostate cancer. "I'm cancer free now, but I have diabetes and need to watch my diet."

We were a force to be reckoned with.

At two in the morning, a scrawny white guy hobbled up to the lunch tables and asked for a cup of milk for his upset stomach. Another mangy white dude circled the room, occasionally refreshing his cup of coffee. A brick house of a black man clasping a three-ringed binder asked, "Can I have one of those sandwich bags full of toiletries?" I gave him one. He shuffled to a table across from me and began writing feverishly in his binder. Sporadically, he looked up and glared at me. I fondled my cell phone, prepared to dial 911. A befuddled old man staggered toward me and asked for directions to the bathroom. "Down that hall," I said and pointed. He stared at me with his mouth agape. I got up and walked him to the bathroom and returned to my chair behind the lunch tables. Minutes later, the old man staggered out, a dark wet saddle-shaped stain between his legs.

"Looks like the poor old guy wet his drawers," Bill said, shaking his head.

"Yep."

I'd ditched Kelly's thirty-ninth birthday party for this. Candy was hosting a chardonnay-tasting party for Kelly, but the homeless shelter had been on my calendar for two months before Candy invited me. I snickered to myself. Oddly, I preferred being here.

[Saturday, April 19]

We went to Reed and Liv's for happy hour to meet Reed's family, who are in town from Des Moines. I had a tennis lesson, so Charlie and the boys went ahead of me. When I drove up, Kelly and Joel's SUV was parked in front of their house. I yanked my tennis skirt down and walked in. Kelly eyed me up and down. The strain between us is palpable. Reed poured me a LaCroix and I sipped fizzy water while everyone else had cocktails. Reed's mother, Celeste, eyed my water.

"You don't drink?" she asked.

"I quit four months ago," I answered. "I decided to take a break."

"I quit for a year," Celeste said.

"Really?"

"My friends said I couldn't do it, but I did. Lost a lot of weight, too."

"But you decided to drink again," I said, nodding toward her martini. I was instantly filled with hope that I might successfully enjoy a martini a year from now.

"I started drinking white wine spritzers," Celeste said. "I just wanted a little something. I started drinking them a month ago. But I decided to have a martini tonight."

A lot of people at meetings talk about how they controlled their drinking after a relapse, but then their alcoholic pattern kicked in and cranked up.

Reed's grandmother sat next to Celeste and sipped her martini. "Liv tap danced for us last night," she said. "She's very good. Have you seen her?"

"Yes," I said and smiled.

I walked into the kitchen and refilled my glass with sparkling water. Reed was at the counter refreshing drinks and Liv walked in and stood next to him.

"Will you put some music on for me?" she asked. "Your grandma wants me to tap dance."

Reed stared at her. "No."

[Sunday, April 20]

We had Easter brunch at our house, and the first thing my father said when he walked in was, "You got any beer?"

"No," I said. "But we have vodka in the pantry."

"You drinking again?" he asked hopefully.

"We had Reed and Liv over for dinner and Charlie picked it up for them."

"You buy booze for other people but not for me?"

"We buy booze when we're having people over for dinner. It didn't occur to me to buy you beer for brunch."

"What about having us for dinner? We watched Van when you were in Savannah."

Apparently he didn't remember the night Charlie and I got back. I'd invited my parents over for dinner after my dad stopped screaming at me. My father had said, "I'm not driving out here for dinner. You can cook for me at my house or take me out to eat."

"You're here for brunch," I told him and took my blintz soufflé out of the oven.

My dad got a glass out of the cupboard, filled it with ice, and grabbed the half-empty liter of Absolut from the pantry. When he left, the bottle was empty.

• • •

I called my cousin, Mike, when the kids were in bed for the night and wished him a happy Easter. Mike moved to California right after we moved to the suburbs. His wife, Susan, had moved to Los Angeles a year before him intending to divorce him. She'd supported Mike in Chicago while he drank and blew off writing his dissertation. When he moved to California, they'd reconciled and Mike landed a good job as a financial analyst. But for some time, Mike's been teetering near the deep end. He's always settling a score with someone, and right now he's out to destroy his next-door neighbors because he believes they catnapped his beloved Patches.

"Before Patches disappeared, my neighbor's fiancé, Nancy,

tells me I shouldn't let my cat out because coyotes will get her," Mike said. "So Susan lets Patches out one Saturday morning and Patches disappears. So I'm upset, very upset, and I'm asking all over the neighborhood if anyone's seen Patches. I see Nancy and she tells me she's sure coyotes didn't get her. Later, at a party, my neighbor Dale pulls me aside and asks me, 'If someone wanted to return your cat, how would they go about doing it?'"

"Weird," I said.

"Yeah. So you know they took her. So I tell Dale, 'They could just bring her to my door, no questions asked,' but no one brings her home. So I confronted Dale. He denied it. Brenda, I know they took her. I even went to a pet psychic and the psychic substantiated my suspicions."

"No way! Really?"

"She channeled for Patches. Patches told me she was catnapped by two guys whose descriptions fit Dale and his friend. Patches said she was taken somewhere in a car and let out and that she'd tried to get home but was run over by a car. Brenda, she's dead."

"Wow," I said, feeling really bad for Mike on many levels.

"I called the cops and reported Patches's catnapping," Mike said. "I told the police Dale appeared to be involved in drug trafficking and offered them my house for stakeouts."

"Do you really think they're selling drugs?"

"No," Mike laughed. "Dale and Nancy think they're getting married on Valentine's Day, but that wedding's never going to happen. I know the church and I'm booby-trapping it with stink bombs."

"I'm really glad I quit drinking," I told Mike, changing the subject. "It's great waking up without a hangover. Reality's way more interesting than being comatose. You should try it sometime."

"Well, good for you," Mike said.

"You really need to let this thing with your neighbor go for your sake, not his," I said. "You're allowing him to consume your thoughts, make you miserable, act crazy. Let it go. Move on."

"That's what my shrink says," he said. "But I can't. They have to pay."

[Tuesday, April 22]

I took Emily out to lunch for her birthday. She and her husband, like a lot of my friends, are having midlife problems.

"You know what Scott did instead of spending Easter with us?" she asked. "Went to Vegas with his friend. I'm tired of going to social functions by myself. He barely talks to me. I don't want to spend the last half of my life like this."

I told Emily about my friend Bea, who left her husband right before Christmas. Somewhere around Thanksgiving, Bea started boxing up her stuff, her children's things, and sent the boxes to her sister in Texas. Remy, her negligent clueless husband, never even noticed. Remy went to a medical conference in Wisconsin and while he was gone, Bea hired movers and she and the kids flew to Texas and moved in with her sister.

"Wow, that's harsh," Emily said.

"Remy deserved it," I said. "Bea was going to leave him eight years ago when she found out he was having a weekly date with a hooker. She was pregnant at the time. But they were involved in a car crash that left Remy partially paralyzed, and Bea felt like she couldn't leave him.

"Remy got deeply religious after that," I continued. "According to him, everything he does is God's will. He left his medical practice to work part time so he could minister. When the bills piled up he told Bea, 'God will take care of us.'

Then he got into computer porn. Bea confronted him and each time he'd tell her, 'It's in the past. I made it right with God,' even if it was only ten minutes ago."

"Oh my God!"

"He's a piece of work. Bea started complaining about Remy's bad career moves, and he told her she was going against God and siding with Satan. He told their daughter her mother was a tool of the devil. 'See how your mother's trying to divide the family? She's going against God and me.'"

"Oh my God!"

"And Remy hasn't been to Texas once to see his kids. Bea served him with divorce papers, but he doesn't believe they're going to get divorced because it isn't God's will."

"I don't think my marriage is so bad after all," Emily said.

"Happy birthday," I said and clinked her water glass with mine.

[Thursday, April 24]

I went downtown to have dinner and see the Joffrey Ballet with Hope. I felt normal until the waiter asked if we wanted a bottle of wine and Hope and I declined. He raised his eyebrows, sniffed, and walked away. I don't know why I should care if a waiter thinks I'm a goober who doesn't know how to enjoy a good meal by ordering the right wine with it. The bastard just wanted to fatten the bill to get a better tip. I looked at the other tables and almost everyone else was drinking wine. Not drinking wine with dinner still feels very foreign to me.

[Friday, April 25]

My friend Libby invited me out with her lesbian pals to see their friend Claudia Allen's new play at Victory Gardens

Theater. Libby lives in Nashville, but she lived in Chicago for a time and we became friends while writing for magazines owned by the same publishing company. Libby quit drinking shortly after we met and when anyone asked her why she quit, she'd give one of two clipped answers: "It was just time" or "I just decided to quit." Her answers annoyed me. She gave nothing away. I wanted an I-knew-it-was-time-to-quit answer I could apply to myself to confirm I was fine. That was thirteen years ago.

I drove to the B&B that Libby and her partner, Nanette, were staying at, and Nanette popped open a beer and offered me one.

"No thanks," I said. "I quit."

"Why?" Nanette asked, looking bummed.

"I was uncomfortable with the amount I was drinking," I said. "And I was sick of the hangovers."

"That'll do it," Libby said.

Nanette wrapped her bottle of beer in a piece of newspaper and chugged it as we walked to a restaurant down the street. Before we walked in, she scanned the sidewalk for a garbage can, sucked down the rest of her beer, and tossed the bottle in. The hostess at the restaurant showed us to a large table full of women. Libby and Nanette sat opposite each other and I sat next to Libby. After a while I nudged Libby and said, "You quit drinking on your own, right?"

"Yeah," she said. "I went to some meetings, but I didn't like them. I know a lot of people who go, though. An old girlfriend of mine called me up to make amends once. It was two years after she dumped me. She told me she was sorry for treating me badly. She said she was young and selfish at the time and that was it. I never heard from her again. I don't know what that was supposed to do for me. She just came out of nowhere and disappeared into nowhere. It was too little, too late."

[Monday, April 28]

I took Kelly out to lunch for her birthday. She started griping about Joel. She's angry he's not freshening up his career skills. She's pushing him to start a side business setting up personal computers and sound systems and she's angry that he's not doing it.

"He's unhappy and unpleasant to live with, and I'm not going to live like this much longer," she told me. Kelly sipped her iced tea and moved on to the night I went out with Libby and the Bacchanal Dinner Club group went to Bin 36 without Charlie and me.

"It was so weird without you two," Kelly said, "but we had the best time ever. The guy from *The Bachelor,* the Firestone guy, was there along with almost every unattached woman from Lake County. The place was packed. You couldn't move. We were smooshed into the bar and they gave us free appetizers. We didn't end up eating until almost ten thirty. We had the best time. I just love Liv and Wendy!"

"Great," I said.

"Whose turn is it to host the next dinner party?" Kelly asked, knowing it was mine.

"It's my turn," I said.

Kelly cocked an eyebrow. "Do you think you can handle us?"

I wanted to smack the bitch.

[Tuesday, April 29]

I was supposed to hook up with Eve and go to a meeting, but she blew me off. I went alone and when I got there Tracy announced, "Deidre's in jail." Everyone gasped. We all knew Deidre could go to jail, but I never believed it would happen.

Deidre was the woman in my First Step meeting who had shaken her finger at me and had said, "In the back of your mind you're planning your next drink." She'd known what was in the back of my head because the same thing was in the back of hers.

Deidre started attending meetings because she was court ordered to. She'd smashed her car into an automobile with two teenage boys in it. The boys weren't wearing seat belts and they'd rocketed through the windshield, lacerating their faces and wrenching their spinal cords. The boys' parents had attended each of Deidre's court dates and she was convicted. During sentencing, the judge gave her two options: She could go to work during the day and get locked up at night for three months, or she could stay in jail around the clock for twenty-four days. Deidre chose the latter.

"Deidre's been incarcerated for three weeks now," Tracy said. "She was so depressed the first week that she was put on suicide watch. She's been writing me letters on ruled notebook paper she decorates with flowery drawings to make the paper look like stationery. She says she's made some friends in jail—no one she'd hang out with on the outside—but having friends has helped. If all goes well, she'll be released in a few days."

On the outside, Deidre looks like a regular suburban mom. She's involved in her kids' schools and activities. She always looks good and has a nicely decorated house. Looking at her is like looking in a mirror. I could be sitting in jail. It scares the shit out of me. Deidre is a tall woman you wouldn't want to pick a fight with, and she's on suicide watch. I'm a five-foot-four, 115-pound blondie. I'd get eaten alive, literally.

[Friday, May 2]

Eve relapsed. Her on-again-off-again relationship with her boyfriend is off, business is bad, and her sister is dying of breast cancer. Maybe I'd drink, too, if I were her.

Eve and I met for breakfast this morning. She said she blew me off Tuesday night because she was getting hammered. My brain began wondering, "What kind of booze did she drink? What did it feel like to buy alcohol after sitting in all those meetings? Did the first sip feel wonderful?" I felt ashamed and confessed my alcoholic thoughts to Eve, hoping she'd give me a vicarious thrill, and she did. Eve said she bought a bottle of vodka and it numbed her up just like she wanted it to.

Sometimes I really miss the numbness vodka gives me. I miss the icy burn on my tongue and the back of my throat. I miss the "Ah" feeling that spreads through my body on the first sip. I miss my wine. The next time I go to Europe, I'm drinking wine. I'll just quit drinking again when I get back home.

[Monday, May 12]

I rented the movie *Monster's Ball* and began watching it after the kids went to bed. The scene where Halle Berry blows up at her fat son for sneaking chocolate, calls him a porker, pushes him, and makes him cough up his candy bar stash hurt to watch. It reminded me of my bad behavior toward Max when he began wetting the bed and peeing on himself during the day when he started first grade. Max had been potty trained since he was three, but for reasons no one ever figured out, he started having accidents—and his accidents went on for more than two years.

I'd taken Max to a pediatric urologist at Children's Memorial Hospital who set us up with an alarm device to pin in Max's underwear. But the alarm would go off at the slightest hint of wetness, like whenever Max sweat, so we didn't use it much. I eliminated certain foods from Max's diet that I learned were diuretics, like cantaloupe, watermelon, and soda. I prevented Max from drinking anything after seven at night. Max eventually got to dry, but it took a while getting there.

I knew Max couldn't help it when he wet the bed. If I found him and his bed wet in the morning, I'd peel off his pajamas, strip his bed, and do a load of laundry. But after four or five mornings in a row like this, I'd sometimes snap. I'd call Max "Baby" and "Pee Pants." I'd make him strip his own bed and carry the sheets downstairs to the laundry room. If he wet his pants during the day, God help him.

Once, when we were in Blockbuster renting movies, Max began fidgeting and wiggling like he had to urinate and I asked him, "Why don't you go to the bathroom?"

"I don't have to go," he answered. He didn't want to stop playing a video game on display.

"I think you should go," I said.

"I don't have to go!" he insisted.

As we were standing in the checkout line, Max really began fidgeting and said, "I have to go to the bathroom, bad." I got the restroom key from the cashier, turned around, and on the front of Max's pants was a huge wet stain. I drove home in a rage. I made Max strip off his clothes in the bathroom. I made him wash his pants by hand in the tub. There was a dinner party for his soccer team in a couple of hours.

"I wonder what your teammates would think if they knew you peed your pants? Should we go? Should we tell them? No, I think you better stay home in case you wet your pants again."

I kept referring to the pee incident all night, rubbing his nose in it. I knew better, I wanted to shut up, but I kept spewing hurtful words. I was afraid Max's classmates and teammates would eventually notice his wet spots and ridicule him mercilessly. So I beat them to the punch thinking my ridicule would stop his wetting problem. I was out of ideas, powerless, frustrated. And I was sick of cleaning up urine.

I continued watching *Monster's Ball* and the phone rang. It was my friend Jason, who owns an art gallery downtown. Jason told me he'd kicked an obnoxiously drunk business associate out of his gallery when the guy began pushing his girlfriend around. A day or so later, Jason sent the guy an email telling him he suspected he had a substance abuse problem. Jason offered to help him, confessing that he himself was an addict who'd sobered up. The guy, outraged and humiliated from being kicked out of Jason's gallery, posted his version of events on the Internet along with Jason's I'm-an-addict confession. Jason was worried sick about it.

"There are a lot of addicts in the art world," I told Jason in an attempt to comfort him. "Who knows, it may help someone else. That guy made himself look like a whack job posting it."

"That guy was scary," Jason said. "He reminded me of me when I relapsed. I was never abusive like that, but it was really bad. I almost died."

"I've heard a lot of people say they'll die if they use again," I said. "But I don't believe drinking will kill me. I think I've got some drinking left in me if I want to do it."

"I go to this really huge meeting where, like, 150 people show up," Jason said. "There's always a story about someone relapsing and dying. Personally, I've known people who've been sober, like, twenty years and started drinking again and were dead in a year. Those people go really quickly. It's a progressive disease, even if you're not drinking."

I have heard alcoholism advances, whether you're drinking or not. As a result, I've contemplated drinking again to keep an eye on my alcoholism and avoid jumping off the deep end should I start drinking years from now.

Right after I told Jason I thought I had some drinks left in me, Deidre popped into my head. I started thinking about all the times I could have killed myself or someone else while driving in a blackout, like the time I was headed for the Ravenswood neighborhood on the north side of Chicago and found myself driving downtown on Lower Wacker Drive, a road that snakes around under the city.

Ordinarily, I didn't drive drunk with my kids in the car. If they were in the car while I was loaded, it was for a short distance to and from a friend's home. Our playgroup, which used to plan field trips to the fire station, bakery, and random parks, had evolved into a moms' happy hour thanks to me. As the kids got older and their interests diversified, I decided to throw a playgroup cocktail hour, and it caught on.

"I dressed up my drinking," I told Jason. "I drank good vodka and good wine out of nice glasses, but I was just a drunk."

"You don't know how much that helps me to hear you say that," Jason said. "My mom and dad are alcoholics, but because they drink the right kinds of booze at the right times of day, they don't think they have a problem."

"My playgroup friends seemed perfect," I said. "They were perfect moms living in perfect houses raising perfect kids. I tried to look like them, too. I thought those five o'clock martinis were a sophisticated release."

"I can't even talk to my parents," Jason said. "I can't have an honest conversation with them even when they are sober. I haven't talked to them in months. Look what you're doing for your kids. It's awesome."

[Tuesday, May 13]

I've been judging Kelly. I think of her as a petty, manipulative, self-centered control freak, and an insecure whacko who needs to believe everyone likes her best. She collects people and tries to be everyone's best friend. She spreads herself around like manure.

The last time I talked to Kelly, she said, "I don't think Fiona likes me. I've been trying to invite her and Carl over for dinner and something's wrong with every night I suggest. I went to Rosy's yesterday and just happened to look at her calendar. She and Fiona have dinner plans for the same night I tried to make dinner plans with Fiona. I asked Rosy when they made those plans, so I know I asked first. I guess Fiona likes Rosy but not me."

Fiona would never slight anyone, so I know there's more to this story.

"Rosy's friend, Sandra, doesn't like me either," Kelly continued. "When I was there yesterday, Sandra was over and she seemed irritated, like I was crashing their little party."

Kelly actually told Liv that Liv's twelve-year-old son, Pete, didn't like her.

[Friday, May 16]

I got the kids and dog in the car and made it to Lakeside, Michigan, by two this afternoon. I've never been to the cottage without Martha. Charlie and his sibs inherited the place when she died last summer, and this is the place I fell off the wagon eight years ago.

I pulled the Jeep into the driveway and started feeling off kilter. Martha was not sitting on the front porch smoking a cigarette and drinking a martini. I loved hanging out and partying with Martha. I'd drive up, and Martha would pour me a stiff one. I'd unpack and we'd sit on the front porch and I'd bum smokes off her. We'd talk and laugh and drink the weekend away.

When I walked into the cottage, the first thing I noticed was a martini cart, a martini shrine, really, that wasn't here the last time I was. Martha must have set it up last summer—silver tray, shaker, triangular glass—before she'd called Charlie's brother, Chris, and asked him to come to the cottage and take her to the hospital. She had spent a month at the cottage painting for an upcoming art show and had started having difficulty breathing. Charlie drove with Chris to get their mother. Chris drove Martha to Northwestern Hospital in Chicago and Charlie drove Martha's car back to her apartment. Months later, Martha died of lung cancer.

I looked at the martini cart longingly. I missed Martha. I missed my martinis with her. I began weighing my options: I could go to the corner store and pick up a bottle of vodka, or I could call my sponsor.

"Let's go to the beach," Max said.

"I want to go," Van said. "I want to go to the beach."

I handed Max a bottle of bubbles, a huge bubble wand, and a dipping tray. "Take Van outside and make some bubbles," I said. "We'll go to the beach in a couple minutes." I looked in the cabinet under the sink. There was a bottle of cheap vodka with a shot or two left in it. I shut the door and called Sara. She didn't answer. I left a message on her voicemail telling her I felt like drinking but was going to the beach. I filled Sturgis's dog dish with water, grabbed some sand toys, and walked to the beach with the boys. Van and I filled pail after pail with sand, and I dumped out crude castles that he promptly smashed with his feet. Max dug a huge trench with a garden shovel. As far as the eye could see, the boys and I had the lake to ourselves.

It was beautiful and peaceful, and I was content. I wanted to freeze us in the moment. Later, when we walked back to the cottage for dinner, I no longer wanted a drink.

[Tuesday, May 20]

Back home, Sara and I met at Starbucks. She told me I needed to go to more meetings.

"You should go to your favorite meetings every week so people get to know you, expect you, worry if you don't show up," she said. "Don't schedule things that conflict with them."

I used to go to a Monday night meeting I liked, but I ditched it for a yoga class. I also blew off the Saturday meeting I used to go to for tennis lessons.

"Hit at least four meetings a week," Sara said.

I don't know about four.

I decided to make the women's meeting tonight my "home group" and I went with Eve. "Is there anything affecting anyone's sobriety that they wish to discuss?" the chairwoman asked. A woman introduced herself and started crying. She said that her mother was in the hospital dying of alcoholism.

"If she lives, if she pulls through, I wonder if she'll get it," the woman sobbed. "I don't understand why some people can get sober and others can't."

"Sobriety's a gift," one woman said. "Nobody knows why some receive the gift and others don't, but for whatever reason, we've been chosen."

"I'm grateful I've been chosen," a woman named Kate said. "I'm grateful I'm an alcoholic. When I first got sober, I'd hear people say they were grateful they were alcoholics and I'd think, *What?! You're crazy!* But I wouldn't have this program if I weren't an alcoholic, I wouldn't have the tools to live the good life I have today."

Deidre, fresh out of jail, said, "I drank last Tuesday. Things were going good, too good, so I sabotaged myself. It felt like good things were happening to me at the expense of other people."

It felt like the air got sucked out of the room.

"Deidre, your going to jail scared me straight, or at least straighter," I said. "What happened to you could have happened to me. It still could if I drink again. I might not be lucky if I drive in a blackout again. I felt untouchable before, but I don't now."

"I'm glad my jail time did you some good, Brenda," Deidre joked. We all laughed, but Deidre's eyes looked sad.

"I still want to drink, though," I continued. "I was at our cottage last weekend and I came close. Honestly, I don't know why I didn't."

Iris spoke next. "You know what's strange? We feel comfortable telling people our drinking war stories, but we're uncomfortable saying we're sober and in recovery. I work in an emergency room and some drunk came in passed out, some young guy. He was a John Doe for a while because he had no ID. When he came to, he had no idea where he was. The nurses were scratching their heads about this blackout thing and I was like, 'Oh yeah, that happened to me all the time. I'd wake up and not remember how I got where I was.' They were like, 'Really?' But never in a million years would I have said, 'But I don't drink anymore. I work a recovery program.'"

That's the paradox. If people know you're in a recovery program, you're sick, but as long as you're still partying, you're okay.

"I'm having a Memorial Day kickoff meeting at seven thirty Friday night, at my house," Tracy said. "Everyone's invited."

Eve and I got into her car. "Why don't we go to Tracy's?" she said. "I know how to get there, sort of. I'll ask Darcy to come. She knows how to get there."

"I'll drive," I said.

"Pick me up at six thirty."

[Friday, May 23]

I was getting dinner ready when the phone rang.

"Hi, Brenda," Eve said all slurry. "How are you?"

"Fine," I said warily. "How are you?"

"Well, I'm not going to the meeting tonight," she said.

"No?"

"No. I, uh, I've been drinking."

"I can hear it in your voice."

"You can?"

"Are you okay?"

"Ah . . ."

"Stupid question. Do you want me to come over?"

"No. I don't want to stop you from going to the meeting."

"If you want me to come over, I will."

"But you really want to go to this meeting," Eve said.

"Do you want me to come over?"

"Me, ask for help?" she asked.

"I'll come over if you want me to."

"Me, ask for help?"

"Do you want me to come?"

"If you want to."

"I'm going to have dinner with my family, then I'll come over. Have you eaten? Do you want me to bring you dinner?"

Eve said she'd eaten, but I doubted it. I hung up the phone and slid to the floor. Shit! I didn't want to go to her house. Charlie walked in and looked at me sitting on the floor. I filled him in and he shrugged. I put dinner on the table and began eating with my family. The phone rang.

"I feel bad making you miss the meeting," Eve said, sounding babyish and sad. "Don't come. Go to your meeting."

"I'm coming over as soon as I'm done with dinner."

"Okay."

I finished eating and called Darcy.

"Hi! What a pleasant surprise," Darcy said. "I'm so glad you called."

Apparently Eve never invited Darcy to go to Tracy's meeting with us tonight because when I told her I wasn't picking her up, she had no idea what I was talking about.

"I hope I'm not breaking any rules," I said, "but Eve's drunk and I'm supposed to go over there in a couple of minutes. I don't know what to do."

"I'm not surprised," Darcy said. "I know her pattern. I've called her every day for the last three days and she hasn't returned my calls. I knew this was coming."

"I'm in over my head here," I said.

"How's your sobriety?" Darcy asked.

"I'm not worried about drinking, if that's what you mean," I said. "I just don't know what I'm supposed to do when I get there."

"I babysat her a number of times," Darcy said. "I pour out her booze, sit with her for a while, then she passes out. Is this about her boyfriend?"

"When she called she said it was about everything."

"She called you?" Darcy asked sounding hurt.

"I'll call you later," I said.

I drove to Eve's and rang the bell to her townhouse. No answer. I turned the doorknob and let myself in.

"Eve?" I yelled, walking in.

A weak little voice floated down from the second floor. "I'm up here."

I glanced around. It was the first time I'd been to Eve's house. It was decorated with southwestern art and mounds of clutter. I climbed the stairs and maneuvered past boxes, stacks of paper, piles of clothing. Eve was sitting in the middle of a king-size bed, cross-legged, her white sweats contrasting with the yellow-stained pillows. Her mauve and turquoise comforter was crumpled at the foot of her bed.

"Hi, Sweetie," she purred. "You came. Why did you come?"

"Because I'm your friend and I'm worried about you."

"Why do you like me?"

"You're smart, funny, you're fun to be around."

"Really? I am?" she asked, cocking her head and grinning. "But why do you want to be my friend?"

"I just told you."

"But I could be your mother," she said pouting like a toddler. "I'm fifty-two. What do you want to be friends with me for?"

"You were thirteen when I was born." We both laughed.

"Am I pathetic?" Eve asked. "Do you think I'm pathetic?"

"No."

"Why do you like me?"

"I already told you."

"But why do you like me?"

I repeated the list and Eve hugged me. She grabbed my hands and kissed them multiple times.

"You're so cute," she said. "Look at you. I used to be you." A nasty gleam flickered in her eyes. "I had everything. I never had to worry about anything. Now I'm broke. And Mel, Mel . . ." She closed her eyes and swayed her head. "You should go home to your little family."

"You're going through a rough patch," I said. "It'll get better."

"This is the first time my business has been bad," she moaned.

"You'll pull out of it," I said. "Business is like that."

She closed her eyes and nodded. "Mel, Mel," she said swaying again. "I haven't talked to him in a week." She opened her eyes and leaned toward me. "Do you know I haven't talked to him in a week?"

"Why not?"

"I haven't called him back."

"That'll do it. You know, you never have anything good to say about the guy. You complain about him all the time. Maybe you should move on."

"Really?" she said, opening one eye.

"Do you love him?" I asked.

She closed her eye and nodded. "I haven't talked to him in a week," she repeated.

"Why don't we call him?" I said. "Do you want him to come over?" I wanted Mel to come over so I could get the hell out of there.

Eve nodded and I picked up the phone. "What's his number?" I asked. Eve recited a number, and I dialed it and an operator came on the line and told me I didn't need to dial the area code. I had Eve repeat the number and dialed it without the area code. The line began ringing before I finished punching in the numbers. I tried again with the same result. It was like using a hotel phone where you need to dial nine to get an outside line. Eve runs her business out of her home. Maybe it was something like that, but she couldn't explain how her phone worked or dial it herself. I pulled my cell phone out of my purse. "What's his number?" I asked again. I dialed it and it was the wrong number.

"Am I pathetic?" Eve asked.

"No," I said, although I was thinking *yes.*

"Look at me."

"You're a drunk," I said lightly. "Just like me."

"Why do you like me?" she asked again, fingering an empty pack of cigarettes.

"Do you want me to get you some cigarettes?" I asked.

"That's okay," she said.

"No, really," I said. "I could use one myself. I'll go and get you a pack."

Eve wanted Virginia Slims menthols. Yuck. I left and drove to the drugstore around the corner. My phone rang and it was Jason. He was in line waiting to see a movie. I told Jason about Eve.

"Are you tempted to join her?" he asked sounding worried.

"Are you kidding?" I said. "She's pathetic."

"Stay away from her," he said.

"That's probably good advice," I agreed.

I left the store and went back to Eve's. She was passed out, so I left her cigarettes on her nightstand and left. I looked at my watch. I was missing Max's soccer game, but I could make the last bit. I drove to the complex and watched Max's team win. I was grateful I wasn't drunk. I was grateful I had a family. I was grateful I wasn't Eve.

[Saturday, May 24 (Memorial Day Weekend)]

I called Eve three times and left messages. I went to a meeting, and Kat pulled me aside afterward.

"I don't know how to say this," she said. "I don't like talking behind people's backs, but I know you've been hanging around Eve and I know a flight attendant who's new in sobriety and

Eve called her—Eve relapses a lot—and Eve got her to drink with her. I've been thinking a lot about you and worrying about this. And Eve's dishonest. I ran into her boyfriend, Mel, at a meeting and I said, 'Hey, I met your fiancé, Eve,' and he said, 'She's not my fiancé.' And you know, Brenda, Eve's been calling me and wanting to get together since I met her. And I liked her. To hear her talk, she has ten years of sobriety. I was even considering her as a sponsor. Then Mel tells me she hasn't been able to string together six months without a drink.

"So I called Eve," Kat continued. "I told her she needed a Fourth Step, she needed to make a searching and fearless moral inventory of herself. I told her she was screaming for it. She got really angry. So I just wanted to tell you to watch out."

"Thanks," I said. "I'll keep my distance."

Kat is intense. She goes off in five directions at once and it's often difficult to follow her train of thought. She has no qualms about telling you what to do, either. But she's super intelligent, insightful, and has a knack for nailing exactly what's going on.

I got home and Charlie told me Eve called. I didn't call her back. I began getting ready for my book club friend Tina's fortieth birthday party.

Tina's party was a retro disco bash at a swanky hotel. Charlie and I walked around, talked to friends, ate appetizers, got drinks. I was okay until people began hitting the dance floor. I really wanted a glass of wine just to loosen up. I pushed the thought out of my head, took a deep breath, and coaxed Charlie onto the dance floor. I felt awkward. The last time I'd danced sober I was a kid at a relative's wedding, ignoring my mother's Adventists-don't-dance glares. But after a few minutes, I hit my groove and it felt good. Nice.

[Sunday, May 25]

I went to a two-hour meditation workshop this morning with Fiona and Fay. We explored breathing and visualization techniques, and as I sat cross-legged on the floor staring at a white card with a Sanskrit symbol on it, I began thinking about the groceries I needed to buy. I refocused on the card and started thinking about the story I was writing. I concentrated on my breathing and noticed my leg falling asleep. This went on for two agonizing hours but, amazingly, I felt a peace and calm afterward that lasted the rest of the day.

We got together at Fiona's later for a barbecue, and Fiona was still riding her peaceful, easy feeling. She was drinking a glass of white wine and Fay was drinking a beer. I grabbed an iced tea from a cooler filled with juice boxes for the kids and felt annoyed that my drinks were in the baby box. There went my serenity. Fiona began carrying appetizers from the kitchen to the screened porch where everyone had gathered, and I followed her to the kitchen to help. My gaze fell on a sweaty bottle of chardonnay sitting on the kitchen counter. Inwardly, I was salivating like Pavlov's dog. I recalled the flavor of chardonnay and how good it made me feel. If I had a glass, I'd have another and another and another. I'd wake up the next morning hung over, vowing not to drink again. I'd find myself shaking up a martini at five. I let out a deep breath and carried a tray of vegetables to the deck. I noticed Fiona and Fay had barely made a dent in their drinks. Drinking like that would drive me nuts.

[Monday, May 26]

I joined a tennis league and played my second match this morning. I got my butt kicked. I called Eve and left a message telling her I needed pointers on my serve. Eve told me, more than once, that she used to be a great tennis player. She said she had many tennis trophies. They must be packed away in one of the many cardboard boxes strewn about her home because I didn't see any.

[Thursday, May 29]

Wisconsin Whitley, a woman I like from the Tuesday night meeting, met me at Starbucks this morning and told me her drunk story. She said her husband had been unhappy with her drinking for ten years, but he'd done nothing about it.

"He'd bring me coffee in bed every morning because I was too hung over to get it myself," she laughed. "I got in a recovery program because 'we' got a DUI. I say 'we' because he got the DUI, but it was my fault. We were both on the Atkins diet. You can't drink beer, but you can drink hard alcohol. We were up in Wisconsin at our cabin and we'd gone out to dinner with friends. We got really lit. My husband wanted to go back to our cabin, which was five minutes away, but I'd told my seventeen-year-old son we'd be home that night. I got nasty and insisted we drive the hour-and-a-half back home. Five minutes away from our house, we got pulled over. The police gave my husband a field sobriety test on the side of the road, and as he was trying to walk a straight line, my son and his friends drove by."

Wisconsin Whitley and I looked at each other and cringed.

"Yeah," she said. "It was bad. The police took my husband to jail and drove me home. My son and his friends were there when they dropped me off. I was mortified. Then my husband had to go to drunk driving school. He started learning about alcoholism and realized how bad I was. He made me get into treatment."

I think I found a normal recovering friend. Yea.

[Saturday, May 31]

I went to a meeting this morning, and a guy named Dave said he'd finished college and gone out with some of his classmates last night to celebrate.

"I was the only one not drinking," he said. "I was fine with it but it felt a little weird. I've been sober eight years and it wasn't like I wanted to drink, but it tweaked my brain in a small way."

That's it. It tweaks your brain, apparently even after eight years.

I called Sara and told her about my Memorial Day barbecue at Fiona's and how I thought about having a glass of wine but thought it through to the hangover and didn't drink. I told her the party tweaked my brain a little but it was refreshing to hang out with light normal drinkers.

"If you keep putting yourself in situations like that, you're going to drink," Sara said. "Most newcomers avoid drinking situations like the plague. Maybe they go to a family wedding or a mandatory work party, but they hightail it out of there early. Most old-timers do the same. You question your motives before you attend a drinking event. If you have a good reason for going, go. If you don't, stay home."

Wisconsin Whitley told me, "I can't bear to go into a nice restaurant with my husband because not drinking would really get to me."

I am sick of being in situations where my brain is constantly tweaked, but I don't want to give up my friends or normal socializing. I don't want to pack my nights with meetings and sober whackos like a lot of people in recovery do.

[Sunday, June 1]

Reed and Liv had us over for a cookout. Before we left, I told Charlie he was damned lucky I was socializing with our drinking friends.

"Don't accept invitations on my account," Charlie said, looking sheepish.

"Well, it doesn't seem fair to screw up your social life," I snapped. "People wouldn't snort lines of coke in front of a cokehead who was trying to straighten out, but people guzzle booze in front of me constantly."

I went into the bathroom and cried. I fixed myself up and Charlie and I went to Reed and Liv's.

Sometimes I think it'd be easier if I were a drug addict. Neighbors don't throw backyard heroin parties. No one offers you crack at baby showers. Magazines aren't full of slick ads for crystal meth. I'm grateful I'm not wasting more precious time being drunk, but sometimes having a drink seems like a really good idea.

[Monday, June 2]

Eve called and left a message this afternoon. She was slurring so badly I listened to the message twice before I realized it was her. I didn't call Eve back.

Later, when I was at a meeting, a beaten-down guy said, "I had a relapse. As a result, I got a DUI, went to jail, and lost my job. I'm thirty-nine and living with my father again. I'm riding my father's bicycle to get around or my dad has to drive me. Shit. I'm thirty-nine. I'd been sober two years then one day, out of nowhere, I decided I could have a beer. I controlled my drinking for a while, but a year and a half later, this is where I am."

"It's weird," I said, when it was my turn to speak, "I can appreciate sobriety so much, love that I'm living a more vivid, rich life, then bam, I feel like having a drink. I constantly have to convince myself that I'm an alcoholic. I'm sick of it. I start thinking, *I wasn't that bad. Everyone in the program is way worse than me.* Then I remind myself I wanted to have a baby so I would quit drinking."

Wisconsin Whitley was sitting across the table from me and looked shocked. When we had coffee at Starbucks, I had gone on and on about how wonderful my life was now that I'm sober.

An old hippie dude spoke. "If you don't think you're an alcoholic, why don't you try some controlled drinking?" he asked condescendingly.

Stupid bastard. Didn't he listen? I called Sara on my way home and bitched to her about the hippie prick. She started laughing.

"You'll run into guys like that," she said. "Those drinking thoughts are totally normal. You're a normal alcoholic. The important thing to remember is what happens after the first drink and where it takes you."

I told Sara about Eve, how I'd gone to her townhouse to help her when she was plastered.

"Don't go over to a drunk's house when they've been drinking," she said. "You don't know what they'll do. Wait until they've sobered up and take someone with you. It's pointless to try to reason with someone when they're drunk. Nothing you say is going to matter. Besides, why's a woman who's been in the program for ten years calling someone like you? Think about that."

[Tuesday, June 3]

I went to my favorite women's meeting tonight and when Tracy, who chairs it, asked, "Is there anything affecting anyone's sobriety that they wish to discuss?" a woman raised her hand and said, "Sue, alcoholic," then began sobbing. She looked familiar. It dawned on me that she was the one who pulled me aside at one of my first meetings and told me her husband was addicted to computer porn.

"My husband went to Indiana on one of those men's spiritual retreats," she said. "He left a week ago. He hasn't called, and I don't know who he's with or where he is or if he's using or if he's dead." She blew her nose and wiped at the tears streaming down her face.

"He's my third husband," Sue continued. "I married my first two husbands when I was young. I was sober thirteen years before I married this one. I met him in recovery. I thought I'd picked a winner."

A recovering winner? Thank God I'm not single. I have not come across one man I find desirable at meetings. Poor Sue. My heart hurts for her.

[Wednesday, June 4]

Darcy and I went out to dinner and talked about Eve.

"My sponsor doesn't think it's a good idea for me to be friends with Eve," I told Darcy. "But if I write her off, what does that say about me? She needs help. I'd be a bad friend."

"So this is about you?" Darcy asked. "The best thing you can do for Eve is leave her alone when she's drinking. I told her I'd be there for her when she wasn't drinking and I hoped she didn't kill herself in the process. Besides, I've got issues with her drinking. I broke up with my boyfriend five months ago, lost my job, and I didn't drink. It pisses me off that Eve gets to drink."

[Thursday, June 5]

Here I go with more Kelly crap. My book club buddies and I went to Margaret's to discuss *The Samurai's Garden*. Fiona, Tina, Nosey Rosy, and Kelly were already there eating appetizers in the kitchen when I arrived. Fiona was telling Tina, "Your fortieth birthday party was a blast."

"Yeah," Tina grinned. "It was fun."

"I loved the CD of disco tunes you burned for party favors," Fiona added.

"Yeah," I said, grabbing a nacho. "The cover of you in a bikini looking like a '70s Barbie doll is hot."

"What CD?" Kelly asked irritably. Kelly hadn't gone to Tina's party. She'd invited Reed and Liv to her Indiana beach house that weekend. "I'd like to see that CD."

"I've got one in my car," Tina said, bouncing out of the house to get it.

"I wonder if she's got extras?" I said. "I didn't get one. Fiona showed me hers on our way to a meditation workshop we went to the next morning."

Kelly turned toward Fiona. "You went to a meditation workshop? I'd like to do that. Where was it?"

"Brenda told Fay and me about it," Fiona said. "It was at the yoga studio she goes to. It was great."

"Let me know if you do that again," Kelly said, shooting me a saccharine smile.

Tina walked in with her CD. Kelly began smirking. Tina handed it to Kelly, and Kelly's smirk faded as soon as she saw how great Tina looked. Kelly tossed the CD on the counter and shoved a nacho into her mouth.

We moved the food into the living room and sat down to discuss the book. I sat on one end of Margaret's couch, Kelly sat next to me, and Nosey Rosy sat on the other end. "Okay, here goes," Margaret said, and began reading discussion questions.

Kelly began whispering something to Rosy, and the two began giggling.

"How do you think the flowers got into Sachi's rock garden?" Margaret asked.

"I think Matsu planted them there as a surprise," Kelly said.

"I don't think so," I disagreed. "Sachi didn't want flowers and I don't think Matsu would have dishonored her. I think wildflowers took root and were a metaphor for beauty appearing in unlikely and inhospitable places."

Kelly snorted and whispered to Rosy.

Margaret read a question that used the word *juxtaposition*. "I'm not sure what that means," she said.

"Me either," Karen said.

"It's when things are put together that don't seem to fit," I said.

"Thank goodness we have a little dictionary," Kelly sniped.

I wanted to shove Kelly off the couch.

"Who's having book club next?" Margaret asked.

"Me," Kelly said.

"What are we reading?" Margaret asked.

"*The Notebook* by Nicholas Sparks," Kelly said. "It's such a sweet book. So well written."

I snorted and went to the bathroom.

[Friday, June 6]

Kelly has always had a cruel streak. I just never noticed it until I got sober. Shitty things she's done keep popping into my head like her "involuntary hand jerk" that caused her to throw a glass of wine down the front of my dress.

Kelly had thrown a party for Rita, one of our playgroup pals who'd moved away but was back in town visiting. It was a hot summer night and I was wearing a long, clingy, lavender sundress. Kelly eyeballed me good when I walked in. After we'd eaten, most of the women clustered in the kitchen and all of a sudden Kelly, who was standing opposite me, jerked her wineglass in my direction, dousing me with chardonnay. Everyone stood there for a long silent moment. Then Kelly put her hand to her mouth and started giggling.

"I, I just don't even know what happened," she said. "Oh my God, I'm so sorry. I don't know . . ." She looked at her glass like it was possessed and laughed harder. I started laughing because I was wasted.

"You're lucky it's not red wine," I said, reaching for club soda to rub into my dress. Everyone else started laughing, too.

Then there was the time the boys and I were at Kelly and Joel's Indiana beach house for the weekend. Kelly and I had done some heavy drinking, and the next day I was nursing a wicked hangover while trying to read a book on her back deck. Joel was chain-sawing tree after tree on a bluff behind their house. He and Kelly wanted it denuded of pesky trees that obscured their view of the water. Their neighbors, aghast, watched and shook their heads. When Joel finished whacking trees, I noticed Max and Ryan playing cops and robbers. They disappeared behind one side of the house, then Max came running around the other side going way too fast and as the bluff dropped off, he tumbled and cartwheeled—thump, crash, thud—down the steep incline like a rag doll. I threw down my book and sprinted toward Max, tripping and stumbling over recently felled trees and stumps. Max hit a fresh stump midway down the hill, flew up into the air one last time, and landed facedown with a sickening thud.

I knelt next to Max, who wasn't moving. I put a hand on his back and gently stroked it. "Max, are you okay Sweetie?" I asked, trying not to sound panicked. "Can you move, Buddy? Does anything feel really bad?"

Max slowly pushed himself up onto all fours and started to cry. I pulled him onto my lap and rocked him.

"Is Max okay?" Kelly called out from an upper deck. She started laughing.

I couldn't believe it. Kelly was laughing. I didn't answer her. I continued to hold Max while he cried and then helped him hobble back to the deck where Kelly was standing.

"You okay, Max?" she chuckled. "You looked so funny coming down the hill. You okay, big guy?"

Max and I ignored her and limped into the house. Kelly followed. I took Max into the bathroom and cleaned him up. I'd planned to drive home with Van that afternoon and leave Max to spend an extra night with Ryan, but there was no way in hell I was leaving him now. "You're coming home with me, Peanut," I told him. "After we get you fixed up, we're leaving."

"Good," he said.

I packed up, thanked Kelly for having us, and told her Max was going home.

"Why?" she asked, putting on her sad puppy face. "Ryan will be so disappointed. Why don't you stay, Max?"

Max just stared at her.

"He fell down a bluff full of jagged stumps, Kelly. He's lucky he didn't break or puncture anything. We're going home."

The day we arrived, Kelly had taken us out on her speedboat. It was Max's first time tubing, and the donut-shaped tube we were dragging was large enough for the boys to ride at the same time. Ryan immediately claimed a spot on one end saying, "This is the side I always take," and Max hunkered down on the other side. Max, not a daredevil, was a little nervous. I gave him the thumbs up sign and held onto Van as Kelly took off. She soon got her boat up to breakneck speed and began slaloming. I could see Max gritting his teeth and hanging on for dear life. I flashed him the thumbs-up sign. Kelly whipped the boat into a tight circle and yanked the tube into a donut spin. Ryan, having experienced the centrifugal force, had claimed the best spot on the tube and was solidly in place. Max had a death grip on the tube while the bottom half of his body flopped on the water. Kelly slowed the boat down, created slack in the towrope, and gunned the engine. The towrope snapped tight and the tube whiplashed forward, sending Max flying. Kelly circled around. Max was bobbing in the water hugging his life vest. He grabbed the tube as it came around and shouted, "I'm done," and gave the throat slashing signal.

I hate Kelly.

[Saturday, June 7]

I called Eve to see how she was doing. She sounded sober, but not good.

"My sisters should be here any minute," she said. "They're worried about me."

"Want to go to a meeting later?" I asked.

"I'm in no shape to go to a meeting. I'm shaking like a leaf. You could come over after my sisters leave. They probably won't stay long."

"I'm home with Van," I said. "Charlie and Max are Rollerblading and swimming. They're coming home so I can hit the four o'clock. I could swing by after the meeting. Do you want me to bring you dinner?"

"I can't keep anything down. I keep throwing up. You remember how that was?"

"Yeah," I said, wondering if she felt like I did in Sarasota, Florida.

When Max was two, Martha took Max and me to Sarasota to escape a cold, damp Chicago spring. We flew, but Charlie said he and his siblings always made that trip by car to visit family. He said that Martha would dope him and his sibs up on Dramamine, wave good-bye to their father, who was staying behind to work, and hit the road.

Charlie was nervous about Max and me going. Every evening he would call at six sharp and ask, "How's it going? Where's Max? Is he on the balcony?" Charlie was familiar with the high-rise condo we were staying at. His uncle had built it, and Charlie was envisioning Max toddling around on the balcony and falling over the railing while Martha and I sucked down martinis.

Martha and I were getting lit, but to a respectable degree, I thought, and I always had my eye on Max. However, one night toward the end of the week, Martha and I (emphasis on "I") polished off half a fifth of vodka before dinner and drank a bottle of wine with dinner, and as we began clearing the dishes and loading the dishwasher, I poured myself another glass of vodka.

"There's no detergent for the dishwasher," Martha mumbled and pulled her head out of the cabinet below the kitchen sink.

"That's okay," I said, grabbing a bottle of Joy off the counter. "I'll use this."

"You think it's okay?" she asked.

"Why not?" I said, squeezing Joy into the dishwasher and turning it on. "I'm taking Max to bed now." I helped Max into his pajamas, brushed his teeth, and read him bedtime stories, even though the words were moving together and doubling up on the page. As I tucked Max into his crib, Martha started shouting, "The dishwasher! The dishwasher!" I turned off the bedroom light and jogged into the kitchen where I found Martha standing in front of the dishwasher ankle-deep in soapsuds. More suds were rapidly oozing from the sides of the dishwasher. Martha threw me a roll of paper towels and I waded in.

"Guess I shouldn't have used the Joy," I said. I put the paper towels on the counter and began scooping suds from the floor onto my arms and scraping the suds off my arms into the sink.

"Yeah," Martha said. She was on all fours trying to push suds into a collapsed plastic garbage bag. I started laughing hysterically then Martha started laughing. We were Lucy and Ethel. That's the last thing I remember that night.

The next morning, I couldn't lift my head off the pillow. Eventually, I rolled out of bed, crawled to the bathroom, vomited, and crawled back into bed—a sequence I repeated off and on for the rest of the day. Martha, miraculously, seemed fine, which I was grateful for because I was physically unable to care for Max. I remember thinking, *Martha can really handle her liquor. What an alcoholic.*

Late that afternoon, I gingerly shuffled into the kitchen to look for crackers. There was a tiny sip of vodka left in the bottle from the night before and I wondered, "How much did Martha drink?"

• • •

I told Eve, "I'll call you when the meeting's over. Maybe you'll feel like eating then." I hung up and started thinking about my high school and college days when I'd go to parties, get drunk, and throw up, and whatever guy I happened to be with would be waiting for me to wipe the vomit from my lips so we could resume making out. One summer night, I was at a rugby party staggering around in tight jeans and stiletto heels. I was talking to a cute rugby player and drinking beer after beer from an enormous plastic cup. All of a sudden, besides having the urge to pee really bad, I knew I was going to get sick.

"I have to go to the bathroom," I told the rugby player and began staggering toward a row of portable toilets. The rugby player followed me. "I'll be back in a minute," I said waving him off. He kept following me. Long lines of people were waiting for the toilets so I took a turn down an alley, braced myself against a brick wall and began vomiting. I finished, wiped my mouth, and unsteadily turned to leave. The rugby player grabbed me and forced his tongue down my throat.

• • •

I went to the four o'clock women's meeting and told Sara what was going on with Eve.

"Don't go over there," Sara said. "It's too dangerous."

"Dangerous?" I said, trying hard not to laugh. "That's ridiculous."

"You don't go over to someone's house when they've been actively drinking like that," she said. "If you take her to a meeting and go out afterward, that's fine."

"She's in no condition to go out. She's shaking like a leaf."

"You know how many meetings I went to shaking?" Sara asked. "Eve's been around long enough. She knows. And the fact that she's calling you and not someone who's been in recovery a long time . . . Don't go."

"So what do I do?" I asked. "She's expecting me to call."

"Call her and tell her you can't come over. Tell her you'd be happy to take her to a meeting, but you can't come over."

I took a big breath and sighed. I got into my Jeep, pulled out my cell phone, and called Eve.

"Hello," Eve answered, sounding drunk. Apparently, things hadn't gone too well with her sisters.

"Eve," I said, "I've been thinking. I really care about you and what happens to you. I want to do what will help you the most. So I'd like to take you to a meeting and maybe go out afterward. I can't come over without doing that first."

"I understand," she said, slurring. "And thanks. Thanks for caring about me."

"Do you want to go to a meeting tomorrow?"

"Why don't you give me a call?"

"I'll call you tomorrow."

Sara was still standing in the parking lot talking to someone. I rolled down my window as I drove past. "I did it," I said.

"Good," Sara said. "Are you going to Caribou for a little bit? Some of us are going for coffee."

"Uh, I could."

I drove to Caribou and spent the next forty-five minutes with six unbelievably boring women who talked about nothing besides drinking and getting sober.

[Sunday, June 8]

I didn't call Eve. I didn't feel like it.

[Monday, June 9]

Sara came over this morning for coffee. She was supposed to be here at ten but showed up just before eleven. I don't know how she runs the adolescent substance abuse program she's in charge of. She's habitually late and in a fog from her bipolar meds. Sara and I talked about my issues with Kelly, which are starting to bore even me. I can only imagine how damned boring my bitching and moaning must sound to Sara. I told Sara I wanted to confront Kelly.

"Why?" she asked.

"To let her know how I feel. To let her know she's been hurting my feelings."

"We don't do things that way," Sara said, shaking her head. "You have to think about what your motives are. What you want to do is make yourself feel like the better person, superior, make her feel bad. Do you really think you can change people?"

"Yeah, in some situations I think what I say might change someone's behavior."

Sara shook her head with a condescending I-know-more-than-you-know smile. "So you're not there yet," she said. "You'll get there."

Her smugness irked me. But I don't really believe confronting Kelly would do any good. Just recently Kelly told me, "Hey, I just went out to lunch with Charlene. She's my new best friend. I hate to tell you Bren, but Charlene is a better singer than you are."

"If you were one of my patients, I'd be an inch away from kicking you out of treatment," Sara told me.

"Why?" I asked.

"Because of all the old friendships you're maintaining, the socializing you're doing with them."

It bugs me how so many people in recovery think you can't hang out with anyone who drinks—like we can't be in spitting distance of alcohol. I don't want to hang out with only recovering alcoholics. A good number of them are loony bores who can't talk about anything other than their alcoholism. I just want a normal life.

[Wednesday, June 11]

The boys and I went to my sister Paula's house for lunch. She spent much of the time bitching about my father because Father's Day is coming up, and she's pissed at him for screwing up Mother's Day.

When my sister and I asked my father what we should do for Mother's Day, he said, "She's not my mother. You take her out. I'm going fishing." My sister and I planned a girls' day out, but when the weather turned foul, my father asked, "So what are we doing for Mother's Day?"

My sister lives in a far southwestern suburb of Chicago. It's an hour-and-twenty-minute drive from my parents' house as well as mine. I had suggested that my sister and I take our vegetarian mother to a vegetarian restaurant near my parents' house before my father horned in.

"Mom loves that restaurant, and Dad won't take her there because they don't serve steak and cocktails," I said.

"Why do I always have to drive the farthest?" my sister complained. "Why can't we meet halfway between Mom's house and mine? Oakbrook has nice restaurants. Mom can find something to eat without meat."

"It's Mother's Day," I said. "Let's go somewhere she can eat anything off the menu. Oakbrook's kind of far for Mom."

"Evanston's far for me. I'm a mother, too, you know."

"I already asked Mom if she wants to go to Blind Faith Cafe, and she wants to go."

Paula emitted a long, huffy sigh. "Next time we do something by me."

"Want to take her to a movie before dinner?" I asked.

"If I have to drive all the way to Evanston, we can't meet for dinner," Paula said. "I have to wake up early for work the next morning, so I want to go to bed early."

"You could be home by eight."

"We'll have to do lunch."

"Okay," I said. "I'll let mom know. Max has a soccer game at nine thirty in the morning in Wilmette. Maybe I'll drive to the game separately and go straight to Mom's since I'll be right around the corner. Actually, she might want to come to the game."

Another huffy sigh. "I guess I'll go to Mom's early. We could give her our presents before we eat. Maybe we could see a movie after lunch."

So that was the plan until my father decided to can his fishing trip.

"Why don't you, Paula, and your families come over here for dinner?" my father asked when I was talking to him on the phone.

"Why, so Mom can cook and clean on Mother's Day?" I asked.

"She doesn't mind."

"Give me a break."

"We could order Chinese food."

"She'd still have to clean up."

"Then why don't we go to your house?" he suggested. "I don't want to go to a restaurant. I'll end up paying the bill."

"Cheap ass," I laughed. "I could make dinner, but Paula's going to have a problem with it. She's not going to want to drive to my house."

"I don't want to drive to her house," he said grumpily. "We can have an early dinner at your house."

"You tell Paula then."

"I'll have your mother call her," he said.

My mother called my sister. My father, overhearing my mother agreeing to Paula's suggestion of going to her house for lunch and mine for dinner, picked up the phone and began yelling. Then he called me.

"Why don't you have everyone over for lunch?" my dad yelled. "I don't want to drive all the fuck the way out there!"

"Fine with me," I said and called my sister.

"He's spoiling everything!" Paula said and began crying. "Dad's ruining Mother's Day. He never wants to come to my house. Mom and Dad go to your house more than mine. Why should I always have to be the one driving the farthest? I'll just spend Mother's Day alone. Mom and Dad can go to your house, and I'll spend Mother's Day alone. No one wants to come here."

"I'd rather not have to cook," I said. "Let's have lunch at your house."

"Okay," Paula said, instantly sounding happier.

"What time do you think?"

"Eleven thirty. Then we can eat at noon."

"Max's soccer game ends at ten thirty," I said. "By the time he gets out of the locker room, it'll be eleven. We won't be able to get to your house till after twelve."

"Rick made plans with his family," Paula said testily. "If I have lunch any later, we won't be hungry when it's time to eat with his family."

"I am so sick of this," I said.

"Yeah, why did Dad have to ruin everything?"

"Have Mom and Dad over for lunch," I said wearily. "I'd actually prefer spending Mother's Day with just my kids," I lied.

"Yeah, that will be nice," Paula said. "Yeah, wow, that'll be really nice for you."

And that's how Mother's Day went.

• • •

"I'm not going out of my way to do anything for Dad on Father's Day," she said, plopping a bowl of salad on her kitchen table.

"He usually wants to go fishing with his friends on Father's Day, so that leaves us off the hook," I said.

"It wouldn't occur to him to take his family out on the boat for Father's Day," Paula said.

"I'm just going to give him a card and a gift," I said. At that moment, I decided to give my dad the two tickets I bought for Charlie and me to see Tony Bennett. I breathed a sigh of relief. It couldn't be simpler.

[Thursday, June 12]

Fiona called and we made a date to play tennis.

"I'm not sure if I'm going to read *The Notebook,*" Fiona mentioned casually.

"I read that drivel years ago," I said. "I already told Kelly I couldn't make her book club because I'm going to be in Michigan."

"Kelly and I have just not been on the same page lately," Fiona said.

"Same here."

"Things have been kind of strained between us," she added.

"Really? Between us, too."

"She's made comments that have been kind of mean."

"What's she said to you?"

"At the last book club I mentioned that Little Carl's Little League team was crushed after they lost their first game," Fiona said. "Carl coaches it, you know. Little Carl loves that his dad is the coach. Carl is great with the kids. The kids love him. They were on this huge winning streak and when they lost their first game, the kids were really bummed. Some of them cried.

Carl pulled the kids together and told them they were great in the field but their hitting was off. He scheduled an extra hitting practice and you could see that it made the kids feel better. I mentioned this at book club and Kelly rolled her eyes and cut me off and said, 'God, they're only nine!' Later, we were talking about something else and I started to say, 'If that was me . . .' and Kelly cut me off and said, 'This isn't about you.'"

I told Fiona a few of my Kelly stories. It felt good to commiserate with a fellow sufferer.

"I'd been wanting to say something to you for a while," Fiona said. "But you and Kelly were always such good friends. Then at book club I noticed things were off between you two."

"They were off, all right," I said. "They've been off for a while."

"I feel like saying something to Kelly," Fiona said. "I want to ask her, 'What's going on?'"

"I've been wanting to do the same thing," I said. "But a friend of mine who's a therapist told me it wouldn't do any good. She said Kelly would just get defensive and deny any mean intentions. I think she's right."

"Probably," Fiona said. "But I want to know if I've done anything to start this behavior."

"Well," I began hesitantly, "since we're having this conversation, Kelly told me she invited you and Carl over for dinner and you cancelled on her a few days later. She said she went to Rosy's house and saw that you and Rosy had dinner plans on the calendar for the night you cancelled."

"Absolutely not!" Fiona said angrily. "That's not what happened. Kelly and I talked about a tentative dinner date two months earlier. She was supposed to get back to me and never did. A week before the date, Kelly called to confirm, but I'd made other plans. Kelly knows what happened. God, I just don't have time for this stuff!

"I noticed Kelly began acting different when Rosy and I

started becoming better friends, like it bothered her," Fiona continued. "I don't know why she would be like that. She has so many friends. When you and Fay and I started seeing movies, she got cool and distant about that, too."

"Kelly didn't like it when I became friends with Liv, either," I said. "Then BAM, Kelly decided to make Liv her new best friend."

"I totally noticed that," Fiona said.

God, it felt good to be validated.

[Saturday, June 14]

Charlie and I went to Ravinia, a swanky outdoor concert venue, for Latin Jazz night with Kelly and Joel and Liv and Reed. Wendy and Tom bailed. It was my way of hosting the Bacchanal Dinner Club without actually hosting it. We all got lawn seats and I brought a picnic-basket dinner of poached salmon with a dill-and-chive sour cream sauce, grilled asparagus, and raspberry pie. Most concertgoers sitting on Ravinia's lawn bring snooty little picnic dinners. Kelly brought an appetizer, Liv brought a salad, and everyone brought their own booze. The food was good, the music was great, but it was cold and miserable. It was only fifty-some degrees and windy.

Reed and Joel had driven their motorcycles with Liv and Kelly on the back. As we sat and listened to the music, Kelly and Joel started pawing each other like two horny teenagers. Whenever Charlie and I went out to dinner with Joel and Kelly, they held hands under the table, made goo-goo eyes at each other, rubbed each other's legs, and God knows what else. They never acted like a couple who'd been sharing the same bed for eleven years and had a child. It was creepy. This evening, Kelly and Joel reclined on a blanket, entwined their legs, and kept rubbing up against each other. I looked at

Charlie sideways. It felt like I was back in high school sitting in the front seat of a car with my date trying to ignore my friend and her boyfriend getting it on in the back seat.

When the concert ended, I desperately wanted to ditch everyone. However, Liv and Kelly asked for a ride home because they didn't want to get on the motorcycles and freeze their asses off. They made inside jokes and giggled in the back seat. It sucked.

[Sunday, June 15 (Father's Day)]

The kids spent last night at my parents' house while Charlie and I were at Ravinia. This morning, I drove to my parents' house and picked them up. My father was out fishing, so I tossed his Father's Day card stuffed with Tony Bennett tickets on the dining room table, hung out with my mom for a while, and left. Back at home, Charlie and the kids and I went to the town carnival and had a ball.

[Tuesday, June 17]

I went to my home group meeting tonight and Tracy gave the lead.

"My neighbors have been irritating me," she said. "We've had issues ever since I put up a fence they don't like. They ignore me. They go out of their way to ignore me. And I've been dwelling on them and their behavior way too much. I have to remind myself not to care about what other people do. What other people think of me is none of my business."

What other people think of me is none of my business. I love that!

Liv and Wendy are cohosting a jewelry party for Kelly to peddle her beadwork. I don't want to go. Liv and Kelly together bug the shit out of me. And it bugs the shit out of me that it bugs the shit out of me. But like Tracy said, I have to not care about what they do, and what they think of me is none of my business.

[Thursday, June 19]

I had an unbelievably bizarre experience with the teachers at Van's preschool. Today was field-trip day, and I'd signed Max and myself up to be chaperones at the farm/petting zoo we were visiting. Max, Van, and I arrived at the preschool ahead of time and found it odd that the kids were already boarding the chartered school buses. I hurried my kids into the building to hook up with Van's class, and his classroom was empty. We high-tailed it out the front door and watched as the buses barreled down the street.

I hustled Max and Van into the director's office and told the athletic director, "We're here for the field trip. I thought we were here early, but the buses just left."

"They changed the time," Randy said. "Didn't they tell you?"

"No."

"They didn't? Wow. Um, I think they put an announcement on the sign-in sheet clip board. Let's see if I can reach one of Van's teachers on her cell phone. Maybe I can get a bus to turn around and come back."

About a week ago, I had overheard Van's teachers, Isabel and Casey, griping to each other about parents not reading their memos. They were always complaining about something or other, and I usually ignored them. Apparently, I shouldn't have. Isabel and Casey had decided to clip a time-change memo to the sign-in sheet in the front hall to reward those who read their memos and punish those who didn't. I'd spoken to them numerous times about Max and me chaperoning, and not once did they breathe a word about the time change.

"I can't reach either of them on their phones," Randy said and frowned. "Tell the program director about this. Please."

"We're not going?" Van asked sadly.

"We're going," I told him. I looked at Randy. "You can bet I'll be talking to the program director about this."

The kids and I drove to the farm and pulled into the lot just as Van's friends were climbing off the bus. Linda, the newly appointed assistant program director, rushed toward us.

"I'm so sorry," Linda said. "I told them to stop the bus. I was sitting all the way in the back with the kids, but they wouldn't stop the bus. I'm so sorry. I should have gotten up and made them stop. I should have done that. I'm so sorry."

I began picturing what happened. Casey and Isabel hated Linda because Casey wanted Linda's assistant director job. Surly, condescending, short-tempered Casey didn't get it. I visualized Linda yelling, "Stop the bus!" while Casey and Isabel smirked at each other and told the bus driver to keep going. As Linda apologized, I began staring daggers at Isabel and Casey. Neither would look at me.

Our group made our way to the cow-milking shelter. Marie, another mom who was chaperoning, grabbed my arm and pulled me aside.

"I just have to tell you," Marie said, "Isabel and Casey purposely left you. I got to school a few minutes before you did. I didn't know about the time change either. My son and I got on the bus in the nick of time, and the kids started yelling, 'Van's here! Van's here!' and Isabel and Casey told the bus driver to leave."

I glared at Isabel and Casey throughout the day. They both

looked really uncomfortable. Not once did they glance my way.

As the kids and I were driving home, I remembered Eve and I were supposed to play tennis. I was never going to make it. I fished around in my purse for my meeting directory, dug it out, flipped it over, and scanned the list of phone numbers I'd written on the back.

"Call before you drink . . ." Max read out loud as he looked at the heading on the back of my directory. "Why is that on there, over these numbers? Drinking wasn't a problem for you."

"It's just something the No Alcohol Club gives everyone," I told Max, feeling prickly heat on my neck and face. "It doesn't mean anything." I called Eve and left a message. I started thinking, *You know, maybe Max is right. Maybe I don't have a drinking problem.*

When we got home, Eve had left a message on my answering machine saying she wanted to meet me at a meeting.

I arrived at the meeting and sat next to Cece, a woman about my age. I told her what Max had said about my not having a drinking problem in the car.

"Wow," Cece said. "Isn't that great he wasn't affected, that he didn't notice? My daughter knows. She knows I have a drinking problem."

"Thanks," I said. "It didn't occur to me to be grateful. You know where my mind went? 'Maybe I'm not an alcoholic.'"

"Typical," Cece laughed.

After the meeting, Eve and I went to Liv and Wendy's jewelry party. It was actually fun. Eve left an hour before I did and as I was getting ready to go, Kelly asked, "Why doesn't Max come over tomorrow and play with Ryan?"

"Okay," I said.

"Good. And why don't you come for lunch?"

"Yeah, okay, thanks."

[Friday, June 20]

Sara came over this morning to go over the First Step questionnaire she'd given me to complete. One of the questions was, "As you have been working on this booklet, you have probably had some strong feelings. What are some of the feelings you are having?" I wrote, "Surprised at how bad I sound on paper."

The booklet had a section titled, "Dangerous Behavior," where I was supposed to list dangerous deeds I'd carried out under the influence. I listed, "Goading my boyfriend to speed down hairpin turns on Lookout Mountain, which caused us to flip the car and almost die."

My boyfriend, Trey, and I were freshmen at Southern College in Tennessee. We'd been hiking and smoking hash all day, and I'd gotten into Trey's car, rolled down my window, cranked up the volume on his stereo, and told Trey to drive faster. He accelerated. I filled my hash pipe, took a hit, passed it to him, and shouted, "Faster!" Trey obeyed. I don't know why I did it, but I kept egging him on until Trey took a corner way too fast and rolled his Honda Accord almost off the mountain. The car flipped onto the passenger side, rolled onto the roof, teetered there on the edge of the mountain, and fell back onto the passenger's side. If it had rolled over on the driver's side, we'd have dropped off the side of the mountain.

When the car dropped back onto the passenger side, it pinned my right hand between the top of the window frame and the asphalt. My head smacked the road pretty hard, too. My hand hurt like hell and I started moaning, "My hand, my hand." Trey climbed out of the driver's side window like it was a submarine hatch, walked behind the roof of the car, squatted down, wiggled his fingers under the window frame, yanked it up a little, and I pulled my hand free. I don't remember getting out of the vehicle, but I do remember sitting on the edge of the road next to Trey as a pickup truck pulled over.

"Ya'll all right?" the driver asked.

"I think so," Trey answered.

"Hop in back," the driver said. "I'll gitchya to a hospital."

I vaguely remember the emergency room and being told to watch for signs of concussion. And I don't know how Trey and I got back to school.

I hated that school. My parents had taken me to Southern College, an Adventist college, the fall of my freshman year. We drove there towing a U-Haul crammed full of my stuff. I sat in the back seat with my sister, occasionally unzipping my purse and looking at the gooey, fragrant brick of hash I was bringing. I knew I was going to need it.

My high school friends were all going to state universities and an Adventist college was the only away-from-home school my mother would send me to. My friends wrote me letters detailing the great parties they were going to while I was incarcerated in an Adventist prison. Sunday through Thursday night, I was on lockdown in the women's dorm at ten thirty. On Friday night, the Sabbath, I had to attend a mandatory church service before lockdown at ten. On Saturday, I had to go to church again, but was allowed to go out on the town after sundown until a whopping midnight. However, I couldn't go anywhere near a nightclub. School employees combed the parking lots of local nightclubs on Saturday nights looking for Southern College parking stickers. The cars they found were reported, and the students who owned them got in big trouble.

I sniffed out other malcontents like me, and Trey was one of them. Trey's parents sent him to Southern College hoping their wayward son would straighten out and find God. The poor guy didn't stand a chance after he met me. I had several run-ins with the dean, and the dean and I came to an understanding: He would let me collect my credits, and I would leave at the end of the semester. Near the end of the semester, I dumped Trey. While we were going out, I had extolled the virtues of dropping acid, and Trey, in a misguided attempt to win me back, began sucking on hits of acid like breath mints. Trey left at the end of the semester, too, in bad shape.

I scanned my dangerous-behavior list. There was the time I lit my hair on fire after dragging my long, permed '80s locks through a candle I was using as a cigarette lighter during an office Christmas party. I showed up at the newspaper I was working at the next day nursing a wicked hangover. Co-workers who'd arrived at the party after I'd left—my friend, Petra, had driven me to her house to sleep it off after she'd clapped her hands to my head and put out my hair—were disappointed that I wasn't bald and scarred. Petra had gotten to me quick, and I looked like I did most mornings.

Further down the list were the numerous cars I'd sideswiped while I was drunk, the strange men I'd met in bars and left with to do drugs (thank God I was never raped), and the time my boyfriend, Jean-Pierre, and I were tripping on mushrooms and having sex while speeding down Lake Shore Drive.

"What problems have you tried to fix with drugs?" the questionnaire asked. I wrote: Feeling edgy. Feeling overwhelmed. Feeling angry. Feeling sad. Feeling inadequate.

Sara nodded as we went over my questionnaire. "Okay, Step Two: Came to believe that a Power greater than ourselves could restore us to sanity," she said. "A lot of people skim right over the 'can restore us to sanity' part. Focus on that before you move onto Step Three."

I wasn't insane. I didn't need to be restored to sanity. But as I looked over my questionnaire, it appeared I was insane.

“Max told me drinking wasn’t a problem of mine,” I told Sara.

“Oh sure,” Sara laughed. “Max knows best.”

“Max made another drinking comment just this morning,” I continued. “We were talking about my grandmother being ninety-four when she died, and Max said, ‘The oldest person living is 122, and she starts every day with a shot of whiskey in her tea. I guess her alcoholic thing is working for her.’”

Sara snorted.

“Hey,” I said, changing the subject. “I think I’ve gotten Kelly out of my head. I think I’m done. Sorry for boring you with her for so long.”

“It wasn’t boring,” Sara said. “Having friend issues is totally normal for people who have friends left when they get sober. You need to talk about it to let it go. I didn’t have any friends left when I got sober. It had gotten embarrassing.”

Max slid open the sliding glass door and walked out onto the deck where Sara and I were sitting. He handed me the phone. “It’s Kelly,” he said. I felt my face flush.

“Hi,” I said, trying to sound nonchalant.

“Hey,” she said. “Are we still on for lunch today?”

“Yeah,” I said.

“Twelve thirty?”

“Yep.”

“Okay, see ya then.”

“See ya.”

I hung up and put the phone on the table. “That was Kelly,” I said sheepishly. “Max is going over there to play later.”

Sara nodded. I couldn’t read her therapist face.

• • •

Ryan and Seth were running around outside Kelly's house when we got there. Ryan had slept at Seth's the night before, and Kelly had invited Seth over to play.

"I made shrimp rolls," Kelly said, walking me out to her patio. The boys ate peanut butter and jelly sandwiches and chicken nuggets at one end of the patio while Kelly and I ate shrimp rolls.

"Liv and Reed were up at our beach house," Kelly mentioned. "Liv was so overly cautious and paranoid about the kids having fun."

"Oh?" I said. Liv had recently told me that Kelly and Joel were letting the kids light fires and shoot BB guns unsupervised until she and Reed put a stop to it.

"Remember when Max put on his 'bulletproof' vest and had Ryan shoot him with his BB gun?" Kelly asked with a laugh. "I told Liv, 'If you're going to have issues with Seth shooting BB guns, you better watch out when Seth goes up to Wisconsin this summer with Max.'"

"What?" I said, not believing my ears. "Ryan never shot at Max. Do you think I would let your kid use mine as a target? I was sitting in the backyard with Max and Ryan the whole time they were shooting."

"Remember? He had on his SWAT team vest and . . ." Kelly started.

"And his SWAT helmet and goggles," I finished. "Max put them on because of ricocheting BBs. He and your son were shooting at Hot Wheels cars they'd lined up on the roof of the plastic Little Tikes car Max used to drive around the yard when he was a toddler. The BBs were ricocheting off of the plastic car and a couple hit him, so Max put on his SWAT gear."

"Well, Ryan said he was shooting at Max."

"That's ridiculous."

Kelly, a notorious story embellisher, stared off into space, apparently trying to sift fact from fiction.

"Mom, will you get Van out of here?" Max shouted. "I want to play with my friends, not him."

"Yeah, we're leaving," I shouted back and carried my plate and glass to the kitchen. I grabbed Van and Kelly walked us back to the car.

"You know," Kelly began, "I'm spending way too much time with peripheral people—my kids' friends' mothers. I hardly get to see my real friends anymore. I was just asking Joel, 'What is it? Everyone from playgroup goes out to lunch, breakfast, to the movies, but no one calls me. It's like they don't like me.' The only time I see anyone from the old playgroup is at book club—and at the last book club Tina was going on and on about her kids and it was driving me nuts. And Rosy, I felt like I was going to crawl out of my skin sitting next to her."

"Really?" I said, remembering how chummy Kelly and Rosy were and how agitated I was sitting next to Kelly.

Kelly nodded and grimaced. "It's like Rosy's mad at me but won't tell me why. She's a grudge-holder. So whatever it is she's mad about she's not going to let it go."

"Why don't you ask her what's bothering her?" I asked, feeling like I was in a Dali painting.

"No," Kelly said. "I asked her one time and she said, 'You just irritate me. It's just you. It's just you being you.'"

I wanted to kiss Rosy.

"I will never forget that," Kelly said, tearing up. "I can still hear it. I'll never forget it. Another time, when Rosy and I were at my beach house for the weekend, she commented on how quiet it was and I told her how nice it was to spend time up there by myself. She told me, 'Maybe you should spend more time by yourself and reevaluate your life and your priorities.'"

"Wow," I said, admiring Rosy.

"You know what it is?" Kelly asked. "She treats me like shit, like her family. She treats her father like shit, her mother like shit, her sister like shit, and I got too close. You know what else? Rosy will ask me, 'Have you seen Fiona lately? No? I just saw her the other day. How about Karen? No? It was so great getting together with her for lunch. When's the last time you talked to Brenda? I just talked to her yesterday.' She tries to hurt my feelings, rub it in."

"Really," I said, wishing I had the guts to say, "Maybe the flaws you see in Rosy are your own."

Kelly shook her head and wiped her eyes. "I think about this stuff all the time and it's making me sick," she said.

"I know what that's like," I said.

"Mom!" Van called from the car seat where I'd buckled him in.

"I gotta go," I said, nodding toward Van. "Hang in there Kelly, and thanks for lunch."

I don't know how many times I'd heard someone in a meeting say, "It's not about you," and it finally clicked. The crap with Kelly wasn't about me, it was about Kelly.

Van and I got home and the phone rang. It was Linda, the assistant director of Van's preschool. She wants me to write down my field trip experience and send it to the director. Linda confided that the preschool wants Isabel and Casey gone, and a letter from me would help. I told Linda I'd write the letter and hung up, but I have mixed feelings. I don't want to be the cause of Isabel and Casey losing their jobs, however much I think they deserve it.

[Saturday, June 21]

I played tennis with Eve this morning. I'd been looking forward to getting serve pointers from her, but Eve was horrible. She couldn't return a ball to save her life. She also wanted to sit down after every few strokes and drink iced tea and smoke.

While we were on one of our many tea breaks, Eve told me she was an art major, a nurse, a pharmaceutical rep, and an interior designer. "Mel and I are closing on a lake house in Antioch," she said. "You want to drive out and see it?"

"I should go home," I told her. "Charlie wants to go bike riding at one thirty. I need to watch the kids."

"Oh, we'll be back in time," she said. "I've got to show it to you. It's a cute little place on the lake. Come on. It's a beautiful day. We'll get a tan while we're driving."

"If you're sure we'll be back by one thirty."

Eve and I hopped into her yellow convertible. I figured her for a fast driver, but Eve was one of the slowest drivers I've ever had the displeasure to ride with. Cars honked at us every few minutes but Eve seemed oblivious.

"Let's stop at Darcy's," Eve suggested. Moments later, we pulled into Darcy's driveway. We were at Darcy's for more than an hour.

"I've got to be home at one thirty," I reminded Eve.

"Oh, then we should go," Eve said.

We got on the road and after a long slow drive, parked behind a house. We walked inside. The house needed a lot of work and the owner was inside painting.

"I'm having second thoughts about renting it," he told Eve. "My family and I enjoy it too much on the weekends." I looked out the front window at the lake and private pier.

Eve laughed. "I'm going to show my friend around."

Eve and I walked out on the pier. "I thought you said you were buying the place," I said.

"Whatever gave you that idea?"

"You said you and Mel were closing on it."

"I never said that."

I stared at her but didn't press it. I looked at my watch. "It's two o'clock, Eve. I wanted to be home at one thirty. I need to go."

I had already called Charlie and given him a heads-up. When Eve finally dropped me off, it was three o'clock. As I got out of the car, I told Eve, "Charlie's going to be pissed."

"He'll get over it," she said and took off with a wave of her hand.

[Sunday, June 22]

Charlie, Max, and I went fishing on my father's boat. I grabbed my father and hugged him the second I boarded. Two days ago, a radiologist told my dad, in a roundabout way, that he had terminal cancer. My dad was diagnosed with prostate cancer early this spring and had surgery to remove his prostate. There was evidence he still had cancer because he still had a PSA count and he began radiation, but two days ago, his PSA count was higher than ever and his radiologist told him, "I'm sorry, there's nothing more I can do for you."

The bright sun glinted off the water as my dad drove his Sea Ray forty miles north of Chicago to his favorite perch fishing spot. He dropped anchor and went below. He emerged with a Bloody Mary in his hand.

"Mom said your PSA count is up," I said.

"Yeah," he said, with a half laugh. "The radiologist looked at me and said, 'There's nothing more we can do.'"

"What does that mean?"

"Means I'm a dead duck."

"There's gotta be something else. There are new drugs, new treatments. Don't jump to any conclusions just yet. Wait until you talk to your oncologist. I'll go to your next appointment with you. When is it?"

"The thirtieth."

"You're gonna be okay," I said, feeling sick to my stomach.

My dad nodded.

We didn't talk about cancer the rest of the day. We got down to fishing and caught thirty-eight fish. Charlie and Max and I got ready to leave, and my father hugged me extra tight and kissed my cheek. I hugged him tight and kissed him back.

"I love you," he said.

"I love you, too."

I looked at my dad and there were tears in his eyes. "I want to see my grandkids grow up," he said.

"Yeah, me too."

[Monday, June 23]

Audrey is back in town. She and I were supposed to go out and do something with our kids today, but instead, Audrey called and suggested coming over to my house for a barbecue.

"Why don't we go out for dinner at a kosher restaurant?" I suggested. "I'll probably use *treyf* ingredients you and your boys can't eat. Besides, you can't eat anything cooked on my grill."

"Some friends gave Nehemiah and me a portable grill for our wedding," Audrey said. "I'll bring it over and pick up kosher meat."

"Are you going to bring all the food?" I asked. "Last time you wouldn't eat my salad because the dressing had vinegar in it and the vinegar had to be kosher. Your kids couldn't drink my juice because it contained grape juice and grape juice has to be kosher. And you wouldn't eat my bread because it had honey in it and honey needs to be kosher."

"Well, you know all that stuff now," Audrey said. "You know what to avoid. Make a salad and corn on the cob. Make sure you get dressing and margarine that has these kosher symbols (she listed several). Make sure the labels don't say dairy. If the label says 'de' that's okay, it just means the plant produces dairy products but there's no dairy in it. And get the kids some popsicles and look for kosher symbols."

Audrey arrived at six thirty with her boys and an unassembled grill still in the box. I helped Audrey assemble her grill and got the kids drinks while keeping an eye on Van and boiling noodles I'd toss with margarine. Audrey had thrown packages of strip steak and chicken into my refrigerator before we started assembling her grill. When we'd put the grill together, she began slapping raw meat all over my countertops. There was enough chicken and steak to feed twenty people. As she unwrapped each steak, she left bloody cellophane wrappers wherever they stuck. I pulled blood-dripping pieces off my sugar bowl, coffee maker, and wall, and began wiping and disinfecting all infected surfaces. Next, Audrey began scraping feathers off the two kosher chickens she'd brought. I opened my refrigerator to get my salad ingredients. There was another package of meat wrapped in a plastic shopping bag on the top shelf. Blood was dripping out of it and spattering my food below. I began cleaning the food and the refrigerator. I looked at the clock. It was seven thirty.

"You started the coals, didn't you?" I asked Audrey.

"Ah, no."

We went outside, threw coals into the grill, doused them with lighter fluid, and torched them. The kids were starving. Max began pulling snack food out. Audrey looked at the boxes and bags of all-natural vegetable puffs and crackers I bought at the health food store.

"My boys can't have these," she said. "They're not kosher."

"My boys can, and they're ready to chew their arms off," I snapped.

Minutes later, I served the children salad and noodles. Charlie came home and put Van to bed. Eventually, Audrey put the chicken and steak on the grill, and at nine o'clock, she gave Max and her boys each a steak. I got juice out for the kids, kosher juice, and went to the cupboard. I reached over the plain plastic cups and grabbed cups decorated with pigs from Famous Dave's barbecue. I poured juice into them and handed one to each of the children. Audrey looked at the cups, raised an eyebrow, but didn't say a word.

Nehemiah showed up at nine thirty after playing a round of golf by himself. He took over barbecuing the chicken, which still wasn't done, and he, Charlie, Audrey, and I ate dinner at ten.

"This is the latest I've eaten dinner in a long time," I said.

"We eat like this all the time," Audrey said. "Sometimes we're at friends' houses until two in the morning."

"Really?" I said looking at my watch. It was eleven o'clock on a Monday night.

When Audrey and her family left an hour later, I looked at Charlie and asked, "Do you think visiting into the wee hours is an orthodox thing?"

"I think it's an Audrey thing," he answered and went to bed.

[Tuesday, June 24]

I went to the Tuesday night women's meeting, and Tracy said, "We will never pass this way again." That rocked me. This part of my life is passing, never to be repeated. It made me realize I need to appreciate what's going on at the moment because it'll disappear fast. Another friend just sent me an email quote that said, "What I do today is important because I'm exchanging a day of my life for it."

[Wednesday, June 25]

The kids and I met Liv and her boys, Seth and Pete, at a bowling alley this afternoon. It was Van's first time bowling. We put bumpers in the gutters—something we all benefited from—and as we began bowling a second game, Liv and I started talking about Seth's upcoming vacation with my family in Wisconsin. My parents have a lake cabin in Minocqua, and Max invited Seth to spend a week there with us.

"My dad brings guns," I told Liv. "He keeps them locked in his car and we shoot them at a shooting range. My mom and Van stay at the cabin, but the rest of us shoot. We don't have to go if you don't want Seth to do it. It won't be a big deal."

"Your dad will be with the kids the whole time?" Liv asked.

"He won't take his eyes off them for a minute," I said. "Charlie and I will be there, too. We allow only one person to shoot at a time."

"Seth will love that," Liv said.

"I had lunch at Kelly's the other day," I said. I relayed Kelly's cockamamie story about Ryan shooting Max with a BB gun.

"I knew something was off," Liv said. "I didn't believe her. When she told me that story, I figured it was just Kelly twisting things like she always does. But she repeated it, like, three times insisting it was true. She brought it up because Reed and I were upset that the boys were running around their beach house recklessly shooting BB guns. Their neighbors are close by, and the boys easily could have shot each other or a neighbor. Reed took Seth's gun away, then Kelly told us that story about Ryan shooting Max. She said we might want to reconsider sending Seth with you to Wisconsin."

"She told you that screwed-up story?" I said.

"Like I said, I didn't believe it," Liv said. "It was so weird, so far-fetched. Plus, I could tell it bugged her that Seth's going on vacation with you. I'm really glad you brought it up."

"She's whacked," I said. Liv and I started laughing.

Who knows how many other people Kelly told this messed-up story to? My sponsor told me not to confront Kelly about the crap she's been pulling, but there is no way I'm letting this one slide. Kelly is bringing Ryan over for lunch in two days and I'm going to lay it on her then.

[Friday, June 27]

Kelly and Ryan came over for lunch. I must have been visibly irritated because when we sat down, Kelly asked me, "Is anything wrong?" The kids were eating with us on the deck in the backyard and I told her, "No."

After lunch, Kelly left and Ryan stayed to play with Max. A few hours later, Kelly called to tell me that Joel would be picking up Ryan at five.

"I have to tell you something," I said. "I'm bothered by your Ryan-shot-Max story. It's a lie. It never happened. It makes me look like a shithead. And you shared it with Liv and God knows who else."

"No," Kelly said, sounding rattled. "I was complaining about my son, that Ryan would do such a thing. It made Ryan look bad, not you."

"No," I said. "Something like that happening under my watch makes me look bad, really bad."

"Ryan was the one who said it," Kelly shot back. "Ryan said, 'Remember when I was at Max's and . . .'"

"You're the one who brought it up," I said, cutting her off. "You brought it up to me at lunch and you brought it up to Liv."

"No, Ryan was the one who brought it up. I wouldn't have brought it up if Ryan hadn't brought it up. Liv and Reed were standing right there when he said it."

"I just saw Liv," I said. "She said that when you told her that story she didn't believe it because it was so absurd, but you kept insisting it was true. I resent that story and I needed to tell you. So I'll expect Joel at five, right?"

"Yeah," Kelly said, "around then."

Kelly was banging on my door twenty minutes later.

"You're here early," I said.

"Oh, well," Kelly began nervously, "Ryan has to go to a birthday party he doesn't want to go to. Every time he gets together with this kid the kid ends up crying. It's really weird. So it's just better if I get Ryan instead of Joel. You know, I never would have said anything to Liv about the BB gun if Ryan hadn't brought it up first. It was no big deal. The boys got into trouble and Ryan said, 'Hey, remember when . . .'"

"You already told me this."

"But that's how it happened," Kelly said, tears welling up in her eyes. "I guess if you think that makes you look bad, then I look bad for how the boys were playing at our beach house."

I didn't say a word.

"It sounds to me like some Kelly bashing was going on," she continued, wiping her eyes. "I don't know Liv very well. We party, but that's about it. I don't know about her, but I know Reed will talk behind anyone's back. I don't want them ruining our friendship." Kelly hugged me. "We've been good friends for six years." She stepped back, her hands on my shoulders. Tears rolled down her cheeks.

Kelly left with Ryan. I plopped down on the wicker couch on my front porch and cried. I hate how things are between Kelly and me. I knew my friendships would go to shit if I quit drinking. Kelly and I used to have so much fun. We used to joke about going to the old folks' home together and hooking each other up to chardonnay drips.

[Monday, June 30]

Sara came over this morning. When I told Max she was coming over, he asked, "Why is she coming over here all the time?"

"She belongs to the No Alcohol Club," I said. "She's been in that club a long time and she's very smart and has interesting things to say. She gives me good advice."

"You know you should never let your friends tell you what to do," Max said.

"Yeah, I know," I said, laughing.

After Sara left, I did several loads of laundry and packed because the kids and I are driving up to the cottage in Lakeside, Michigan, tomorrow. Charlie came home early to watch the kids so I could go to my dad's urologist appointment. When I walked into the office, my parents were already sitting in the waiting room. I hugged and kissed them both, sat down, and began making small talk about going to Lakeside.

"Why do you keep calling it Lakeside?" my father asked testily. "You're not even on Lake Michigan. You're going to be there for what, two weeks?"

"I call it Lakeside because it's in the town of Lakeside," I said. "The cottage is a five-minute walk from the beach, and the beach is awesome. It's got soft white sand that stretches as far as the eye can see. It's like being in Florida but better because it's fresh water."

"What's there to do there?" my dad asked irritably.

"Go to the beach."

"That's it? There's nothing else?"

"Shop, go to restaurants, go to art galleries, hit antique malls."

"I bet the kids love that," he said nastily.

"You should come up sometime," I said, trying not to snap back. "The cottage is really cute. Martha decorated it."

"I should drive there in my car, through all that crappy city traffic?"

"You could take your boat," I suggested. You could dock in New Buffalo. I could pick you up. Might be a fun trip for you and Mom."

"And burn up all that gas? That would cost me an arm and a leg."

A nurse appeared and called us into an examining room. Minutes later, Dr. Wheeler walked in and got straight to the point. He said my dad's prostate surgery and radiation hadn't worked and that his cancer was spreading.

My mother had visited the Johns Hopkins Web site and printed out an estimate of how long a guy with terminal prostate cancer has to live. I had read the article at my parents' house a few days earlier. The best-case scenario was for a guy who had a Gleason score of less than eight (my father's was seven), didn't have a PSA score for two years post-surgery (my dad had a PSA score right away), and when a PSA score developed, it wouldn't double within the first ten months (my dad's had already doubled). The report said cancer might not appear on a CT or bone scan for seven years in a guy with the best-case scenario, and once it appeared, he could live for another seven years. This fourteen-year best-case scenario somehow convinced my mother that my dad might have another twenty years.

My mom sat in a little plastic chair in the examining room clutching the Johns Hopkins report. My dad sat with one haunch on the examining table. I stood against the wall holding a report I'd printed out from the National Cancer Institute's Web site.

"You have three choices," Dr. Wheeler began. "To do nothing, in which case you could be fine for several years."

"What do you mean by several?" my dad asked.

"Three, four years," Wheeler said. "But I don't know. I can't say. Could be longer, could be shorter. We don't know. Medicine is an art, not a science. We don't know these things for sure."

My dad nodded grimly.

"Two," Wheeler continued, "you could do hormone therapy. It's not a cure, but it could stop it for a while. How long it stops it is anyone's guess. Some people respond to hormone therapy well, some don't respond at all. Basically, the therapy blocks the hormone that the cancer cells feed on. But eventually the cancer gets smart and starts spreading. There are also side effects."

My father went ramrod stiff.

"Three, you could get into a study and try experimental treatments," Wheeler said. "But these are very toxic, a lot of side effects, and you could get into a placebo group."

"I pulled this off the National Cancer Institute Web site," I said, waving my papers. "Here are some experimental drugs that look promising."

I handed the report to Wheeler. He skimmed it and nodded.

"You'll have to shop around for an oncologist who'll go off-label if you want to try this stuff and not be in a study," he said.

"What about diet?" my dad asked. "Can I do anything to lengthen my life?"

Wheeler told us about Dr. Locke, a holistic MD. "My father-in-law tried that approach," he said. "But he started in very late stages, and on his deathbed he complained that it had taken away his pleasure for eating and he regretted it. But I know people whose lives were extended by changing their diet."

"Who are the top oncologists?" I asked. "Who would you send your dad to?"

Wheeler gave us three names. "You're going to have to weigh the amount of time treatments may give you with your quality of life—decide if the side effects are worth it," he said.

"So basically what you're saying is I'm fucked," my dad said.

"Oh, don't say that," my mother said. "It says right here," and she rattled her papers, "that you could live for twenty more years. This is from Johns Hopkins."

"I don't know what you've got there," Wheeler said, and turned to my dad, "but you could have a number of good years left, we just don't know how many. Again, this isn't a science, it's not exact."

Wheeler looked at me. "I know you want your dad to go on some new drugs," he said and turned back to my father, "but I'd go fishing first. Get on the boat, do some thinking, then see the oncologists right away and get started on something. And take your daughter with you."

The four of us left the room single file.

"I have to go to the bathroom," my father said. "Let's go down the elevator. I don't want to go in here."

“We’re on the first floor,” my mother laughed.

“Oh.”

After my dad went to the bathroom, we walked outside and I sat on a bench in front of the medical center and copied the doctor referrals onto a slip of paper and handed the slip to my mother. My dad stood next to the bench staring off into space.

“Okay, here’s what we’ll do,” I said. “We’ll make appointments with these oncologists, interview them, and pick one to fight for us. This is fucking war. We’re not giving up.”

“Do you have to swear?” my mother complained. “You don’t need to swear.”

I ignored her. “You know what I’m saying dad?” I asked. “We’re fucking going to war. We’re going to get you as many fucking years as possible.”

“I’m fucked,” my dad said. “I’m a dead man.”

“I don’t believe that,” my mother said with a smile and rattled her Johns Hopkins report. “You could have twenty more years.”

I got in my car and cried all the way home. God, a stiff vodka would be nice.

[Tuesday, July 1]

I loaded up the Jeep around eleven last night, and at five thirty this morning, the kids and I pulled out for Lakeside. When we arrived in town, we pulled into the parking lot of the Blue Plate restaurant, which is literally around the corner from our cottage. The second after we walked into the restaurant, Van vomited all over the floor. A waitress rushed over with a bucket and a mop and began cleaning the entryway. I wiped Van off and fed him breakfast. After that, he was fine. Riding in the back seat for an hour and forty-five minutes on an empty stomach apparently hadn't set well with him.

I started unpacking when we got to the cottage and began figuring out where I was going to put everyone. Hope and her two boys were on their way up. They were staying for a few days. Charlie was coming up for the weekend, and my sister and her two boys were coming up after that. I was starting to stress.

Max had brought his BB gun, and while I was unpacking and making shopping lists in my head, Max kept pestering me to let him shoot.

"No," I told him repeatedly. "Please watch Van. Take him outside. Blow some bubbles, play ball, help me out, please."

Max took Van outside and, moments later, was screaming at him for spilling all the bubble solution. He yanked the bubble paraphernalia away from Van, and Van began screaming at Max and shoved him. Max screamed back at Van. Van snatched one of Max's toy guns and whipped it on the ground, smashing it. I hurried outside, packed the boys into the car, and headed for the grocery store.

We walked into the grocery store, and I sat Van in the grocery cart seat. Max jumped on the back end of the cart and I began pushing it. Max yanked his body from side to side, making the cart sway with his body weight.

"Stop it," I snapped. "Get off! You're making it hard to push."

Max jumped off. He jumped back on. He jumped off. He jumped back on.

"Knock it off," I yelled. I began picking through a pile of cantaloupe. Max grabbed the shopping cart and ran down an aisle with it. Van began screaming and laughing. Max slalomed around the produce, cutting people off. He skidded to a stop and left Van and the cart in the middle of another aisle and ran over to a Twinkie display. I marched over to the cart with my cantaloupe and pushed it past glaring shoppers.

"Can we get these, can we get these?" Max asked running up to the cart with a box of Twinkies.

"No. Put them back."

Max put the Twinkies back, ran to the cart, and trailed after me making siren sounds and flailing his arms. I seriously wanted to smack him. We checked out, hopped back into the car, and drove back to the cottage. Hope's SUV was in the driveway, and she and her boys, Sid and Robin, were unloading their stuff. Max jumped out of the Jeep as soon as I put it in park and hopped on his bike. He wove his bike in and out of tight spots between the two vehicles and the cottage. He careened toward Van, skidded to a stop, and hopped off before hitting him. Max ran to the Jeep while I was unloading groceries and pulled his BB gun out of the back. He began waving it around and I snatched it from him and threw it back in the Jeep.

"That's where it's staying for a week!" I yelled. "You don't touch that thing without permission. And waving it around little kids, are you nuts?"

"Wow, he has a BB gun?" Hope said. "If you had a BB gun in my neighborhood you'd be ostracized."

"That's why I live with the gentiles," I snapped.

Hope clucked her tongue and stared at me with her mouth hanging open. I knew I shouldn't have said that, but I was at my limit.

Hope and her boys put their stuff in the cottage and I put the groceries away. We headed down to the beach, and Lake Michigan looked like a sea. Huge waves were crashing on the shore and I knew before putting my foot in that there was a strong undercurrent. Max jumped into the water and began swimming away from the shore. I screamed at him to swim back. He slowly turned and swam back. As he neared the shore, I felt like yanking him out by the hair. I was acutely aware that I'd been yelling at Max since Hope arrived. I could feel her silent judgment. In a calm, measured voice I told Max how dangerous the lake was and gave him parameters for where he could and could not swim.

My friends never seem to yell at their kids. Even when their kids are behaving hideously they pull them aside and say, "Now Sweetie, you know you shouldn't blah, blah, blah. Please don't yadda, yadda, yadda, okay Sweetie?" Maybe it's a bullshit show they put on for nonfamily members, but I'd have to be on happy pills to act like that. God, I want a drink!

[Wednesday, July 2]

I'm almost done reading the book *We Need to Talk About Kevin* by Lionel Shriver. It's a fictional story about a teenage boy, a nasty little seed, who murders his classmates like in Columbine. Hope's son Robin is a nasty little shit, and I couldn't stop comparing him to Kevin.

Robin is three and constantly scowls. We went to the beach today, and Robin sat on the sand and refused to step foot into the water. Hope jumped around Robin like a moronic court jester, and Robin screamed at Hope to stop, so she did. Van was playing on the sand with a beach ball.

"I want that ball," Robin shouted.

Hope asked Van if he wanted to play ball with Robin and walked Van over to her little angel of darkness. "Throw the ball to Robin," she told Van. Van threw the ball to Robin and Robin grabbed it and ran in the opposite direction. Van stood there for a moment then walked off toward a shovel and pail and began digging in the sand. Robin saw what Van was doing, threw down the ball, ran over, pushed Van, and took his shovel and pail.

"Hey, those are mine," Van wailed. "I was playing with them."

Hope sat on the sand next to Robin. "Robin, Van was playing with those," she said cheerily. "It's not nice to push." Robin ignored her and kept digging. Hope sat there for a moment then began helping Robin build a sand castle.

I was thoroughly disgusted. "Let's play ball," I told Van.

I grabbed the beach ball and Van and I waded into the water and tossed it back and forth. I looked over at Robin to see what he was doing. He had stopped digging. He was sitting with his arms crossed over his chest scowling at us. I saw Hope flapping her arms and jaws. Robin got up, walked across the beach, and began climbing the stairs to leave.

"Robin, come here," Hope shouted. "Robin! Come back here! Robin!" She got up and jogged to the stairs and ran up. Moments later, Hope reappeared with Robin. "Sid!" she called. "Come on, we need to go up. We need to go with Robin."

"Why do we always have to leave because of Robin?" Sid yelled. He turned to Robin. "Robin, why are you so mean?"

"You know what?" I said looking at my watch. "It's time for lunch anyway. We'll go up and eat and come back down."

The six of us climbed up the stairs from the beach to the top of the bluff. We walked back to the cottage and I made grilled cheese sandwiches. Robin wouldn't eat his. Sid finished his sandwich and began eating Robin's. Robin started screaming at Sid saying he wanted his sandwich.

Throughout the day, Robin continued to abuse Van. I saw him slap Van; push Van. When I started to intervene, Hope would pull Robin aside, quietly talk to him, and make Robin apologize. One of the times Robin pushed Van, Robin looked at me first, looked at Hope, and shoved Van anyway. The little brat knew his mother would step in and wouldn't do jack shit. The icing on the cake was when Robin spit at Van and gave him the finger. I didn't see it, but Max came running up yelling, "Mom, Mom, Robin spit at Van! And he gave him the finger! I hate that kid! What's wrong with him?"

I gave Hope a very pissed-off look. Hope said, "Robin, why would you do that?" She turned to Van and said, "Sorry, Van." She turned toward me. "What can you do?" she shrugged.

I looked at her incredulously. Hope winced and turned away.

[Thursday, July 3]

It was a hot, windless day and Robin didn't want to go to the beach.

"I heard about this big playground in Three Oaks," Hope said. "Let's go there. You want to go there, Robin? Yeah? Let's go!"

"Can we stay here?" Max asked me, motioning to Sid and himself.

"Yeah, can we stay here?" Sid asked. "We want to go to the beach."

"I want to go to the park with Robin," Van said.

"We're all going to the park," Hope said. "Come on, let's go."

"You guys can't stay here by yourselves," I told Max. "We'll go to the beach later, okay?"

"But they're leaving later," Max said.

I looked at Max and shrugged.

Max and Sid disgustedly got into Hope's SUV.

The Three Oaks playground, an enormous community-built structure erected in a treeless field, sat baking in the sun. Waves of heat danced off of it as we walked toward it. The kids climbed on, but minutes later, Max, Sid, Van, and I were sitting in the shade under a wooden platform.

"It's too hot," Sid moaned. "I want to leave. Everyone wants to go, Mom," Sid wailed.

"Robin doesn't want to leave," Hope said.

"Four against one," Sid said.

"Four against two," Hope said. "And I'm driving." She turned toward Robin, "We're having fun, right Robin?"

Robin was sitting in a corner near the top of a slide, pouting as usual. But as soon as Sid began complaining, Robin jumped up and slid down the slide.

"Come on, Mom," Sid complained loudly.

"This sucks," Max groaned.

"Hope, let's go," I said. "This is miserable. I've had it."

We left the inferno, and as Hope drove back to the cottage with the air conditioner cranked, I called my mom.

"Hey, how are things going? How's Dad? Did you make those doctor appointments?"

"I made one with Dr. Locke."

"That's it?" I said. "He's the holistic MD. He's not an oncologist."

"He's not? I thought he was. His office sent over a twenty-page questionnaire. Can you believe it? I don't know why they need so much information."

"Doctors like that do exhaustive case histories. Your lifestyle has a lot to do with your health. You need to make appointments with those oncologists. We need to pick a cancer doctor and get Dad started on treatment."

"I was on the phone and computer all day yesterday with this stuff and I don't feel like spending another day on it," my mother complained.

"Well, you have to," I said irritably. "Make those appointments today."

I hung up. Hope was playing a sappy children's CD, still trying to make Robin happy.

"What's this shit you're listening to?" I snapped.

Hope gave me a shocked look. "It's Robin's favorite. We love it!"

"I'd be on Prozac, too, if I had to listen to this crap."

Hope had confided in me that she took Prozac. She stared at me in disbelief and I stared out the window.

We ate lunch at the cottage, then Hope and her kids packed up their SUV and left. Van waved and cried as they drove away.

"I don't know why Van likes Robin," Max muttered.

"Van likes being around another kid his age, even if he is a mean little so-and-so," I said. "Let's go to the beach."

We went to the beach and Charlie arrived at the cottage before dinner. At dusk, we drove to the little town of Baroda for a fireworks show. Everyone was parking in the middle of a large open field. We put a blanket down and watched the fireworks explode, literally over our heads. Ash and soot drifted down from the sky and tapped our bodies lightly after each close-up explosion. It felt good to be present and not floating in an alcohol haze.

[Friday, July 4]

I called my mother. She told me she had made an appointment for my dad with a doctor at Evanston-Northwestern.

"Make an appointment with the oncologist downtown, too," I said.

"I've been emailing my cousin Pat," my mother said. "You remember him? We usually see him at the flea market in St. Germaine when we're in Minocqua? He says doctors are full of it and I agree. He sent me a link to a Web site for nutritional supplements that are supposed to change your body's PH and cure cancer. Some doctor has been curing his patients, all thirty of them, with this stuff."

"Bullshit," I said. "Kelly came across a miracle drug on the Internet when her mother was dying of cancer. She got all excited about it, but after digging around she found out it was made out of airplane fuel."

I hung up. I picked up the phone book and looked for a recovery meeting. I called a number and left my number on someone's answering machine. A while later, a man called back. "This is the Program Police," he said. I laughed. It felt good to laugh.

[Saturday, July 5]

I went to a meeting this morning and the man who spoke was the kind of guy my dad would like. He was a blue-collar guy about the same age as my dad and funny as hell. He said he'd never met his father, but his dad would send him a card every five years or so while he was growing up.

"My dad was an unsuccessful bank robber," the speaker said. "The kind of bank robber who would walk into a bank, pull a sack over his head, but have forgotten to cut the eyeholes out. That part is true. He really did forget to cut the eye holes out."

After he finished, we took turns commenting. One woman said she was sober three weeks and having a rough time watching her family drink at her cottage. When it was my turn, I said I was having trouble dealing with my dad's terminal cancer. A chic woman approached me after the meeting.

"I lost my dad to cancer right after I got sober," she said. She wrote her phone number on a piece of paper. "Here," she said, handing it to me. The number was to an upscale clothing boutique in New Buffalo. "Just tell them you're my friend and they'll put you through to me."

I thanked her and left. Later, Charlie and the boys and I went to see *Lilly's Orchid Show* in Three Oaks. *Lilly's Orchid*

Show, a collection of talented and not-so-talented musical and performance acts, is usually geared for adults. I'd seen it years ago in Chicago when it showcased the Blue Man Group before the Blue Man Group was famous. But tonight, it was a family show. Square dancers, plate-twirlers, and Kurt Elling singing jazz. It was cool.

We drove back to the cottage and my cell phone rang.

"I don't want to alarm you," Reed said, "but a tornado ripped through your neighborhood. They're calling it a micro-burst, but I'm calling it a tornado. A humongous box elder was knocked down and is covering the whole back three-quarters of your yard. The maple tree by your brick patio, the whole top and middle section got ripped out. There's a five-foot-high, ten-foot-wide barricade of branches and trees piled up in your street. It looks like a war zone."

I called Judy, my next-door neighbor.

"Branches from your maple tree fell across the alley onto your neighbor's car," she said. "But I don't think the car was damaged. Dennis and I cleared the limbs off your garage roof and we cleaned up the alley and put the branches in the street. Your telephone wire was ripped off the front of your house and took some fascia with it. But otherwise, everything else is okay."

"Thank you," I said. "We'll be home tomorrow."

"Don't cancel your vacation," Judy said. There's nothing to do that can't wait until you come back. But you might want to call a tree removal service. The tree guys are really busy. I'll get you the number for the guy we used."

[Sunday, July 6]

Instead of returning home, we drove to Saugatuck. Saugatuck is a lovely little town full of arty clip joints. After a day of poking around in the shops, we drove back to the cottage and I flipped on the news and began cooking dinner. The news anchor reported that librarians were destroying library patrons' checkout histories so the federal government couldn't get them under the Patriot Act.

"I checked out books on Hitler and Osama bin Laden," Max said. "Do you think the government might come after me?"

"Don't forget all the books you checked out on guns," I said.

Charlie started laughing. "Didn't you check out some books on bombs?"

"No!" Max snapped, looking worried. He sat back on the couch, arms folded, deep in troubled thought.

"You're fine," I told Max. "You're ten. Ten-year-old boys check out that kind of stuff. But you shouldn't have to worry about the government looking over your shoulder while you're reading. That's sickening." Secretly, I wondered if my family was on the government's watch list. Maybe Max's reading history was a red flag. I also donate money to Greenpeace and Planned Parenthood.

[Monday, July 7]

Charlie left and my sister arrived in Lakeside with her kids. We went to the beach, and when we returned to the cottage, Paula began drinking a wine cooler she'd made by mixing red wine with some off-brand citrus soda. I'd told Paula I didn't want her bringing anything I wanted to drink, so she complied. But her liquor consumption is starting to make me feel edgy.

I called my parents' house. My mom said she made an appointment for my dad to see the oncologist downtown at Northwestern. They were going to see the Evanston doc in three days.

"Ask the doctor if there's a study Dad can get into with no risk of getting into a placebo group," I said. "Ask him if he's willing to go off-label—prescribe drugs that haven't been approved."

"I think the supplement Pat told me about on the Internet sounds promising," my mom said. "Sounds like it can cure him. I'm going to ask the doctor about that."

"How's Dad?" I asked.

"He's here. You want to talk to him?"

"Yeah."

I began telling my dad what I'd just told my mother.

"I can't think about this," my dad shouted. "I can't figure anything out. What the fuck's a placebo? I don't know what the fuck that is. I don't know what the fuck they're saying or what the fuck to do. I wish you were going to this doctor appointment with me. I can't think about this. When I do, I just go fucking nuts. This drives me fucking crazy. I can't think about it, Brenda. Everyone has to go sometime. Maybe I'll just do nothing. When I just put it out of my mind I'm fine."

[Tuesday, July 8]

We went to the beach and after the kids were in bed, Paula and I talked for a while about our dad. She, like my mother, is carrying false hope.

"He's not going to get better," I said. "And he's not going to feel well much longer."

"Stop that!" Paula snapped. "Don't say that."

"He's going to get sick and the cancer treatments are going to make him feel like shit."

"Well, maybe he should just do hormone therapy," Paula said. "I talked to a guy on a plane who told me his prostate cancer had spread so much that when they opened him up, they just closed him right back up. He's been on hormone therapy for six years and he's doing fine, I think."

"Doesn't sound right," I said. "The cancer is going to kill him. Dad's only hope is an experimental drug."

"You said there was no hope, that the cancer would kill him."

"Nothing so far cures cancer."

Paula looked deflated. I felt bad. But I don't want to be the only one not in denial.

[Wednesday, July 9]

Paula, the boys, and I climbed mountains of sand at Warren Dunes. We swam at the beach, and as I was flicking sand off my towel my cell phone rang.

"It's going to cost $1,210 to trim our trees and remove the downed box elder in our yard," Charlie said. "Removing the box elder is $800. The neighborhood is pretty cleaned up, but both of our phone lines are out. The phone cable is coiled up on the neighbor's grass across the street. I've got a lot of work to do, but I'll come back to Lakeside late Friday or early Saturday."

[Thursday, July 10]

Paula and her kids left this morning. It was nice having a quiet day with just my kids to myself. After Max and Van went to bed, I stayed up and read. I've been craving alone time, but now that I've got it, it's making me uncomfortable. I'm noticing how spidery the cottage is. I'm feeling uneasy with myself in general. There are people who can't stand being by themselves, and I've always prided myself on not being one of them. But I'm feeling edgy, restless, pretty much crawling in my skin.

I loved living alone before I got married. When Charlie and I were dating, he wanted me to move in with him and I wouldn't. When we got married I missed having my own space. But I smoked a lot of pot back then. It wasn't like I was being introspective.

As a kid, I used to spend long periods of time lying on my closet floor thinking about how weird it was that I existed, that my parents had picked each other, that out of all the possible combinations everything had lined up for me to be here. I'd look at myself in the mirror and feel like I was looking at myself from outside my body. It felt supernatural, interesting. I tried doing it again recently, staring at myself in the mirror to see if I could look at myself from the outside, but I got too creeped out and stopped.

[Monday, July 14]

We drove back home and I began doing loads of laundry. Darcy called.

"I'm not feeling comfortable around Eve, not safe," she said. "I think drinking is still working for her and I can't be around that."

"Sometimes it's best to drift away," I said, thinking about Kelly.

[Thursday, July 17]

More psycho Kelly crap. The kids and I went out to lunch with Liv and her boys and I told Liv about calling Kelly on her bad behavior and dragging Liv's name into it.

"I'm so glad you're bringing this up," Liv said. "I've wanted to talk to you about this, but Reed was like, 'This is between Kelly and Brenda. Stay out of it.' You were out of town, but at Kelly's book club, she pulled me aside and wanted to talk about the conversation she had with you."

"What did she say?"

"Kelly said you were mad at her because, and these were her words, 'I supposedly told you Ryan was using Max as a BB gun target.' Then she started crying and kept saying, 'Ryan was the one who said it. Don't you remember?' I told her, 'No, I don't remember it that way,' but she wanted me to tell you that's how it happened. I told her I wasn't going to do that and she wasn't too happy with me. She was pretty irritated."

"She's lost her mind," I said.

"What am I going to say when she calls me and asks how it went when I talked to you?" Liv asked. "Kelly is expecting me to talk to you."

"Kelly's been leaving a lot of messages on my answering machine since I got back from Michigan," I said. "Now I know why."

Yesterday, I swung by Kelly's to pick up a belated wedding present for Audrey and Nehemiah that I'd ordered from Kelly's friend Lexi, who runs a corporate gifts business. When Kelly opened the door, she had a sad look pasted on her face.

"You never called me to tell me how your dad's doctor appointment went and it hurt my feelings," she said.

I ignored her and opened the boxes and pulled out the hand-painted platter and bowl I was going to give Audrey. "Look at this," I said. "I feel like keeping this stuff."

"I need to get something for my mother-in-law's birthday," Kelly said. "Will you bring me those catalogs Lexi gave you?"

Kelly left me a message today saying she needed to stop by and get those catalogs.

"I'm not calling her back," I told Liv.

[Friday, July 18]

I went to my dad's appointment at the holistic medical center. While I was in Michigan, my parents met with an oncologist in Evanston, Dr. Chevron, and they said Dr. Chevron wanted to do nothing until my dad started feeling bad, then he'd start him on hormone therapy. I don't like that.

A nutritionist at the holistic center came into the room we were waiting in and told my dad he needs to radically change his diet and eat a lot of deep Atlantic fish, vegetables, and only whole-grain carbohydrates.

"No meat, dairy products, or sugar—and stop drinking alcohol," the nutritionist said. "Sugar feeds cancer and so does animal fat. Alcohol converts to sugar in your body."

"So I should give up all the pleasures in life?" my dad asked testily. "I gave up smoking. I can't have sex because I've got a limp dick from surgery and radiation. Now I should give up drinking and meat?" My dad snorted and laughed.

My father walked out of the clinic agitated but hopeful that he could lengthen his life by changing his diet. He's not going to change his eating habits. It's never going to happen.

[Monday, July 21]

My parents and I went downtown to see Dr. Benton, the Northwestern oncologist Dr. Wheeler recommended. I initially liked Benton because he's aggressive. He said he wanted to start my dad on hormone therapy right away.

"How much time do I have?" my dad asked Benton.

"I could arrest the cancer with hormones for three to four years if the cancer is visible on CT or bone scans. And I can arrest it for up to seven years if it's not. I want you to get CT and bone scans right away."

My dad went ashen. "What about changing my diet? Can I help myself by changing my diet?"

"That won't do a thing," Benton said. "It's a lot of smoke and mirrors. There's some evidence to suggest that diet affects your health before you get sick based on the different types of cancer people get. But your house is on fire and you can't rebuild a burning house."

After the appointment, as we waited for the elevator, my dad said, "That guy's a fucking asshole. I don't like him. He's not going to be my doctor."

We got in the elevator. "Did you hear what he said?" my dad asked. "I've got seven years tops, but probably three to four. Prick. But at least he told me I can eat and drink whatever I want."

[Tuesday, July 22]

I was cooking with Max when the phone rang and I let the answering machine pick up.

"Brenda," Kelly sing-songed. "I need those catalogs."

I picked up the phone and told her to come over. I couldn't avoid Kelly forever. Kelly was over in five minutes. I walked her into my kitchen and we chatted for half an hour, then I walked Kelly out onto my front porch.

"Bren," she began, "I just want to reiterate that I didn't bring up that BB gun story. I reminded Liv that Ryan had been the one to bring it up, but Liv couldn't remember a thing. It was weird, like a *Twilight Zone* episode." Kelly's voice began to shake and her eyes filled with tears. "I'm not about to let Liv, a new friend, get in the way and mess up our friendship." Tears rolled down Kelly's cheeks and she swiped them away. "In the six years we've been friends, you've never been mad at me, and I'm not about to let Liv screw things up."

"I didn't like your asinine story," I said. "I had to tell you how I felt and I did. Now it's over. Okay?"

Kelly hugged me, and I hugged her back. She tearfully told me she valued my friendship and loved me. I got teary and told her, "Back at ya."

[Thursday, July 24]

I've got mixed feelings about leaving for Minocqua tomorrow. I met with Sara this morning, and we talked about how I was going to handle being with my parents and watching my dad drink all week. Things get ugly around mid-week every time I stay with them. This time around, I wanted to avoid making barbed comments like the one I skewered my dad with before seeing Dr. Benton.

While we were in Benton's waiting room, I asked my dad if he was changing his diet.

"Your father's been drinking as much as ever, maybe more," my mother tattled.

I glared at my father. "Every time you pour booze down your throat you're feeding your cancer. If you're going to keep boozing and bringing on your death, let me know so I can try not to care."

"I feel bad about that," I told Sara. "I don't want to say anything like that again. But we push each other's buttons."

"Don't nag," Sara told me. "Don't push. Just be supportive. Tell your dad, 'I love you, I'm scared for you, and however you want me to help you I will.' Don't count his drinks. Try not to get upset when you see him drinking. Remember, drinking used to be fun, that's why we did it. Just look at it as your dad having a good time and handling things his own way. And go to meetings up there."

[Friday, July 25]

I'm up in Minocqua already blowing Sara's good advice. My dad and I went grocery shopping this evening, and as we meandered down the aisles, I told him I'd been working a recovery program for six months and that it was helping me a lot and he should try it.

"I'm friends with this older dude called Playboy Pete," I told him. "He was a friend of your childhood buddy Leo. You'd like Pete. He has poker parties at his house, lives on a lake, has a boat."

"Leo was a big alcoholic," my dad said. "His wife was going to leave him if he didn't quit drinking. He quit drinking then died of cancer."

"Pete wanted me to give you his card," I said and fished Pete's card out of my purse and held it out to my dad. "He'd love it if you called him."

"I'm not going to call him," my father said. "I can quit drinking anytime I want. If I want to, I'll quit by myself. I don't need a recovery program."

I stuffed Playboy Pete's card into my dad's shirt pocket. "Hang onto it, just in case."

Back at the cabin, I started counting my dad's drinks. He had five huge manhattans in an oversized rocks glass. I reminded him that he needed to stop drinking. Then I forced myself to shut up. Later, when it was dark, my dad went outside and sat on the deck with another manhattan. I went out and sat with him.

"You don't know how it feels to have cancer, Brenda," he said. "I think about it all the time. I can't sleep. It keeps me up at night. I don't want to die. I don't want to leave you, the boys, your mother. Who would have thought this would happen to me? Sometimes I think I'll just buy a Harley and drive it into a fucking wall. I see myself in a coffin already, so why not? Everyone's going to die. Why not make it sooner than later? I really think I'll buy a Harley. It would make me happy. But your mother won't hear of it. She says it'll cost too much money. She's got enough money to live on very comfortably after I'm gone."

"She's afraid you'll ride it all fucked up and kill yourself," I said. "If you quit drinking, I'll lobby for you to get that bike."

[Saturday, July 26]

I woke up feeling sick to my stomach worrying about my father. I rolled out of bed and sat on the couch in the loft area outside my upstairs bedroom while Charlie slept. The kids got up and I cooked breakfast. When we finished eating, my dad and I took Seth and Max tubing.

My dad recently bought two tubes and we drove one out to the middle of the lake. Max hunkered down on top of the tube. His only experience tubing was getting whiplashed behind Kelly's boat. Remembering his violent jerking, Max kept the tube in the wake behind the boat. Seth, having tubed a ton, signaled for my dad to speed up, fishtail, do donuts. My dad, who loves a daredevil, began whipping Seth around.

"Seth's doing a great job out there," my dad shouted for Max's benefit. "Look at him. He's really hot-dogging it. You were just hanging in the wake."

Max looked like he'd been slapped. I knew exactly how he felt. My dad pulled that on my sister and me. "Look at Paula," or "Look at Brenda." Max got onto the tube again and hit it hard, but I could tell he wasn't enjoying it.

While my dad was tying his boat to the dock, I said I wanted to take out the dinged-up piece-of-crap community boat the other cabin owners use. My parents own the cabin with eight other couples and my dad bought his own boat rather than use the dilapidated piece of garbage everyone else drives.

"Why?" my dad asked.

"I want to be able to take it out if I want to," I said. "I should learn how to maneuver it in and out of the boathouse."

"You can't do that. Just go out with me."

"That piece of garbage is perfect to learn on," I said irritably.

I lowered the boat, drove it out of the boathouse, drove it around the lake, and brought it back to the dock. The wind had picked up and there was a strong current. As I approached the boathouse, the boat swung out at a funky angle and I aborted my attempt to pull the boat into the house. I reapproached. My father started screaming, "Throw it in reverse! Throw it in reverse!" I got flustered, threw the throttle forward, and rammed the boat into a metal pole holding up one end of the boathouse.

"Look what you did!" my father screamed. "Look what you did! You dented the boat. Everyone's going to be pissed!"

"What dent? What fucking dent? Which one of these fucking dents is new?"

"Just get out of the fucking boat and let me pull it in."

I got out of the boat and stalked off.

[Sunday, July 27]

I've been trying to find a recovery meeting for two days. On Friday, I called a number in the phone book, left a message on someone's answering machine, and no one called me back. On Saturday, I called the number again, someone picked up, and it sounded like the phone was tumbling around in the bottom of a purse while a hand fished for it. An older woman laughed then the phone went dead. I called back. The old woman answered.

"Hi," I said. "I'm looking for a meeting but I'm not sure I have the right number."

"Oh hi," she said. "Yeah, this is the right number. I'm not at home so I'm not by my meeting list. Could you call back at four thirty when I'll be home?"

I called back at four thirty and got her voicemail. I left another message and left the cabin number and my cell number. She didn't call back. I called a local treatment center thinking they might have a meeting list. What sounded to be a very old woman answered. "There's a meeting going on here right now, but it's almost over," she said.

"Great. Is there another one this week?"

"Oh, this is the only one here," she said. "It's once a week on Saturday."

"There have to be other meetings," I said. "Do you have a list?"

"I work at the hospital as a greeter," she said. "I don't have any of that information. Call me back tomorrow. I'll be at work at ten on Sunday. I'll see what I can find out for you from the men as they leave tonight."

I called the hospital greeter this morning.

"Oh, I didn't get a chance to ask," the woman said. "They went out a different door."

I was livid. I called Sara. I told her I felt like drinking.

"Look how hard you've tried to find a meeting," Sara said. "Look how much you want to stay sober. That's awesome. So you couldn't find a meeting, you're talking to me. Just think how lucky we are to have all the meetings we have at home. Those poor people up there—it's got to be a lot harder for them. Keep calling me."

[Tuesday, July 29]

I miss getting loaded. I've been wanting to drink all week. When I arrived at the cabin on Friday, I went directly to the kitchen to get a martini then remembered I wasn't drinking. It felt weird not grabbing the vodka bottle and pouring myself a stiff one. Saturday night, while we were having dinner, my dad asked, "Where's the wine?" I'm the wino who always supplied it. My dad doesn't drink wine if I'm not around. I wanted a glass of pinot grigio so bad I could feel its icy dryness on my tongue. I made a trip to buy groceries on Sunday and my dad said, "Pick me up some vodka," as I was walking out the door. I didn't buy him any, so yesterday he purchased a liter of vodka. Before dinner last night, my dad took the kids and me for a boat ride and on our way back, he said, "I'm gonna fix Charlie and me a nice martini. Charlie's about ready for one, I'm sure." This morning, my dad and I went out on the boat and docked at a restaurant to check its dinner hours. "Last year we stopped here for Bloody Marys," he said. "Remember?"

My father has been grinding me down for four days. He'd love to have me back as his drinking buddy. Part of me feels guilty for not drinking with him, like it's the least I could do for a dying man.

When my dad and I got back to the cabin, Charlie and I loaded our bikes on our Jeep and took Seth and Max biking in Boulder Junction. We rode to Cathedral Point, a gorgeous secluded lake spot, and ate a picnic lunch there. We waded into the water, and Seth and I decided to swim. Seth, Max, and I were wearing quick-dry shorts. Charlie was wearing heavy cotton ones.

"Take them off and swim in your boxers," I told Charlie.

Charlie, for whatever reason, was in one of his pissy moods. He shook his head, and I turned away from his crabby face. Max was agitated, too. Seth was riding a brand new bike that was twice the size of Max's, and Max was pedaling twice as hard as the rest of us to keep up. Max said he didn't want to swim either.

"Come on Max," I said. "A swim will feel good. Go into the woods, take your underwear off, put your shorts back on, and come in. You'll be all nice and cool during the ride back. It's not going to be fun sitting here like a bump on a log with Dad watching Seth and me."

"I'm going to swim in my underwear," Seth said, peeling off his shorts and wading in.

Max shook his head at Seth and reluctantly walked into the woods to change out of his underwear. I walked to a different spot in the woods, took off my underwear, put my shorts back on, removed my shirt, and walked out in my shorts and bra.

"Mom!" Max shouted. "What are you doing? Are you crazy?"

"What? Pretend it's a bathing suit top."

The water felt great. Charlie sat on the bank fidgeting irritably. I continued to ignore him. Fuck him. On the ride back, the boys and I were cool and refreshed, and Charlie was sweaty and grimy.

We got back to the cabin, showered up for dinner, and hopped into my dad's Suburban. We drove to the Norwood Pines restaurant, but there was an hour wait for a table.

"You got all these tables here," my father said to the hostess and gestured at a closed dining room. "Can't you open this up?"

"We can't do that to our waitstaff or our kitchen," the hostess answered. "We don't have enough people tonight."

"Well, we're not waiting an hour," my dad snapped. He was already lit.

"Would you like a menu to take with?" the hostess asked. "You could call for a reservation next time."

My father waved his hand at her in disgust and stalked out the door. My mother took the menu.

"Whoever heard of a reservation on a Tuesday night?" my father growled. "If they know they're going to be busy, plan for it. No reason they couldn't open a fucking table for us."

We had dinner at The Plantation instead. Charlie paid the check and we piled back into my dad's Suburban. Charlie, Van, and I climbed into the back seat, and my dad opened the hatch for Max and Seth to hop in the cargo area. My dad drove off. We were on the road two minutes when police lights began flashing. My father, who'd had many cocktails, began yelling for someone to give him a piece of gum. My mother had given Charlie a stick of gum at the restaurant and was frantically digging through her purse trying to find another piece.

"Fuck!" my dad shouted. "Give me the piece in your mouth Charlie." Charlie spit his gum out and handed it to my dad. My father popped it in his mouth and got out of the car. "What did I do?" he asked the officer, who was standing next to the Suburban.

"I need to see your license, your vehicle registration, your proof of insurance," the officer said.

My father stalked around the front of the Suburban, opened the passenger side door, and started rifling through the glove compartment. After handing the documents to the officer, my father and the cop exchanged some testy words I couldn't make out and the officer told my dad to get back in the car.

"Fucking asshole," my father ranted from the driver's seat. "Said I improperly entered the highway, that I pulled out right in front of him. He's giving me a warning for that and writing me up for the kids in back. Cocksucker! The cocksucker was laying for me. Son of a bitch. Fucking asshole. 'How many drinks have you had tonight?' my dad mimicked. I'd tell him where to fucking go if I didn't have drinks in me."

"So you could go to jail, spend the night in jail?" my mother asked sarcastically.

"That's right," my father spat. "Because I'm in the right here and I'd tell him where to stick it."

"Jerry, calm down," Charlie said. "You're going to make this worse. You just don't say anything. When a policeman gives you a ticket, you say thank you and drive away."

"Shut up," I hissed at Charlie.

"Thank you!?" my father shouted. "I'm going to say thank you to that cocksucker? I don't fucking believe it."

"You don't say thank you," I snapped. I looked at Charlie like he was a moron. "But don't get upset. Don't let the cop have that kind of power over you."

We sat in silence for a few minutes.

"What the hell is taking that asshole so long?" my dad asked. "He's just fucking with me now. I'd like to fuck with him."

The cop was sitting in his vehicle parked behind us. The windows of the Suburban were all open.

"Somebody else better get in the back because I can't leave here with minors in the cargo area," my father growled.

"It's okay if adults are back there?" I asked.

"Yes," he snapped.

Charlie and I traded places with Max and Seth. The cop walked up to my dad's window and gave him the ticket and we drove off.

"Cocksucker," my dad muttered.

[Wednesday, July 30]

Things got ugly today, just like I knew they would. My family and I have been coming up here every summer for years, and my father always has a meltdown. As the days tick by, my father dwells on instances when he wasn't thanked sufficiently, tallies up the money he's spent, figures out how many meals or drinks he should have been treated to. He comes up with ways his ass should have been kissed but wasn't.

Tonight, my dad started picking on the kids. He yelled at them for monopolizing the TV, not picking up enough, not spending enough time fishing, wasting food. He had begun the day, like every other, with Bloody Marys after breakfast. He'd moved on to beer by lunch, and by early afternoon he was pouring manhattans. By dinner, my dad was tanked and cranky. We were having dinner at The Ribber, the lake restaurant my dad and I had checked out yesterday morning. We all hopped in his boat, put our name on the waiting list, and ordered drinks on the patio. Max and Seth ordered kiddie cocktails.

"I hope our drinks come with umbrellas," Seth said.

"Why? Are you a girl?" my dad sneered and made a limp-wristed gesture. "Only girls want to play with umbrellas in their drinks."

A few minutes later, Seth pulled out a stack of business cards he'd collected from the places we'd been.

"What do you want with those?" my dad asked nastily. "You want business cards? Here, take these." My father fished three cards out of his wallet, his fishing charter business cards, and said, "You can give these to your father. Tell him this is the guy who took you tubing, shooting at the rifle range, put you up in Minocqua for a week."

The hostess sat us at a table twenty minutes later. I ordered Van chicken fingers and asked the waitress to bring them before the rest of our meal. Fifteen minutes passed. Our waitress delivered a basket of rolls and left. Fifteen more minutes passed. The waitress brought our soups and salads but no chicken fingers. Finally, the waitress delivered Van's meal, and almost twenty minutes later, the rest of us got our dinner. Max and Seth were bouncing off the walls. While we were waiting, Seth and Max had pulled up the hoods of their jackets, yanked the strings tight, poked their noses out of the tiny hood openings, and dangled spoons from their noses. When their ribs came, they yanked their hoods off and ripped into their food. Van, however, barely nibbled at the chicken because he'd eaten loads of rolls before his food arrived.

"I don't know why you order him food," my father snapped at me. "You know he's not going to eat anything."

"He stuffed himself with rolls and crackers because it took forever for his food to get here," I snapped back.

My dad scanned the table with a nasty look on his face. He was mentally tabulating what the meal was going to cost him. Charlie and I had bought dinner last night, but I could see my dad was feeling entitled to another meal. Fuck him. Charlie looked at me when the bill came and I shook my head.

We hopped into my dad's boat and drove back to the cabin. I put Van to bed and Max popped *Psycho* into the VCR. We'd started watching *Psycho* a couple of nights ago, but Seth had fallen asleep before the shower scene so Max rewound the tape to the infamous whacking.

"It's always the kids, everything's for the kids," my dad bitched. "What about me? What about what I want to watch?"

"What do you want to watch?" I asked him.

"Not this."

We watched the shower scene.

"That wasn't scary," Seth said. "I wasn't scared at all."

"These kids, all the shit they see and this is nothing!" my dad howled. He wagged his head disgustedly and drained his manhattan. He got up to get another drink. I let the kids finish watching *Psycho* and told them to go to bed. My dad put on *David Letterman*. Just then, my geriatric German shepherd, Sturgis, farted.

"Hey Mom, when did the dogs go out last?" I asked.

"Now your mother's supposed to take care of your dog?" my dad growled. "She's supposed to let your dog out? That's her job?"

My parents have a Labrador retriever, and we all let the dogs in and out of the cabin constantly.

"What are you talking about? I just want to know . . ." I started.

"You don't even know when he's been out last," my dad spat. "Your mother's been picking up his shit, too. Yeah. That's her job. Let her do it."

My mother started to say something and my father cut her off. "You know it's true. You're the fucking maid."

My mother attempted to speak again and my father shouted over her.

I looked at my mother. "Don't get sucked into this. He's drunk. It's pointless." I got up and went upstairs. Charlie had fled when the boys went to bed. I put on my pajamas and sat on the loft couch attempting to read. My parents were sitting in the living room below still watching *Letterman*. I could see them out of the corner of my eye through the pine log railing.

"What the hell's wrong with her?" my father muttered to my mother. "Can't take a little criticism? She brings Max's friend along, and I'm supposed to feed him, take care of him for a week? What kind of shit is that? The gas money I burned dragging him around the lake, what the fuck?!"

I wanted to chop my father's head off his stubby neck. I took some deep breaths and told myself, "Detach, detach, don't get sucked in." During my dad's meltdown last year, he and I had a screaming match. I attempted to remain calm this time but in the end I got up off the couch, grabbed my purse, scribbled my father a check for $200, and penned a note that said, "Dad, even though we bought most of the groceries, this check should cover any food or boat expenses. Thanks for being a gracious host." I marched downstairs. The door to the downstairs bathroom was open, and my father was in there brushing his teeth. I walked in, slapped the check and the note down on the sink, and stalked back upstairs.

"Would you look at this," my dad screamed at my mother. "What the hell is wrong with her?" I entered the upstairs bathroom and slammed the door shut. I began washing up but could still hear my dad screaming over the running water. "I'm gonna wipe my ass with this check and give it back to her," he bellowed.

I looked in the mirror. My adrenaline was pumping. The bathroom seesawed as my heartbeat banged in my head. I heard my mother tell my father to calm down, go to bed, everything would be better in the morning. Their bedroom door slammed shut. I could hear my dad bitching behind it. I went to bed and lay rigged for at least an hour before falling asleep.

[Thursday, July 31]

I woke up and made my way to the bathroom. I could see my father sitting on the living room couch downstairs. That was unusual. My father hops on his boat and goes fishing at the crack of dawn every morning. But there he was. The boys got up and went downstairs.

"We're going to Paul Bunyan's for breakfast," I called to the boys over the railing.

"Yea!" Max yelled.

"Paul Bunyan's!" Seth shouted.

The kids love the log cabin all-you-can-eat restaurant. My father hates it.

"Woo hoo!" Max shouted.

The boys ran upstairs to get dressed. I wanted nothing to do with my father. My plan was to avoid him and leave tomorrow morning. I was making my bed and my mother walked in.

"Your father feels really bad about last night," she said. "Here." She handed me my check. She'd voided it. "You know what he's like. He says stupid things when he's had too much to drink. Then he's sorry. I was so mad at him last night I wouldn't touch him or talk to him when we got into bed."

"Charlie and I have bought almost every grocery in this place," I said.

"I know. He knows it, too. But you know how he is. Otherwise he's a very generous person."

"He's not a generous person," I said. "He wants people to think he is but he's not. Whenever he helps someone out, he reminds them of it and mentions it in front of other people. He 'helps' people to make himself look like a big shot."

"I don't think he had a very happy childhood," my mother said.

"Well neither did I," I snapped. "We spent plenty of Christmas Eves waiting for him to show up, and he'd show up drunk. Then you'd cry."

"I know," my mother said grimly.

"Like I've said before, I wouldn't come up here if it weren't for the kids. Max loves it here. He loves shooting, fishing, boating, spending time with you two. These ugly episodes with Dad, I've been sucking them up because I know you guys aren't going to be around forever and I want the kids to build memories of you."

"I know," my mother said. "When it's just me and him up here, there are times I hate being here, too."

"This is going to sound terrible," I said, "but I'm glad he's dying first. I love him. I don't want him to die. But I think you're going to enjoy life without his nastiness."

My mother nodded.

"He wants to go to Paul Bunyan's," my mother said. "It's his way of making it up to you."

"I don't want him to go," I said.

"I know," she said. "I'll tell him he can't go."

"No, don't do that," I said. "That'll just make me feel like a shit."

I hurried the kids along, got them in the Jeep, and Charlie and I took off. My parents followed behind in their Suburban. We pulled into the parking lot and my father found a parking spot by the front door. By the time we parked and got all the kids out of the Jeep, my parents had gone into the restaurant and were standing in line to prepay. I jogged into the building. Two old ladies were working the cash registers and I squeezed in line behind my father and shoved money at the second old lady. She looked at me funny and glanced at the woman in line behind me. The woman behind me shot me a dirty look.

"Oh, I'm with him," I said pointing at my father. "I just don't want him to pay." The second old lady took my money. My dad tried to give the first old lady his credit card and I told her, "Don't take his money. I already paid." My father glanced at me, shook his head, and put his credit card away.

We were shown to a big log picnic table. My father sat at one end of the table and I sat at the other. Everyone chatted happily, wolfing down donuts, scrambled eggs, pancakes, and bacon; everyone except my father and me. Neither of us ate or said much and we left the restaurant without having spoken to each other.

Charlie and the boys and I piled into the Jeep and drove to the town of Eagle River, where we went rafting down the Wisconsin River. Van sat between Charlie and me in the back of the inflatable raft, and Max and Seth sat up front on the sides, occasionally dipping an oar in. We bounced over rocks and warm water sprayed us. Max and Seth laughed as we bumped along and caught air. At times they nearly flew over the sides into the hip-high river. Eventually, we hit a huge rock and Max went flying into the water. He stood up, completely soaked. We all laughed, except for Max.

"Really funny," he said. "I could have been killed and you're all laughing."

"I'm going in, too," Seth said and jumped over the side.

The boys splashed each other and giggled.

"Come on you guys, get back in the raft," Charlie shouted.

Max and Seth climbed in, but every time we hit a rock they flew overboard.

"Enough you guys," I said after about the tenth time. "I think there are leeches in the river. You might want to start checking yourselves. Be sure to check down in your pants. That's where they like to go." That put an end to their flying off the raft.

We stopped for lunch and went go-carting. I was trying hard to think of more things to do to avoid going back to the cabin, but I was out of ideas.

We arrived at the cabin around dinnertime and I started making a meal for Van. My dad walked into the kitchen and started making himself a manhattan.

"You know, I can be a real asshole," he said.

I nodded and walked out of the kitchen with Van's dinner. Van was sitting on the living room couch watching cartoons, and I set his plate on the coffee table. I walked back into the kitchen, and my father hugged me.

"You know I love you," he said tearing up.

"I love you, too," I said. "Even though you can be a fucking asshole."

My father and I laughed, and everything was back to normal.

[Saturday, August 2]

We drove home from Minocqua yesterday, and today I chaired my first meeting. I reluctantly volunteered to chair this meeting for a month because no one else stepped up to do it. I sat behind a big table at the head of the room and watched as women filed in. One minute before four, I nervously wondered if I should wait for the chitchat to trail off, or if I should shout and call the meeting to order. Most of the women have been coming to this meeting a lot longer than me. I hoped they'd notice it was time to start and quiet down, but a minute later, I was yelling and calling it to order. After following a prewritten format, I announced Anita, the lead speaker.

Anita said she could pinpoint the moment she became an alcoholic. She said she was in her early twenties working as a performance artist in Los Angeles and, one night, she went to a job and was raped. She returned to the Midwest and began drinking with a vengeance.

"I married a really nice guy, albeit a fellow alcoholic, and we had a son," she said. "We had many good years together, but then I got sober and ended up having an affair with a guy in the program. The affair was serious. I told my husband about it and asked him for a divorce. My husband didn't want a divorce but he eventually gave me one. One year later, he killed himself."

Anita fidgeted with her hands. She pursed her lips together and tried not to cry. She sat in silence for many moments before saying, "It's very hard to live with that. He was a good man. My son and I have a very strained relationship because of it. My son barely talks to me." Anita swiped at tears, didn't speak for a moment, and switched gears. "I'm an egomaniac with an inferiority complex," she said.

Anita's random last comment hit me like a ton of bricks. I, too, am an egomaniac with an inferiority complex.

[Tuesday, August 5]

I went to a meeting and bitched about my dad. It elicited some big laughs. I think I'm done being pissed off at him for now.

[Wednesday, August 6]

Charlie is going to a conference in Budapest. We have enough frequent-flier miles for me to go, too. Max will stay at Liv and Reed's house so he can go to school. Van is going to my parents' house. My mother said she would come to our house and watch both boys if my father didn't mind, but my father minded. Big surprise.

Charlie and I will leave for Budapest on September fifteenth. I checked out several Hungarian travel books at the library and when I got home, I opened one and turned to the wine section. I never planned on staying sober while I traveled. Charlie flies to Europe a lot for work. I usually pick a destination and go with him once a year. Last year we went to Sweden and Finland and took Max along. The year before, Charlie and I went to Cannes, Provence, and Paris. I still think about the delicious wine we drank there. As I skimmed the section on wine, a part of me hoped Budapest would have horrid wine, and according to the guidebook, much of Hungarian wine is swill. However, the wine that is good is considered to be some of the best in the world. Maybe it's time for a wine break.

[Thursday, August 7]

Charlie had hernia surgery today. We got up early this morning, piled into the Jeep, and I dropped Van at Hope's house for the day so he could hang out with Robin. Charlie, Max, and I proceeded to the hospital, and we checked Charlie into a stark little hospital room. He put on a gown and sat on the bed looking nervous.

"Boy, I bet you're hungry," I teased. "I bet you wish you could get pancakes with Max and me."

Charlie, always ravenous, hadn't been able to eat anything for twelve hours. "You got that right," he said.

I looked at my watch. "When the heck are they going to wheel you out of here so Max and I can go eat?"

"Mom!" Max said.

"You can go," Charlie said.

"I'm joking," I laughed. I looked at Max and loudly whispered, "I'm trying to keep Dad from worrying. Look how nervous he is."

"You do look nervous, Dad," Max said.

"Well, I am a little."

"Don't worry. You'll be back at home in a few hours," I said. "You want me to get you an apple pancake from Walker Brothers?"

"No, they're too sweet."

There was a knock at the door and two orderlies wheeled a gurney into the room.

"Well, you're going to the show," I told Charlie.

Charlie chuckled but looked like he wanted to throw up. I kissed him. "You're going to be just fine," I said. They began wheeling him away. "I love you," I yelled after him.

"Love you guys, too," he said shakily.

Max and I had breakfast at Walker Brothers and I took Max to the park before returning to the hospital. When we got to the room, Charlie was already lying in bed. He looked at us but didn't see us. He muttered something and Max looked at me, worried.

"Anesthesia," I said. "Dad's fine. We've just got to wait for the anesthesia to wear off. He's all drugged up."

Charlie mumbled again.

"What did he say?" Max giggled.

"I don't know. What did you say Charlie?"

"Yeah, good, do mumble, mumble, mumble."

"What if anesthesia is a truth serum?" I asked Max. "Should we ask him some questions?"

"Yeah."

"Charlie, do you secretly want to take belly dancing lessons?" I asked.

"Airplane, mumble, mumble."

Max doubled up laughing.

"Dad, do you have stinky feet?" Max asked.

"Here, okay, mumble, mumble," Charlie muttered.

"We should probably let him rest," I told Max. "Let's go to the gift shop."

When the drugs wore off, Charlie got a pep talk on wound care and we left. I drove to Hope's and picked up Van.

"Thanks for having Van," I said. "It was a big help."

"Van and Robin had a great time," Hope said.

Van was sitting in the kitchen eating a bowl of Lucky Charms. Robin was nowhere to be seen.

"Robin, Robin," Hope called. "Say good-bye to your friend. Van's leaving."

Robin never appeared. Van and I left.

[Saturday, August 9]

I chaired the meeting again, and this time Kiki gave the lead. Kiki is cute, petite, and articulate, but there's a screw loose. Her facial expressions are manic. She has those too-wide-open eyes. She stands too close to me when she talks and studies me like she's trying to read my mind. We both have ten-year-old boys, and she often says, "We should get them together. When's good for you?"

"Yesterday," I think.

Today, Kiki's lead was about how no one in her family thinks she's an alcoholic.

"I am an alcoholic," she said. "Like Brenda, I just hid my alcoholism well, too well, so now my family thinks I'm crazy. They think I claim to be an alcoholic so I can hang out with you people. Well they're right about that. I want to hang out with you people because you're my true family. You understand me. I belong here. I am an alcoholic."

When she finished, I scooted my chair an inch further away from her and said, "Because this is a big meeting, let's keep an eye on the clock and keep our comments short. We have until five o'clock."

The first woman to comment droned on and on. When the first person speaks forever, the people who follow usually talk forever, too. Five o'clock came and went. People actually began their comments by saying, "I know we're running late but," and gave long-winded monologues anyway. I squirmed in my chair until it finally ended at five thirty, which is when this meeting usually ends. The more I attend this meeting, the more I hate it.

I had a wicked headache by the time I got home. I went to the bathroom to take something for it. Charlie's Vicodin was there. I looked at the bottle, opened it, and popped one. I could have taken an ibuprofen, but to hell with it. I'm seriously considering ditching this recovery program and the whackos in it.

[Sunday, August 10]

I took Max to his swimming lesson this morning and when we got back home, I looked at Charlie's stitches.

"I feel great," he said, "like nothing happened. I think I'll take Max and Seth to the skate park this afternoon."

"Why don't you take Van, too," I said. "You can play with him at the park while Max and Seth skate."

Charlie made a face. "I'm not supposed to pick him up."

"You don't have to pick him up. He can walk. Just bring a stroller."

"You know he'll want me to pick him up."

"Don't. He walks for me all the time. Van will feel left out if you don't take him."

Selfishly, I wanted everyone out of the house so I could garden and sit on the deck and read in the sun.

Charlie grimaced. "Okay, fine," he grumbled, throwing up his hands and walking away.

I was lying in the sun and reading when I heard the Jeep pull up. The boys were back.

"How was it?" I asked, shading my eyes and watching them walk through the gate into the yard. Charlie was holding his abdomen and limping.

"I think I did too much," he said. "I carried Van. I'm gonna take some Vicodin and lay down." He limped away.

I looked down at my tan stomach and legs. I felt guilty, then angry. *Moron,* I thought. Why did the idiot lift Van? He probably injured himself on purpose so he could say, "See, I told you this would happen." What an asshole. I hate martyrs.

[Tuesday, August 12]

Darcy and I attended a Mozart concert at Ravinia. I brought two reclining beach chairs, a candle lantern, and a picnic basket packed with brie, olive hummus, a baguette, plates, cutlery, glasses, two bottles of sparkling water, and lemon wedges. Darcy was supposed to bring fruit and vegetables. She brought a bag of Subway sandwiches and individual snack packs of celery sticks with peanut butter. It irritated me.

A couple sitting on a blanket in front of us appeared to be on their first date. The guy put his arm around the woman, whispered in her ear, kissed her cheek, pecked at her mouth. The woman sat ramrod straight, staring straight ahead. She flinched periodically. They got up during intermission and walked past Darcy and me. The woman looked at our baguette, brie, and hummus.

"Yum," she said. "You guys want some sub sandwiches? He brought a bunch of sub sandwiches that we're not eating." Turning to her date she said, "You should have brought stuff like theirs." Turning back to us, the woman made a sweeping gesture with her hand and sarcastically asked, "Will you watch our crème brulee while we go to the bathroom?"

"Sure," I said.

"I don't know how much more of this I can take—him all over her like that," Darcy said.

When the couple returned, Darcy jealously watched the guy nuzzle his iceberg of a date. I couldn't help but feel sorry for the woman. I'd been stuck on many dates with guys I didn't like. She stiffened as her date glided his fingertips up and down her back and pecked at her mouth. My skin crawled for her.

As Darcy and I slowly drove out of the busy parking lot, she said, "I wish I wasn't affected like that, but when I see people all over each other, it bothers me because I don't have that."

"I felt sorry for the woman," I said, and explained how I saw it.

"Yeah, yeah, you're right," Darcy said gleefully. "I didn't see it but you're right. The way she complained about the food and made that snotty comment about the crème brulee. I totally see it now. Thanks for pointing that out."

It's interesting how our baggage influences our vision. I wonder how often we see things for what they really are.

"I sort of have a boyfriend," Darcy said suddenly. "But I think it might be over. He said something insensitive about my unemployment situation. (Darcy has been unemployed since February and is getting more depressed about it.) "I told Dave his comment was insensitive, he told me I was too sensitive and, well, you get the idea. I dated him two years ago for five months back when I was still drinking. I blew him off. Two months ago, he called because he got a DUI. I think it was an excuse to give us another try." After a long pause, Darcy said, "He's been a perfect gentleman. He puts his arm around me in movies, holds my hand, kisses my cheek when he walks me to my door."

"He hasn't tried anything in two months?" I asked.

"No," she said. "But it's not like we don't make out. We'll be at my house or at his house lying on the couch kissing a lot."

"And he doesn't try to take it further?"

"No."

"Don't you think that's odd? I mean, you're an attractive woman. I think it's weird he hasn't tried more."

"We had sex when we dated two years ago," Darcy said. "We did it twice toward the end. I think he just wants to take it slow this time."

"He waited five months before you guys had sex the first time? You guys have already done it and he still hasn't tried anything?"

"He's very spiritual. He's a born-again Christian."

"A born-again with a DUI."

"He did tell me he loses interest in women as soon as they have sex with him."

"That's a problem."

Darcy nodded sadly and pulled up in front of my house.

"Thanks for driving," I said. "I had fun."

"Yeah, me too," Darcy said, smiling faintly.

[Wednesday, August 13]

The boys and I drove to Milwaukee, Wisconsin, with Hope and her boys to take a tour of Miller Park. I'd called the ballpark a week ago to make sure they were giving tours today, but when we got there the place was deserted. We walked through the empty parking lot and empty building and finally bumped into an employee.

"There's a terrorism drill going on," the woman said. "No one knew about it. So no tours today, sorry."

The kids began complaining that they were hungry so I suggested going to Mader's, a Milwaukee institution that's decorated with expensive beer steins, suits of armor, and autographed celebrity photos. The heavy German food is served by a lot of stout middle-aged waitresses who've worked there for years. But today we got a skinny twerp in his early twenties. Our waiter took our order, brought us drinks, and we waited and waited for almost half an hour before he came back. The kids began squirming in their seats. Max tipped his chair over and fell on the floor. The other kids laughed, so Max hung a spoon from his nose, put a napkin on his head, and gargled with his water.

"Stop it!" I hissed. Fellow diners who all had their food were glaring at us.

Van grabbed the salt and pepper shakers and began sprinkling seasoning into his water. He grabbed his water glass, took a gulp, and let it cascade out of his mouth and down the front of his shirt. "You baby night-night ba-ba," he screeched, pointing his finger at patrons. People were really glaring now.

"Let's get out of here," Hope said. "I don't blame the kids for acting like this."

We got up to leave and the waiter brought our food.

"If I wasn't so hungry, I'd leave," Hope said and sat back down.

We scarfed down our food and left our waiter a lousy tip.

[Thursday, August 14]

Liv invited the Wendts and us over for cocktails to meet her parents who are in town from Arizona. Reed doesn't like Liv's parents and gives her a hard time when her family visits. He's the first one to admit it. Reed reminds me a lot of my cousin Mike, who enjoys being contrary and saying outrageous things to screw with people. I figured Reed would be in rare form tonight and I was right. He started up by telling his liberal mother-in-law that he supported the Iraq invasion.

"What about the American casualties?" Liv's mother asked, appalled. "What about the kids who are being sent home in body bags?"

"Who cares about them?" Reed asked. "Those guys had nothing going for them in the first place. They had to join the armed services to get a life."

Liv's mother's jaw dropped.

"He doesn't really think that," Liv laughed, shaking her head and giving Reed an incredulous, semi-pissed look. "He just has to say something."

Liv's mother changed the subject and started talking about the great clothes she just bought on sale.

"I don't buy anything on sale," Reed said. "If it's on sale, it means no one else wanted it."

I started laughing and said, "That's what Max said when he was four." Everyone laughed except Reed. "Max and I were in a children's store looking at flannel shirts. One rack was full price, the other was half price. Max said he liked the shirts and I grabbed two off the half-price rack. I asked the saleswoman, 'Why are these cheaper than the other shirts?' She said, 'They're from last fall. They have slightly different colors and patterns.' I bought the two sale shirts and the next day, when I tried to get Max to wear one, he refused to put it on. 'You liked this shirt yesterday,' I said. 'Why won't you wear it?' 'Because it's ugly,' Max said. 'No one else wanted it.'"

"Max had it right," Reed said, leaning back in his chair and stroking his chin. Everyone laughed. Reed shifted uneasily and looked uncomfortable. I felt sorry for Reed and regretted sharing my story. I could tell Liv's parents liked Reed as much as he liked them, and I didn't want to help them gang up on him.

[Friday, August 15]

Today was gorgeous, hot, and sunny. Hope and I took the kids to a new water park, and as soon as we paid the entrance fee, Max and Sid took off for the big slides. Hope and Robin ran into the shallow water toward the water sprayers, and I helped Van slide down the tongue of a small whale. Time after time I sat Van at the top of the whale's red tongue and caught him as he splashed into the water. My mind began to wander. I started thinking about Kelly and how it was Kelly who'd invited Max and me into playgroup when we moved to the suburbs. It was Kelly who'd helped me plant a lovely shade garden in our front yard. And it has been Kelly who's been pursuing our friendship since I got sober. I stopped calling her, and she's been the one reaching out and trying to stay in touch. If the tables were turned, if Kelly had been the one to quit drinking, I don't think I'd be pursuing our friendship.

The last time Reed was at her house, he said Kelly answered the door looking like a wreck. He'd gone over to ride motorcycles with Joel, and when they left, Joel told Reed, "Kelly's been crying her eyes out. This thing with Brenda and Liv has got her really upset."

When Reed shared this information with me, I said, "She's just feeling sorry for herself because she got caught." But I know Kelly cares about me in a warped way, and I feel bad about the whole screwed-up mess.

Last year, I had season tickets to the Joffrey Ballet and took Kelly to one of the performances. Since then, she's been bugging me to get season tickets for the two of us. When I got home from the pool, I called the Joffrey and got us tickets. I called Kelly and left a message on her answering machine, telling her that we were going to the ballet.

[Saturday, August 16]

I took Max to his swimming lesson at eight o'clock this morning and afterward, a guy who does carpentry work for my dad and his friends came over to give me an estimate on the damage done to our house from the microburst.

"Is the insurance company coming out?" he asked as we stood in front of my house looking at the soffit and fascia that had been ripped off.

"No."

"How much over do you want the quote?"

"I have a $500 deductible that I'd prefer not to pay," I said and immediately felt guilty.

I never would have batted an eye over getting my insurance company, a company we've paid megabucks to over the years, to cover the damage. But now I'm working a recovery program and trying to be honest all the time, and this is bothering me. I wish I could stop the nagging voice in my head telling me, "Your character defects may be your destiny." Screw it. I'm going to push this thing out of my head and not think about it.

• • •

This afternoon, I chaired the women's meeting I hate. The woman who was supposed to give the lead didn't show up and since no one else volunteered, I was stuck being the talking head.

"What book should I read out of?" I asked the group. "Is there a topic someone wants to discuss?" I thought about making honesty the topic and discussing my carpentry dilemma, but then three women said they wanted a meeting on the First Step, which is the Step that we admit we're powerless over our addictions and that our lives had been unmanageable. Since I'm seriously kicking around the idea of drinking in Budapest, I figured it was a pretty good topic for me, too.

During my lead, I fessed up and told the women that from the time I'd gotten sober, I'd planned to drink whenever I was in Europe.

"This back and forth thing—should I? shouldn't I?—is driving me crazy," I told them. "I went out to dinner with my husband and told him what I was thinking. He frowned and said, 'That's up to you. I'm not going to tell you what you should or shouldn't do.' But his face said it all. He doesn't want me to drink. And I've been thinking that, no matter how good the bottle of wine is, no matter how expensive, I'd be selling my hard-won sobriety cheap if I took a drink. I haven't had a drink in almost eight months and it's been hard. There have been many times I wanted to drink but didn't. I haven't been numbing out every night with booze. I'm not drinking in front of my kids. I haven't been hung over in a long time. I don't want any of that back. If I drink in Budapest, I know I'll find more good reasons to drink when I get back. I know myself. I'll be right back where I started. So there, I'm glad I just worked that out. Thanks."

I can't believe how relieved I feel. There's something very therapeutic about hearing yourself say what's running around in your head. It's cleansing and clarifying. It's bizarre.

I went home and finished fixing dinner. We'd invited Liv, Reed, and Seth over and I'd made a beef tenderloin stuffed with a creamy horseradish sauce laced with bacon and mushrooms. I'd also purchased some nice red wine to go with it earlier in the week. Buying the wine had tweaked me a little, but uncorking it tonight didn't bother me a bit. Watching Liv drink a martini and a glass of wine while Charlie and Reed got tanked didn't bother me, either. I felt fine. Purging myself at that meeting had done wonders.

[Monday, August 18]

Max had his friend Walter over and the two of them spent a lot of time on the computer researching how to get a patent for a four-way pencil Max "invented": four pencils of different colors poking out of a hub like spokes. After poking around, Max found himself on the Paper Mate site and clicked on a link to a patent attorney in Virginia. Ten minutes after Walter left, the phone rang.

"Hi, I'm looking for Max," a man said.

"May I ask who's calling?" I asked.

"I'm Steve Littleman, a patent attorney, and Max contacted me about a four-way pencil he invented and I'm getting back to him," he said.

"Do you know he's ten?" I asked.

"Ah, well, hmm. He did a good job filling out the patent form on my Web site."

"Do you still want to talk to him?"

"Ah, I can talk to you," he said.

In a nutshell, the attorney wanted $400 to do a search to see what other similar ideas were out there with patents pending. If we wanted to pursue a patent for Max's pencil, it would cost about $3,000.

"You might just want to go ahead and do the search," the attorney said. "It would be fun and educational."

"I think Max needs to come up with a better idea if we're going to spend four hundred dollars on it," I said.

I told Max about my conversation with the patent attorney.

"God, what a rip-off," he said, looking angry and disappointed.

[Tuesday, August 26]

Sara came over this morning, and we talked about starting my Fourth Step, which entails making a list of the people I resent and how I behaved badly toward them.

"I think you should wait until you get back from Budapest to do it because I don't want it ruining your vacation," Sara said.

I was actually jazzed about doing my Fourth Step. I have been treating myself like a science experiment, and I wanted to get on with the dissection process. I've glimpsed parts of myself I don't like. I haven't been as honest with myself as I thought I had. I haven't been good at seeing myself for who I am. I justify and rationalize everything I do. I rarely examine my motives.

My grandmother used to tell me, "You've got an answer for everything," and it was true. I also judge others to feel superior, make myself feel like Queen B. And Queen B's about to find out what an insecure self-centered little shit she is, but not until I get back from Budapest.

Sara and I were sitting on my deck sipping tea and watching Max and Van play in the yard. Max climbed out of the sandbox, walked over to us, and asked if we wanted another pot of tea.

"Thanks," I said. "That would be great."

Max took the teapot off the table and disappeared inside the house. He came back a short time later and placed the pot on the table. I poured Sara and myself a cup. It tasted horrible.

"The tea tastes coffee-ish," I told Max. "How did you heat the water?"

"I ran it through the coffee maker."

"Ah," I said, putting my cup down.

Max slid a piece of paper in front of me. It was a bill for $1.25. Under the amount, he'd listed all the things he'd done for me that morning: "Gave Van water. Put a video on for Van. Helped Van down from the monkey bars. Made tea."

"What about all the things your mom does for you in a day?" Sara asked Max. "What would that list look like if your mom wrote down everything she did for you and came up with a dollar amount?"

"That's her job," Max said.

• • •

Later, Kat and I went to Playboy Pete's house for a meeting. It's Playboy Pete's twenty-fifth sober anniversary. Twenty-five years without a drink. Unbelievable. More than forty people showed up to celebrate his anniversary with him.

I owe Playboy Pete. When I first started going to meetings, I felt like a fish out of water and I wanted to be a fish out of water. I didn't want to be an alcoholic loser. I wanted to keep my distance. Playboy Pete came up to me after a meeting one Saturday night and asked, "What's a nice girl like you doing in a place like this?" We both started laughing. He hooked his arm around my shoulders and started steering me around the room. He introduced me to a lot of people that night and jokingly avoided others saying, "You don't want to meet that guy, he's a, well, you don't want to know what he is." He invited me to go out with him and a group of people who were going to a steak house afterward, and it was the first time I felt normal in weeks. I didn't feel like a sicko hanging out with other sickos.

[Wednesday, August 27]

Max started fifth grade today and, officially, I haven't had a drink in eight months. I can't believe it. It's actually gone by surprisingly fast.

I took Sturgis, my arthritic thirteen-year-old dog, to the vet because his teeth are rotten and his gums are infected. My poor old boy can't even eat now. I helped him into the back of my Jeep, drove him to the vet, and he limped into the vet's office. The vet did blood work to see if Sturgis could survive being put under for dental cleaning and tooth extraction. She also wants to see if Sturgis should be on heart meds and steroids. I love that dog. I hope I can keep him alive and feeling better a while longer.

[Thursday, August 28]

I went to Liv's house for book club tonight. Kelly just got back from a fabulous family vacation, and she and I talked about it for a good long time. It felt like we were back to normal. The entire book club meeting felt normal. It was nice.

[Friday, August 29]

I've been trying to potty train Van, but it hasn't been going very well. After I worked out at the gym this morning, Van and I went to the toy store to purchase a potty-bribe present. Van picked out a Leap Pad, and I paid for it and we went home.

"Do a good job of going potty for one week and you can have the Leap Pad," I told Van and let him watch me put the potty present in my closet. Van looked like he wanted to push past me and tear the box open. Experts say you're not supposed to bribe your kids, but bribery helped me potty train Max, although he relapsed into pants-wetting behavior four years later.

Max wasn't interested in using the toilet until I told him I'd buy him a police car with flashing lights and a siren. In three days, Max was using the toilet and playing with his police car. He had just turned three. Van will be three October fifteenth, so I figured it was time to get started.

"Do you want to go potty?" I asked him.

"No," he answered.

"Let's just sit on the potty and see if you can go."

I sat Van on the potty and he peed a little. I asked him throughout the day if he had to go, and although he always said no, I'd sit him on the potty, remind him of the Leap Pad, and he'd go a little.

During dinner, I smelled flatulence coming from Van's direction. I asked him if he needed to poop and he said no. I took him to the potty anyway and reminded him about the Leap Pad. Still nothing. We pulled up his pants, washed hands, and sat back down at the dining room table. Moments later, Van stood up on his chair, grunted, and loaded his pants.

[Saturday, August 30]

My parents saw Tony Bennett tonight using the tickets I'd given them for Father's Day. They were good seats in the pavilion. I bought lawn tickets for Charlie and I, as did Liv and Reed, and we coordinated a picnic dinner for the concert. At six thirty, Liv and Reed picked up Charlie and me for the eight o'clock show. Hoards of people were going to see Tony Bennett. By seven thirty, we were somewhat near the concert but sitting in bumper-to-bumper traffic, and Reed was getting pissier and pissier by the minute. I started laughing. I poked fun at our situation, trying to lighten the mood. Liv and Charlie joked back. Reed muttered expletives. We turned onto Green Bay Road, almost at Ravinia, and inched our way closer and closer. The parking lot was full. We continued driving north on Green Bay Road flagged on by Ravinia workers directing us toward remote parking. We approached another lot. Full. Lot after lot was full, and we continued on through downtown Highland Park, a fair distance from Ravinia, and drove until we were in neighboring Highwood. I tapped Liv's arm.

"Good thing we have our pack mules," I said. "My picnic basket's heavy. I'm not carrying it."

"Brenda!" Liv laughed, shooting a look at Reed and cringing.

"Fuck it!" Reed said angrily, yanking the steering wheel and turning the car west toward the highway. "We're bagging it and going back to our place. These fuckers have been out here waiting since four o'clock (which I later found out was true). They fucking oversold the lawn."

"I'm with you," Charlie said. "Let's bag it."

"Yeah, I think so," Liv agreed.

"By the time we park and haul all this stuff and get on a shuttle bus and try to find a spot to sit, not to mention trying to get on the damned shuttle later," Reed said, "fuck it. I'm not doing it."

Reed sped back to his house. The moment we walked in, he began pouring drinks. He began shaking a martini for Liv and I wanted one bad.

"I wouldn't mind a martini," I said, hoping Reed would offer me one, but he ignored me. Liv and I set out the food, and I watched the three of them drink. I talked myself into and out of having a drink for the next twenty minutes. We sat around the island counter in Liv and Reed's kitchen and ate shrimp, sushi, bruschetta, and pâté.

"Back in college," Reed said, "my buddies and I had an eight-ball. It was some good cocaine. We went to a forest preserve to get high. We were underage and having trouble getting booze, and we came across a biker party. I walked up to the first biker I saw and asked to see his leader."

"Sounds like something Frankie and Annette would have asked in *Beach Blanket Bingo,*" I snickered. Liv and Charlie laughed.

"No, really," Reed said. "I asked to see their leader and when he was pointed out to me, I offered to turn the guy onto coke if he let me and my buddies drink at his party. He and I bonded. I ended up riding around with him on his bike all night doing blow. We snorted the last of it beside a donut shop at dawn. It was great."

I remembered that jagged, edgy, coming-off-the-rails feeling when the coke ran out and the sun was coming up. People were beginning their day and there I was, skin coated with a clammy narcotic film, barely able to function, going to someone's dark apartment to wait for sleep. It sucked. I hated the ugly aftermath. Maybe that's why coke was never my thing.

The last time I got really high on coke was at an overnight

bachelorette party, and I came home all wired and haggard to a two-year-old Max. It was a new low for me, and I decided never to get wasted on coke again. I did a line or two here and there on New Year's Eve if someone offered it to me, but that was it.

"I'll never forget that night," Reed said, smiling fondly at the memory.

"Yeah, sounds awesome," Liv said sarcastically.

I no longer wanted a drink. I was glad I was sober.

"I was just on a motorcycle trip with Joel and his friends," Reed continued. "We got busted. We were camping and drinking in a state park that didn't allow alcohol, and the cops came by and made us dump our booze. After the cops left, the guys started chopping down trees for a campfire, but they were green and wet. They kept trying to light a fire and I kept telling them it wasn't going to work. It was hysterical."

"Wow, sounds like fun," Liv deadpanned.

"Did you see *Bowling for Columbine*?" I asked Reed, changing the subject. "You're a big fan of George's. You should see it."

"I hate Michael Moore. The guy's a smug, fact-altering prick."

"The guy's got bigger balls than anyone I know," I said. "How 'bout I buy it for you? It just came out on DVD."

"Don't."

[Sunday, August 31]

I went to a meeting this morning and mentioned wanting to drink last night. Old Baseball Bob, who'd had visions of playing pro ball, was there, and when it was his turn to speak he said, "Brenda and I were just at Playboy Pete's for his twenty-fifth anniversary." He turned to me and continued. "It made my heart drop when I heard you say you wanted to drink. I really want you to stick around."

It made me feel good.

[Thursday, September 4]

I've been in a depressed funk the past few days and I'm not sure why. I can be driving my car, fine as can be, and all of a sudden I start crying. I don't understand it.

Van and I went back to Van's old preschool today. After the bad field trip incident, I pulled him out, wrote a letter of complaint documenting what happened, and as a result, Casey and Isabel were fired. The director asked me to re-enroll Van, so he and I visited today to check it out because Isabel's sister, Aliyah, is still there.

"Aliyah has really blossomed now that she's out from under Isabel and Casey," the director told me. "She has no hard feelings about what happened. Bring Van in, let him play, and talk to Aliyah. We hired another new teacher for the room who I think you'll love."

Van and I got to the school at nine thirty, and Van was happy to see his friends. Jenny, another new teacher, seemed great. She just got back to the States after being on a mission trip in Africa, and she and Aliyah were on the playground with the kids.

"Hey Aliyah," I said.

"Hi, Brenda," she said and gave me a hug.

Surprised, I hugged Aliyah back. "I'm thinking of re-enrolling Van," I said. "You're great with the kids, but I've been a little worried that you might have hard feelings about what happened between me and your sister."

"Not at all," Aliyah said. "What happened on that field trip was wrong. I was actually happy to see them go. Casey used to say mean things and make fun of me all the time. Isabel used to boss me around and take credit for things I did. We should go out to lunch sometime when Van's back in school."

"That would be nice," I said.

I re-enrolled Van.

[Friday, September 5]

I dropped Sturgis off at the vet to have his teeth cleaned and two rotten molars extracted. When I picked him up later, the woman running the office gave me the two molars they yanked, a bottle of antibiotics, and an enormous bill. But my boy is worth it.

[Tuesday, September 9]

Sara came over this morning and I told her I've been feeling very bitchy toward Charlie. I resent that he's a workaholic. I resent that everything to do with the house and kids is on me. I resent that he wants to live in his little work bubble and have me do everything else. I feel like a single mom with financial support—which is better than being a single mom without it. Kat is a single mom and she's got it rough. I have friends who are married to control freaks, too. And when I think about my two grandmothers, I thank God I don't have their lives.

My mother's mother, Mary, gave birth to fourteen children on her dairy farm. Two died as young children, and she raised the other twelve in a house that was heated by one wood-burning stove and had no indoor plumbing. She washed dirty diapers and clothes by hand, grew and canned her own vegetables, and slaughtered and plucked chickens for dinner. My grandmother hardly ever stepped foot off her farm.

My father's mother, Alice, had an *Angela's Ashes* kind of marriage. My grandfather drank with his friends after work and spent most of his money in taverns. My grandmother had to hunt him down on paydays and grab what she could before it was gone. When my dad and his three sisters were all enrolled in school, my grandmother got a job as a school lunch lady.

Comparatively, my life is good. I dismiss my negative feelings and problems and tell myself I'm a whiny jerk. But the same shit keeps coming back at me. I keep getting twisted up about the same old stuff.

[Thursday, September 11]

I drove up to Minocqua with Van and Sturgis. Paula and her family have been vacationing at the cabin with my parents for a week, and I'm dropping off Van and the dog because Charlie and I are leaving for Budapest on Monday. I'm going to stay a couple of nights and drive home on Saturday.

[Friday, September 12]

My father posted an ad to sell his fishing boat, and this afternoon a couple and their adult son came by to look at it. My mother never liked my dad having this boat. She couldn't see why he wouldn't just motor around the lake in the rickety piece of crap the other cabin owners use. All morning, before the prospective buyers showed up, my father was unhappily lost in thought. Periodically he'd comment that he needed to sell the boat so my mother wouldn't have to sell it when he was dead or dying. After lunch, the couple and their son showed up, bought the boat, and drove away with it. My father looked miserable. He looked at me and frowned. My mother walked through the living room and he looked at her disgustedly. "I'm regretting it already," he said and shook his head. He spent the rest of the afternoon drinking. By evening, he was in a nasty mood.

During dinner, I made small talk and said, "Charlie's taking Max to Lakeside tomorrow. Charlie's brother, Chris, and little Charlie are going, too. It's good they're hanging out."

"You never invite me to Lakeside."

"Yes I have," I snapped.

"Why are you going to Budapest?" my father asked. "What's there to do there?"

"Uh, let's see, visit a beautiful, former-communist city," I said sarcastically. "Experience another culture. See the world. If we had enough frequent-flier miles for Max, we'd bring him, too."

"You'd take him out of school for a week to go there but you won't take him out of school for a week to come here?"

"There's no comparison," I snapped. "Budapest would be a broadening experience. Max has been coming here for years. He was here this summer. He should come again and miss a week of school?"

My father snorted and no one spoke for a while.

Later, after Paula and I put our kids to bed and the grown-ups were sitting around watching TV, my dad blurted out, "You girls want our Minocqua time shares? You'll have to pay the yearly taxes and maintenance fees and let your mother come up whenever she wants to."

"Of course!" Paula responded gleefully. "I definitely want the place."

I looked at my mother. She was staring straight ahead at the TV saying nothing.

"I only hear one of you saying you want it," my father said, looking at me.

"Have you discussed this with Mom?" I asked him.

"No."

"Maybe you should before you offer us your shares."

"Well, we definitely want it," my sister said, looking at her husband.

My father said nothing. My mother said nothing. My brother-in-law, Rick, said nothing.

"Really, we want it," my sister said.

[saturday, september 13]

My dad was watching a hunting show on TV this morning when I got up. The hunters were in South Africa. I'd spent three weeks in South Africa in December and January of 1987 and 1988. My then-boyfriend was from Johannesburg and we spent a week on safari, a week at the beach, and a week in Johannesburg with his family. I sat down next to my father and watched the show for a couple of minutes.

"You and Mom should go there this winter," I said. "It'll be summer there. It's fabulous. You should go while you're feeling good."

My dad nodded and kept watching the show. I packed my bag and threw it in the Jeep. When the kids were awake, we piled into our vehicles and had breakfast at Paul Bunyan's. I thanked my parents for watching Van and the dog and gave Van a big hug and kiss and left.

[sunday, september 14]

Charlie's high school buddy, Sean, and I went to a meeting this morning. He mentioned wanting to get sober again when Charlie and I had dinner with him and his wife back in February.

"It's been pretty bad," Sean said as we drove to the meeting. "It's a pot problem this time. I've been smoking every day all day for the past three months and I can't stop. I've been feeling like I'm going crazy, literally nuts, so I know it's time to do this again. You know I had a coke problem a while back, right? I haven't picked that up again, but I'm binging on alcohol, and this pot thing I've always done. But lately I've been smoking first thing in the morning and throughout the day until I go to bed. Then I lay in bed unable to sleep with my heart hammering and crazy thoughts racing through my head.

"When you and Charlie and Marcy and I went out to dinner in February and you told me you were sober and going to meetings, I was jealous of you," he continued. "You got the monkey off your back." Sean sighed and looked defeated. "I gotta stay away from my other high school buddies," he said.

"That's probably a good idea," I agreed. Most of Charlie and Sean's high school buddies are affluent drunks and addicts who never grew up.

We went to the meeting and before we parted ways, I told Sean that Charlie and I were leaving for Budapest tomorrow, but that I hoped to see him at meetings when I got back. I wonder if I will.

[Monday, September 15]

I called my mother this morning to check on Van before leaving for Budapest. She told me a shitty little story that brought up all sorts of resentments for me. I believe my mother shared this story to gauge my reaction, to see if what she did was okay, because I think deep down she knows what she did was wrong.

My mother told me Van said he wanted a peanut butter and jelly sandwich. She made him one and when they sat down to eat, Van told her he wasn't hungry. So my mother said she made Van sit at the dining room table for one hour until he ate his sandwich.

"I showed him who's boss," my mother said.

"I don't like what you did," I told her. "Don't do that again." I wanted to cry. I wanted to shake her. I wanted to drive to Wisconsin to pick up Van and bring him home, but I was leaving the country in a few hours.

"He didn't cry," my mother said. "He just kept looking down at his sandwich and looking at me with a sad face. Finally, after an hour, he ate his sandwich and even licked the jelly off his fingers. He said it was good."

"You should have put the sandwich in the refrigerator and given it to him later," I said.

"Well, he needed to eat. It was after one o'clock, and he hadn't had lunch."

"He'll eat when he's hungry. If he doesn't feel like eating, don't force him."

I got off the phone and cried. I remembered the day I bought a chocolate bunny after school and when my mother saw it, she said, "You didn't ask me permission. Give it to me," and she whipped the bunny into the garbage.

My mother often pulled my long blond hair into two tight, painful ponytails. I started pulling my hair loose at school, but my mother didn't appreciate that. "I put those ponytails in your hair and I expect to see them when you walk out of school," she said. A few days later, I pulled my hair out of my ponytails and got spanked for it.

When my mother spanked me, she used a wooden paddle that used to have a red rubber ball attached to it by a rubber string. It used to be my toy before she ripped the ball and string off and began using it to punish me.

I pictured Van, head hung low, looking up at my mother's tight-lipped glare and eventually eating that rotten sandwich.

At three o'clock, I picked up Max from school and we packed his suitcase. I gave him a portable CD player and let him pick out a bunch of my CDs to take to Liv's. I gave Max a great big hug and said, "I'm really going to miss you, Buddy."

"I'm going to miss you, too," he said.

"I'll be back before you know it, probably before you want me to. I know you're going to have fun at Seth's house."

"Yeah, it'll probably be fun," Max said.

I took Max to Liv's and we carried his things to the guest bedroom. Max sat down on the bed, put his headphones on, and began listening to CDs. We kissed good-bye, and Liv walked me out the front door.

Liv smiled. "He's going to be fine," she said. "He'll have a good time. Don't worry about him. Seth's so excited that Max is staying here."

"Thank you so much," I said. "I really appreciate you."

I went to the airport, my plane took off, and I was on my way to Budapest.

[Tuesday, September 16]

One of the travel guides I've been reading warned that the taxis in the taxi queue are notorious rip-offs and recommended calling a cab company. So after I got my luggage, I changed some American money for Hungarian forint and spent several minutes staring at a pay phone trying to figure out how I was going to do that. Fortunately, no one else needed to use the phone while I stood there looking like a dolt. I put some money in and dialed. The phone rang and rang. I was about to hang up when someone answered in Magyar.

"Uh, hello. English?" I said.

"Yes. Little," the woman answered.

By the time I got off the phone, I was pretty sure I'd reached a taxi company and fairly certain a cab was coming. I yanked the handle up from my suitcase and rolled it to the reserved taxi stand. I watched other tourists hopping into the rip-off taxis and felt smug. Several minutes passed, and a swarthy gray-haired man walked toward me and motioned for me to get into a cab that was parked across a median two lanes over. I got in and arrived at the hotel. Charlie was in the room waiting for me.

"How much did you pay for your cab?" I asked him right away.

"About 5,500 forint," he said.

"Ha! I paid 3,600," I said.

Charlie had paid ten dollars more than me.

"I'm starving," I told Charlie.

"The concierge recommended a restaurant nearby," Charlie said. "We have a reservation. Let's go."

The restaurant, Nostalgia, was gorgeous. It was art nouveau with domed ceilings, arched windows, and sunken and raised dining rooms. The walls were pink and trimmed with elaborate white moldings. Huge chandeliers hung from the ceiling. A gypsy trio played music from a corner. And the food was delicious: crusty rolls with herbed butter, fish soup with hot paprika paste, grilled goose liver and apples in plum sauce, and for dessert, a dense wedge of a ricotta-like cheesecake laced with raisins and topped with an apricot sauce. Charlie had a gin and tonic and a beer. I looked at the other tables and their sparkling crystal wine decanters and glassware. It actually didn't bother me. Huh.

[Wednesday, September 17]

Charlie attended a conference today but before he trotted off, we walked around the city a bit and found Café Gerbeaud, which was highly recommended in guide books for coffee and pastries. Like Nostalgia, Gerbeaud was extravagantly lovely. Charlie had a big puffy cheese pocket and I had a chestnut croissant. They were heavenly. I walked Charlie back to the hotel for his conference and started off on my own.

Before I'd left the States, I checked out five travel books

from the library and cross-referenced their recommendations. Soon after I left Charlie, I stumbled on a tourism office and picked up a detailed map of the city, a brochure for organ concerts at St. Anne's church—which the guidebooks said were fabulous—and an opera house schedule. I began perusing one of the guidebooks I brought with me. A nearby attraction I'd highlighted was an ancient train that was on display in a subway. I descended a flight of stairs into the subway and saw nothing. There was a short escalator and I rode it down to the next level. Nothing. I walked across a platform to the top of another down escalator and stepped on. Holy shit! It was the steepest, tallest, longest, fastest escalator I'd ever seen. If the escalator had been a building, it would have been something like twenty stories high. My hair flew behind me as I plummeted hundreds of feet down a seemingly endless gray chute at what appeared to be a thirty-degree angle. Halfway down, I began feeling dizzy and nauseated. If I tripped or was pushed, I was a dead woman. The handrail was moving at a slower rate than the stairs and I adjusted my grip. I looked across at the people flying up the up escalator and started to giggle. It was a ridiculous wild ride that smacked of the communist era. I got off the escalator and in front of me was a train platform but no antique train. Screw it. I stepped on the up escalator and watched people flying past on the down one. A mother and her daughter, a girl about Max's age, were hurtling toward the train platform below. It made me wince. I got off and took the short escalator up to the next level. I walked toward the stairway and a man began yelling at me in Magyar. I quickened my pace and the man ran in front of me. "Ticket, ticket!" he shouted. I took out my guidebook and pointed to the paragraph of the antique train.

"You need ticket!" he shouted. "Passport!"

"I didn't ride the train," I said. I tapped the guide book with my finger. "I was looking for the old train."

The man began aggressively moving toward me, weaving from side to side, backing me toward a wall. "Passport, I need passport!" he demanded. "This is fine!" He flapped a book of tickets in my face.

I looked at the two laminated ID badges hanging from a cord around his neck and hoped he was legitimate. I fished around in my purse and handed him my passport.

"Where do you buy a ticket?" I asked. "I never saw a ticket booth."

He swept his arm toward a tiny booth in a dimly lit corner. He waved his arms over an almost-worn-off red line painted across the width of the floor. "Need ticket to cross," he said. He scribbled up my fine and demanded money. I pulled a bill out of my wallet and handed it to him. He handed me some change and my passport and left. I walked out of the station.

Budapest is two cities: Buda and Pest. Buda is the old side, Pest is the new side, and they are separated by the Danube River. I walked the Pest side, which is full of impressively ornate buildings, and popped into a health food store and bought a wedge of eggplant pie for lunch. I carried it out in a brown paper bag and ate it on the steps of the Hungarian National Museum. I entered the museum and viewed the Hungarian history of Turkish occupation, Hapsburg rule, Nazi occupation, and communist rule. I headed to the opera house and bought two front-row tickets to the ballet for Saturday night. I walked back to the hotel, freshened up, and changed for dinner.

Charlie showed up and we walked down to the Danube River and boarded a boat aglow with festive white lights for a conference dinner cruise. We were directed to the top deck where waiters dressed as monks, turbaned Turks, and Hungarian folk dancers served cocktails on silver trays. I sipped water for an hour and stood next to Charlie as he schmoozed with clients. Music began floating up from below and people started streaming down the boat's stairwells to go inside.

Two floors down, waitstaff had begun serving people food from three stations: traditional Hungarian, medieval times, and Turkish. Hungarian folk dancers skipped and twirled. Dancers dressed in medieval garb circled. Belly dancers jiggled next to the Turkish food.

Upstairs, white linen-covered tables were topped with miniature mirrored staircases supporting bite-sized Napoleons, chocolate tortes, and orange sponge cakes. It was heaven. I stuffed my face, and Charlie and I climbed back up to the top deck of the boat for a gorgeous view of Budapest all lit up. As the boat cruised down the Danube, warm wind floated through my hair, and I was thrilled I wasn't numb from booze. The night was glorious. Everything was vivid and sharp. I'm not going to wake up tomorrow with a hangover.

[Thursday, September 18]

I went to the enormous, gorgeous, and opulently tiled Central Market for a Hungarian cooking class arranged by the conference for spouses of attendees. We made Hungarian goulash and for dessert, thin pancakes stuffed with raisin-laced sweet cottage cheese. I ate lunch and ditched the other spouses who were getting on a tour bus for a tour of Pest, which I'd seen yesterday on foot. I hung out at the market and started shopping. I toured stalls filled with lace tablecloths, gaudy crystal goblets, touristy imitations of Herend china, and real Herend porcelain, which the Queen of England is rumored to drink tea from. I bought Max a petrushka doll of the American presidents and Van some wooden animal jigsaw puzzles. The shops rimming the walls of the top two floors of the market overlooked the ground floor, which was loaded with fruit and vegetable stands, pastry shops, meat markets, and paprika kiosks. Locals grocery shopping scurried from stall to stall. I made a mental note to come back when I was hungry and took a leisure walk back to the hotel to get ready for tonight's putska.

A putska is a Hungarian cookout. I freshened up, changed into jeans, and Charlie changed into casual clothes. We walked down to the lobby and Charlie shepherded me toward some of his business buddies and their spouses, and we got on one of three enormous tour buses. Charlie leaned over me from his aisle seat and pointed out the window.

"Look at that," he said. Two police officers on BMW motorcycles had pulled up next to our bus. The cops blared their sirens and began stopping cars. The tour buses pulled out into heavy rush-hour traffic. More motorcycle cops were in front of and in back of our motorcade. They swooped around, stopped traffic, and pushed our buses through stoplights.

"This is embarrassing," Charlie said as we peered out the window at angry drivers stopped in their cars.

The event planner, noticing our shocked faces, picked up a microphone and said, "You might notice we have a police escort to get us through rush-hour traffic. We were concerned we wouldn't be able to meet our train in time."

"We're getting on a train?" I asked.

"I guess," said Charlie, still looking out the window, thoroughly appalled. "I can't believe they're doing this."

"Oh, lighten up," I said. "It's obnoxious, but it's kinda cool. This would never happen in the States. I wonder how many palms they had to grease to pull this off."

We traveled through the city and suburbs, and began driving through the countryside, which was dotted with clusters of shack-like homes. Eventually, the buses stopped in the middle of nowhere and parked. We got out and walked around the bus. There was a posh antique train and Charlie grabbed my hand and we entered one of the dining cars. Charlie's friend, Lawrence, and his wife, Ann Marie, were already seated at a table covered with a white linen tablecloth, and Charlie and I joined them.

"My grandfather used to live in one of those small country houses," Ann Marie said.

Waiters brought wine, mineral water, soda, and dense cheese biscuits to the tables. The train began clattering down the track. We heard music and, minutes later, accordion players were strolling down our aisle. Waiters brought party sandwiches to our table and a beer was plunked down in front of every passenger.

"It would be rude to refuse," Lawrence said and popped open his beer.

My guidebook said Hungarians take offense if a man refuses a proffered alcoholic beverage, but if a woman graciously declines a hard drink in favor of a soft one, it's okay. God help the alcoholic man trying to stay sober in this country. I pushed my beer in front of Charlie and drank mineral water.

We rattled through more Hungarian countryside and rolled to a stop about an hour later. Horses and wagons were stationed alongside the track, waiting to take us to a ranch. I'd had my fill of mineral water. God, I was tired of drinking water. And I had to go to the bathroom. Ann Marie said she had to go, too, and we found a restroom at the end of a dining car.

"Go ahead, you first," I told her.

As Ann Marie exited, she said, "I don't know what you have to do, but I wouldn't relieve myself of both things in this toilet. It goes straight outside."

I shot her a puzzled look and went into the bathroom. As I sat down, I noticed daylight shining through the bottom of the toilet. I looked down and saw train tracks. I took a quick pee, wiped, and walked off the train. Charlie, Lawrence, and Ann Marie were standing a few feet away laughing.

"We saw it all come out," Charlie laughed. I looked at the train and saw two wads of paper on the track below and urine dripping onto the tracks.

"Oh my God!" I said, laughing.

"I can't believe it," Ann Marie said. "You wouldn't want to take a romantic walk along these tracks."

We walked toward the horses and wagons where men clad in Hungarian cowboy costumes were handing out shot glasses and filling them with apricot brandy. I avoided the cowboys and got on one of the wagons. Ann Marie, who'd been handed a shot glass, held one out to me."

"No. She doesn't drink," Charlie said urgently.

"Yeah, I don't drink," I said, shrugging.

Ann Marie looked at me quizzically and put her shot glass under her seat. I felt like kicking Charlie.

After a short ride, we arrived at the ranch and the horse-drawn wagons dropped us off near a pavilion where an enormous ox was roasting on a spit. Several open bars were serving drinks and waiters roved with trays of more drinks. I was shocked that the alcohol swirling around wasn't tweaking me. I was totally fine.

Each of us was handed a piece of paper with a number on it, and an event organizer grabbed a microphone and announced that the numbers indicated which teams we were on and that we should get ready to play games. The first game was Find the Needles in the Haystack. Several tarps were spread out on the ground and on each was a large mound of hay full of sharp needles. The organizer yelled, "Go!" and each team swooped down on a haystack and began sifting madly for needles. I happened to be on a team of über-competitive Germans who were sifting as fast as they could. They periodically shot me dirty looks because I was sitting on the tarp laughing. "Look, look for the needles," one of them yelled at me and motioned toward the stack. I started sifting and giggling. When our time was up, I'd contributed one measly needle.

Next came a wagon race, where each team piled onto a wooden horse-drawn cart and four of the burliest most testosterone-pumped members acted as horses and began pulling and pushing the creaky hernia mobile toward the finish line. After that, six men on each team were strapped onto one pair of ridiculously long skis mounted on wheels. Then came the wheelbarrow race.

I was the smallest woman on the team and was elected to sit in the wheelbarrow. I shifted uncomfortably as I prepared for each of the eleven members on my team to run me down the field, round a pole, and run back before handing me off to the next person in the relay. The first teammate to grab the handles of the wooden wheelbarrow was a large German dude. At the sound of "Go!" he ran down the field as fast as he could go, rounded the pole, and ran me back. I laughed good-naturedly as the wheelbarrow bumped and bounced over ruts and lumps loosening my kidneys. He handed me off to a female teammate who ran more gently around the field. The next guy to grab the wheelbarrow ran as fast as he could, didn't slow up as he careened around the pole, lost control, and dumped me on the ground. I quickly got back into the wheelbarrow while he apologized profusely and ran me back. The next three guys in line whipped me as fast as they could up and down the field and I was thinking, *fuck, fuck, fuck* with every bump and hole I hit. A female teammate grabbed the wheelbarrow, ran me around the field, lost control at the pass-off point, and dumped me on the ground while swinging the wheelbarrow around to pass to the next person. Charlie was last in line. I got back into the wheelbarrow, and he wheeled me away, taking it easy, which caused us to come in second and disappoint our teammates, who saw me as nothing more than a pile of rocks.

"You okay?" he asked, helping me out of the wheelbarrow.

"I think so," I said, rubbing my behind.

We began walking to the last event, a bullwhip contest, to see who could crack the whip and knock a wine bottle off a stump in the fewest number of tries. As we watched the contestants and waited for our turn, one of our teammates leaned over and said, "Did you hear what happened to Hans?" Apparently Hans had bullwhipped the bottle, broke it, and a jagged piece of glass had flown back and sliced his hand open. He was on his way to a Budapest hospital to get stitched up.

Charlie took a turn at the bullwhip and, like most people, kept missing the bottle. We walked off with a large group of people headed for a large corral where a cowboy show was about to start. A team of five horses—three in front, two in back—was led into the corral by a cowboy who climbed onto the two rear horses, stood with a foot on each of the horses' behinds, and drove the team around the ring at breakneck speed. I looked at Ann Marie, who was sitting next to me. We stared at each other, our mouths hanging open.

We headed to the pavilion for a dinner of goulash and roast ox, and as we ate, I noticed a little hut where a line of people were waiting.

"What's over there?" I asked Bobbie, one of Charlie's co-workers.

"A real gypsy fortune-teller," she said.

"Have you seen her?" I asked.

"No, but he has," she said motioning to her husband, Jonathan.

"Was she any good?" I asked Jonathan.

Jonathan shrugged and smiled. "She said some interesting things."

"Like what?"

Jonathan shrugged and smiled and wouldn't elaborate. "Go see for yourself."

I got in line and after a short wait entered the hut. A wizened old woman sat behind a table and an interpreter motioned for me to sit down next to him. The fortune-teller had me shuffle a deck of tarot cards and began reading them. Through the interpreter, the gypsy told me my writing career was going to go well. She said I had a very good marriage. Then she mumbled something to the interpreter.

"She asked me if she saw anything bad, should she tell you?" the interpreter asked me.

"Yes," I said, feeling anxious and worried.

"Someone else is either in love with you or going to be in love with you," she said. "You are going to have to choose who to be with."

"Really?" I said, relieved she didn't say I was going to die.

"Is there anything else you want to ask her?" the interpreter asked.

"My father is ill," I said. "Ask her how that's going to turn out."

The gypsy said my father was going to be fine, that he didn't have anything serious like cancer. Ha!

I left the hut and the next person entered. A small group of people standing outside was discussing what the gypsy had told them. According to the gypsy, one guy was going to become seriously ill. Another man was told someone was trying to sabotage his job. A worried-looking woman said the gypsy told her that a brunette was after her husband. That gypsy was one little ray of sunshine.

[Friday, September 19]

I got up and took a long walk along the Danube down the Pest side, turned onto the Szabadság híd (Liberty Bridge), and crossed it to Buda. Two days earlier, I'd crossed the Széchenyi lánchíd (Chain Bridge) and seen a very pathetic gypsy beggar. He was hunched over a tiny metal crutch that was only a foot long. As I walked past, he groaned, muttered something, and shook a cap full of change at me. I kept walking and felt guilty for not dropping a few forint in. As I crossed the bridge today, another beggar was pulling the exact same tiny-crutch act. I blew off the second beggar and crossed the bridge to the Hotel Gellert.

The Hotel Gellert opened in 1918 as an enormous art nouveau hotel and renowned spa. It has a huge Greek-influenced swimming pool surrounded by ornate white columns. Sculptures and fountains rim the pool spilling water onto the backs and heads of bathers.

I walked into the lobby of the once opulent and gorgeous Gellert, which is scruffily long in the tooth, and got in line to purchase spa services. There were mudpacks, salt baths, and various curative massages that require a doctor's prescription. Across the lobby and down the stairs in a dingy little office was the staff doctor who did the prescribing. I got up to the counter and the cashier spoke no English. I pointed to the swimming pool/thermal bath/massage package because I was incapable of ordering à la carte. I left the counter, tickets in hand, with no idea of where to go. I wandered around for ten minutes, went up some stairs, and stumbled onto the women's locker room. The cream-colored room was lit by overhead skylights and rows of dark-paneled lockers lined the walls. Stout older women were milling around naked or draped in white sheets. I stood near the doorway looking for someone who could tell me what to do. An attendant finally approached me and pointed to my receipt. I handed it to her. "Wait," she told me and handed my receipt to an attendant who was sitting at an old high school desk reading a Hungarian celeb magazine. The attendant lowered her magazine and motioned for me to stand next to a couple of husky old women. She wiggled out from behind her desk and handed my receipt to a third attendant who motioned me over and walked me past many dark-paneled lockers before pointing me at a dressing room cubby. "Change," she said, and pulled a curtain closed across the entrance of the cubby. I pulled a swimsuit out of my purse, changed into it, and emerged from behind the curtain.

"Swimming pool first," the attendant said. "Remember locker number." She ripped off part of my receipt and handed me a small green square stamp. "For massage," she said. "Put in locker." I put the square in the locker. The attendant locked the locker with a key hanging from her wrist and handed me a numbered tag attached to a loop of string. The attendant led me to a door and pushed it open. We walked through a small bathroom to another door and the attendant pushed it open. She pointed to the right. "Swimming pool," she said. She pointed to a doorbell next to the door. "Ring when done," she told me and walked away.

The pool, although showing its age, was still grand and impressive. Men and women were swimming and lounging along the sides chatting. I swam several laps and sat in the hot tub at the shallow end. I positioned myself under a water-cascading sculpture. The warm fresh water flowing over me felt wonderful. When I was done, I walked back to the door, rang the bell, and was taken back through the locker room to the women's thermal bath room. Fifty percent of the women sitting in one of the two baths were naked. I kept my suit on and got into the warmest one. Back in the locker room, an attendant opened my locker, grabbed my green stamp, and said, "Massage."

She took me to a waiting area, handed me a white sheet to wrap myself in, and left. I took off my wet bathing suit and wrapped myself in the sheet. A plump old woman sitting at another high school desk motioned for me to sit in a chair around the corner. A sheet-clad woman, like myself, was sitting in one of several chairs lining the wall. I sat down near her and we faced a massage room that looked like it came out of a black and white horror movie about hydrotherapy treatments in a mental institution. Hoses, white tile, grubby grout, and a gurney were partitioned off from us by a hospital curtain. I could see a masseuse kneading oil into the fat shiny thighs of a client through an opening. After about ten minutes, the attendant walked over and said something in Magyar. The other sheet-clad woman got up and followed her. The attendant turned and motioned for me to follow, too.

We walked into a long, narrow room where I could see the legs of five or six masseuses poking out from under hospital curtains as they massaged clients on gurneys. A long line of chairs ran along the wall facing the curtained massage chambers, and the other sheet-clad woman and I sat down and waited some more. For fifteen or twenty minutes we watched feet shuffling behind the curtains and listened to groans and American songs sung in Magyar from a portable radio. An oil-slicked woman emerged from behind a curtain and the woman I was waiting with was taken behind it. A few minutes later, my masseuse came and got me and walked me back to the freaky hydrotherapy room. The masseuse, an attractive redhead about my age, took a sheet, laid it on the gurney, and

I lay down on top of it. She sprinkled me with talcum powder and went to work gently kneading my muscles.

I walked out of the Gellert feeling like a million bucks.

I hiked up to the citadel and eventually made my way to Szilagyi Dezso ter, a neo-gothic Calvinist church dating back to the end of the nineteenth century. The Danube bank near the church was where the Arrow Cross, the Hungarian Nazis, massacred thousands of Jews in 1944 to 1945 by tying them together in small groups and throwing them into the icy river. Today, the church has stained-glass windows adorned with stars of David in remembrance.

I slowly walked back to the hotel and began getting ready for dinner. I put on an evening gown, Charlie dressed in a suit, and we joined other elegantly clad conference couples in the lobby of the hotel. Conference organizers directed us outside to a train, and the train dropped us off near the Néprajzi Múzeum (Ethnographical Museum).

"Wow," I said as Charlie and I strode up a tall flight of red-carpeted stairs leading to the front doors of the museum. Uniformed men were holding tall pillar candles along the stairway's edges. Inside, the magnificent hall was lit by thousands of candles. Linen-covered tables were topped with gorgeous floral arrangements dripping with blossoms and tea light candles. When everyone was seated, a Cirque du Soleil-like entertainer entered the room wearing a harlequin suit covered in diamond-shaped mirrors. The human glitter ball threw sparks all over the room as he pranced about making music by rubbing the rims of water glasses and playing the flute. A waiter came to our table with a bottle of sherry, and Charlie's hand shot up over my glass as the waiter was about to pour. "No," he said too loudly.

"I can handle it," I hissed. "You're so damned conspicuous."

Appetizer plates of foie gras and bottles of white wine were set on the table. I held my hand over my white-wine glass as waiters frequently tried to fill it. Salads were brought out with red wine. Our very attentive waiters attempted to fill my red-wine glass constantly, and if my hand didn't shoot over it quickly enough, Charlie shot his over the rim of my glass. Other couples seated at our table looked at us quizzically.

"Let the next waiter fill my damned glass," I muttered to Charlie, "Then we won't have to keep telling them no."

"Yeah, okay," Charlie said, looking a little uneasy.

The next time a waiter came by, I let him fill my glasses with both red and white wines and let them sit there. They didn't bother me one bit.

When the dinner ended, everyone went back to the hotel bar. Charlie got a scotch and a club soda with lime for me. Charlie's co-worker, Bobbie, who'd been seated at our dinner table earlier, said, "I hope it doesn't offend you that we're drinking. I noticed you don't drink, and I hope it doesn't bother you."

"I used to drink but I don't anymore," I said, shooting her a get-my-drift look. "Don't worry about it. I don't mind if you drink, it's just better that I don't."

"Ah," Bobbie said, nodding, looking a bit taken aback and at a loss for words.

I still haven't told anyone besides my sister and parents that I'm in recovery, but I'm becoming less and less concerned about people finding out. I finished my club soda, gave Charlie a kiss, and went up to our room, leaving him behind.

[saturday, september 20]

Charlie and I were married twelve years ago today. The conference over, Charlie and I went sightseeing in the Castle district of Buda. We toured the castle's eerie labyrinth, walked the oldest streets of Buda, and I threw out tidbits of interest from my guidebook. Charlie feigned interest for a while and, before noon, said he was hungry for lunch.

"I'm tired," he said when we'd finished lunch at an outdoor café. "Let's go back to the hotel."

"Fine," I said, mystified that he'd rather have sex than see Budapest. We can have sex anytime, but we may never get here again. Later, we took a dip in the pool, sat in the sauna, showered, and got dressed for the ballet. We walked to a restaurant a short distance from the Opera House and ordered dinner. When the waiter arrived with our food, he placed a mountain of raw ground beef in front of Charlie.

"You ordered steak tartar?" I asked, surveying his plate disgustedly.

"I didn't know it was raw," he said.

I looked at the chalkboard specials menu Charlie had ordered from.

"It says right there that it's raw," I pointed out.

"Guess I didn't look at it carefully," he said, shifting uncomfortably in his seat.

"Are you going to eat that, with all the mad cow disease going on in Europe?"

"I don't want to send it back," Charlie snapped. "I hate when people do that."

"Whatever."

"I ordered it, I'll eat it," Charlie said, fidgeting irritably.

"It's your brain, but I'll have to take care of you when it looks like Swiss cheese."

Charlie ate a forkful. "It's actually good," he said.

"I'm happy for you."

We walked to the Opera House and took our front row seats at the edge of the orchestra pit. An attractive cellist wearing a red bandana on his head kept looking at me, and

I liked it. The ballet began. Every expression on the dancers' faces, the sweat glistening on their bodies, their muscles trembling with exertion, was visible. It was incredible. When we broke for intermission, Charlie and I climbed the stairs to the top floor of the Opera House for refreshments. Champagne in crystal glasses and pastries on china were beautifully displayed for purchase. It put all the ballet intermissions at the Auditorium Theater in Chicago—candy bars, drinks in plastic cups—to shame. Charlie purchased a glass of champagne for himself and a pastry for me, and we walked out onto the rooftop terrace and looked out at the city below. It was fabulous.

The second half of *Onnegan* sucked me in and I got lost in it and cried. I looked at Charlie. His head was bobbing and his eyes were fluttering. It was an incredible anniversary, for me anyway. It's lucky we remembered it.

Charlie and I usually don't remember our anniversary until a day or two before it. Two nights ago, during our train ride to the putska, Charlie and I were sitting at a table with Ann Marie and her husband, Lawrence, when I asked Charlie, "Hey, did you remember it's our anniversary on Saturday?" Ann Marie and I'd been discussing how long we'd been married, and it registered that our anniversary was in two days. It hadn't occurred to me when I was purchasing ballet tickets that the performance was on our anniversary.

"Oh, yeah," Charlie lied. I rolled my eyes at him.

"Brenda said you'll be married thirteen years," Ann Marie commented.

"No, twelve," Charlie said.

"Oh, yeah," I said, flushing. "I got our anniversary mixed up with our dog's age. We got Sturgis right before we got married, and Sturgis will be thirteen."

Ann Marie and Lawrence looked at each other and then at Charlie and me.

[Sunday, September 21]

Charlie flew home this morning, but I'm flying home tomorrow because we booked our trips separately. I walked to Buda and spent three hours in the castle's Hungarian National Art Museum, which I'd planned to visit yesterday with Charlie. I walked to the largest Jewish synagogue in Europe, the second largest in the world. Its massive Moorish exterior was stunning, and behind it was a courtyard full of headstones and feral cats. Many of the headstones were stacked together like books in a bookcase. The headstones belonged to Holocaust victims who'd taken refuge in the synagogue before it was taken over by the Nazis. Behind the courtyard was a metal sculpture of a weeping willow tree, its silver leaves engraved with names of victims. Goosebumps covered my arms.

I left the synagogue and meandered through gray narrow streets bordered by apartment buildings and headed for a recovery meeting I'd found online before flying to Budapest. Sara had suggested attending one here, and weirdly enough I was actually looking forward to it. It was dusk and the streets were mostly deserted. Occasionally voices floated through open windows, and I dodged mounds of dog shit littering the sidewalks. Eventually, I bumped into the little street I was looking for and began searching doorways for address numbers. I stumbled on a small recessed area tucked back on the street with a couple of buildings on it, and the building set furthest back was the one I was looking for. I opened the door to the dingy gray building and stepped into its grubby entryway. I stood there for a minute or two feeling totally creeped out. I heard muffled voices coming from the floors above and began to ascend the stairs toward the second floor. I couldn't tell if the building was residential or offices. I walked down a poorly lit hallway and heard voices coming from what appeared to be an office door. I opened it and found three more doors behind that one. I shut the door and stood in the hallway debating whether I should follow the voices or leave. A man in shorts walked up behind me.

"You here for a meeting?" I asked him.

"Yes I am," he said and opened the door I'd just closed. I followed him through it, and we passed through another door. The room we entered was brightly lit and coffee was brewing.

"Hello," said a woman with red hair and an Irish accent. She appeared to be about my age. She scanned me thoroughly. "This is a closed meeting," she said.

"That's my kind of meeting," I said and smiled.

She looked at me warily and offered me coffee and a seat.

"How did you find us?" she asked.

"On the Internet before I left Chicago," I said. "This is the only English-speaking meeting I found."

The woman gave me a big smile and immediately lightened up. She started the meeting. "I came to Budapest because of the booze," she said. "It's so cheap here. This is where I hit my bottom."

A young Dutch guy spoke next. "I rode my bike here all the way from the Netherlands. Riding through Germany was fucking something. It was like traveling through one long beer ad."

A German man sitting next to the Dutch guy started laughing and shaking his head. "I'm here hiding out from my successful alcoholic parents who live in Munich. They want me to come back to the family business, but I don't know. I don't want to go back, but I'm unemployed, and things are not going so great for me and my family here."

I told the group about all of the glitzy alcohol-studded events I'd been to in the past week. "Booze was pushed on me night after night, but it was oddly easy to pass up. It was incredible really. I still can't believe it. I don't know how you guys feel about the God thing, but God was definitely doing for me what I could not do for myself. It was wild."

The American I walked in with spoke next. "I'm going back to Arizona, and I'm really worried about how I'm going to handle the cocktail circuit. It hasn't been easy for me to turn down glasses of wine and cognac."

When everyone had a chance to speak, I said, "I have something I'd like to add. I may have given you the wrong impression that not drinking has been a cakewalk for me. I got sober planning to relapse whenever I traveled out of the country. After I booked this trip, I tortured myself for two weeks going back and forth on the 'should I, shouldn't I,' question. The first thing I looked up in the guidebooks was what kind of wine was produced here. Finally, I went to a meeting and admitted what was rocking around in my brain. I don't know why or how, but as soon as I started talking about what was plaguing me, the urge to drink left me. So if I gave you the false impression that this has been easy, it hasn't."

After the meeting I chit-chatted for a bit with an old Irishman, looked at my watch and told him, "I've gotta go. I'm going to an organ concert at St. Anne's that starts in an hour, and it's an hour's walk from here."

"Ah, ya better get goin' then," he said.

I shook his hand and bolted. I was walking at a fast clip down the dark streets when I heard a man's voice shouting from behind, "Hey Chicago, Chicago Brenda." I stopped and turned. It was Steve, one of the Americans from the meeting. Steve was tall, lean, about forty-five, and ruggedly good looking. He began jogging and caught up with me.

"Hey, you mind if I walk with you?" he asked. "This isn't the safest area. You mentioned your hotel, and I live a couple blocks away."

"Yeah, sure," I said. "I'm not going back to the hotel, though. I'm crossing the Chain Bridge to Buda and going to an organ concert at St. Anne's."

"Mind if I tag along?"

"Not at all," I said. "How come you're living in Budapest?"

"I've been here two months," Steve said. "I'm a carpenter. The company I work for is building the new American Embassy. I don't know how much longer I'll be here, though, because my company's about to lose its contract. There've been so many delays and setbacks. A lot of deadlines missed due to poor management. Building materials have to come from the States for security purposes and it's been a nightmare."

"Where's home when you're not here?" I asked.

"I move around a lot," Steve said. "I lived in Hawaii, the Marshall Islands, but I'm from Indiana. Unfortunately, I haven't seen much of Budapest since I've been here."

I started blathering on about the highlights I'd seen and what he should check out. When we got to St. Anne's, a beautiful baroque church, we slid into an antique pew and I told Steve, "Franz Liszt played this organ."

The concert was incredible. Steve and I sat with our eyes closed and let the dark, moody organ music reverberate through us as it filled the church. Tears rolled down my cheeks.

We walked back toward the Chain Bridge, and Steve bumped into an old man he knew from recovery meetings. The old man was with an old woman.

"Everywhere he goes he runs into someone he knows," the old woman said about the old man, who turned out to be her brother.

"My sister and I come here for three weeks every summer," the old man said. "We come to get goulashed out. Our parents were from Budapest. Hey," he said elbowing Steve, "you're not going to let her go back to the States now, are you? Pretty girl like that. No. And none of this handshake business tonight. Gotta be a kiss good-bye."

Steve laughed uncomfortably.

"You can't leave," the old man said to me. "Why you gotta go?"

"Well," I said, "I've been here a week with my husband and he left this morning. I got an extra day and I ran into Steve at a meeting."

The poor old guy, totally embarrassed, fumbled for words and apologized. "You don't look like someone who'd be at a meeting," he said. His sister whacked him in the gut, and they ducked into the hotel we were standing in front of. Steve and I walked across the bridge, shook hands, hugged, and said good-bye.

[Monday, September 22]

I left Budapest and landed in Munich. My plane from Munich to Montreal was delayed three and a half hours, so when I got to Montreal, there were no more connecting flights to Chicago.

I'd picked up a Hungarian salami and two tins of expensive goose liver foie gras at the Budapest airport even though I remembered reading in a guidebook that you can't bring food out of Europe. I'd bought a prized salami at the Central Market and made Charlie pack it in his suitcase before he left because I didn't want my clothes to reek of it. I was toting my new food purchases in a plastic duty-free bag and while heading for Canadian customs, I began filling out a document declaring what I was bringing in. I began to worry. I'd spent a tidy sum on these delicacies and didn't want to give them up. What if I quickly stashed the food in my suitcase after I yanked it off the conveyor belt and proceeded through customs pretending I didn't have anything? What if there were dogs? What trouble would I be in? I decided to declare the food.

The first customs officer I approached looked at my papers. "What kind of food are you bringing in?" she asked me.

"Salami," I said, the duty-free bag with the salami and goose liver pâté hanging from my arm.

"Oh, you're not allowed to bring in meat from Europe. Here," she said, handing me a document about SARS. "Go through there after you get your luggage," she said and pointed toward a doorway.

I walked to the luggage conveyor belt debating what I should do. Should I hide the pâté in my luggage? I placed my purse, my carry-on bag, and the duty-free bag of food on the floor and nonchalantly transferred the tins of pâté into my packed carry-on. My luggage snaked toward me. I pulled it off the conveyor belt and lugged my belongings through the door I'd been directed to.

"You brought a salami?" the customs agent asked. "You can't bring any meat over." She handed me a leaflet on foot-and-mouth disease that I stuck into my purse and I began feeling guilty for not checking the box that asked if I'd been to a farm during my visit. We'd been to that ranch for the putska.

"Do you have anything else?" the agent asked.

"No," I lied.

"No other meat or food products?"

"No," I lied again. "What are you going to do with my salami?" I asked, directing her attention back to the one piece of food I was admitting to. "It's a salami that's considered by many to be the best in the world." I took it out of the bag and handed it to her.

"We have to burn it," she said.

"Really? No one's going to take it to a back room and eat it?"

"We have to burn everything."

"What a bummer."

"Do you want the bag?" the agent asked, holding up the empty plastic duty-free bag.

"No," I said glumly, hoping to convey that she'd taken my only piece of illegal contraband.

I grabbed my things, walked to a ticket counter, and waited behind two men who were also re-booking flights to Chicago. I complained to the guy in front of me about my customs incident.

"They don't burn that stuff," he said. "I'm sure someone got a nice loaf of bread and they're eating it now."

"Maybe I should have tried to sneak it in," I said.

"If they catch you, it's a $400 fine," he said.

"But if I hadn't declared it, they probably wouldn't have noticed."

"We have to go through American customs before we get on the plane tomorrow," the man said. "We're not done."

I began worrying about the pâté again.

I checked into a hotel near the airport, opened my suitcase, and wedged the triangle-shaped tins of pâté upright against the ends of my suitcase, hoping that when my bag was X-rayed, the tins would appear to be a structural part of the luggage. The paranoid part of me wanted to leave the pâté in the room for the maid. The honest part of me felt guilty about being dishonest. And the thrill-seeking part of me was enjoying the risk. Years ago, I routinely hopped on planes with pot in my purse and never gave it a second thought. Now I was twisted up about a couple tins of goose liver pâté.

I got into bed feeling tired and edgy. I tried to sleep but couldn't. My mind was reeling. During my years of religious training, I remembered reading that to God, sin is sin. It's all the same. Smuggling in two tins of foie gras, blowing someone's head off, it's all the same. I got up, went to the bathroom, and popped a Vicodin that had been prescribed for Charlie's hernia. I'd brought a Vicodin in case I had trouble adjusting to the time zone change in Europe. I hadn't needed it in Budapest, but I was in need of sleep now. I got back into bed and prayed. I had the audacity to ask for his protection as I smuggled the pâté through customs.

[Tuesday, September 23]

I successfully smuggled the pâté. I got home and kissed and hugged my kids like crazy. Van said he had fun with Nana and Papa, and Max said he had a good time at Seth's house.

"There was a tornado warning while you were gone," Max said. "It was serious. We had to hide in the crawl space."

"That must have been scary," I said. "Were you scared?"

"Not that much, but Seth was. You should have seen him."

I went over to Liv's later to thank her for watching Max and give her the gifts I'd bought her in Hungary.

"Did Max tell you about the tornado warning?" Liv asked. "You should have seen him. Seth was so scared, and Max put his arm around him and kept telling him it was going to be okay. He's a great kid."

[Thursday, September 25]

I went to a meeting this morning, and Krissy was in bad shape.

"I haven't been taking care of my basics, I haven't taken care of my basics," she kept saying. "I let myself run out of my medication. Yesterday, I was thinking about steering my car off a bridge. I don't have money for my medication."

After the meeting, I saw Krissy in the parking lot and walked over to her.

"I'll help you get your medication," I said. "How much do you need?"

"My prescription's three hundred dollars."

I blanched.

"Uh, I have a couple other options to try in the next couple of days," Krissy said.

"If you're in trouble and need your medicine, I'll go to the pharmacy with you and get it," I said and gave her my phone number. We parted ways and I hoped she wouldn't call.

[Friday, September 26]

I went to a meeting tonight and hung out with Henry afterward. I love flamboyant, witty Henry. He told me he used to own a restaurant and, waxing nostalgic, said, "Oh, the coke we used to do."

"I waitressed my way through college and almost got caught in a sting operation," I told him. "An undercover FBI agent tried to get me to line him up with some blow, said he'd turn me on, but the bartender didn't have any that night, thank God. The next day I found out they busted a bunch of people at the bar down the street."

"You should have partied at my restaurant," Henry said. "We partied like rock stars. One night, there was a drug dealer in my place we didn't like. We called the police on him while we were snorting big fat lines of his coke in a back room."

Henry and I laughed hysterically.

"I walked into a police station tripping on mushrooms to report a hit-and-run to my car," I said, still giggling. "My friends and I were at a Violent Femmes concert. We went to a punk bar afterward and a guy sideswiped my car right in front of the bar. I got his license plate number, went to the police station, and filled out a report while I was tripping my brains out. I was a waitress at the Playboy Club at the time," I continued. "Did I tell you I used to be a bunny?"

"Really? You were a Playboy bunny?" Henry said, smiling, clearly impressed.

"Yeah. One night I got so drunk after work I couldn't find my car. I thought someone had stolen it. So I'm walking down the street and this police car cruises by and I flag it down. I tell the cops I think my car's been stolen. They tell me to hop in and they start driving up and down the streets looking for my car. I spot my car, right where I had parked it, and tell them, 'Stop, there it is.' I get out of the squad car and thank the officers profusely. 'Drive safely,' the cops tell me and drive away."

Henry and I laughed hard again.

"How about this one," Henry said. "One night, we got all coked up, closed the bar, and drove to the lake. I was driving. We were doing lines on a cookie tray while I was driving. All of a sudden, splash! I drive my car into the lake and all we're worried about is snorting the rest of the coke before the car goes down."

"I can't top that one," I laughed.

"Then there was the time I decided to go cliff diving," Henry said. "Only I jumped and missed the water and went splat on the rocks. But I was so drunk and pliable I only got scratched."

I love Henry. I drove home and called Sara to let her know I was back in the country. She sounded strange.

"Are you okay?" I asked her.

"A sixteen-year-old patient of mine OD'd," she said. "Her mother found her in her bedroom this morning. She didn't make it."

"Wow," I said, stunned. "Are you okay? How do you handle something like that?"

"You learn to detach," she said, not sounding detached.

We got off the phone and I sat on the couch for a while feeling paralyzed. Why do some of us get to careen through life driving cars into lakes and jumping off cliffs while others die?

[Sunday, September 28]

Olivia might be getting kicked out of the women's shelter she's living at, for having a fling with another woman living there.

Olivia started coming to meetings recently. She's a cute young blonde I've given rides to a few times. We were both at the same meeting tonight, and afterward, I gave her a ride back to the house she lives in.

"I grew up in an affluent suburb, I have a BA from Loyola, and I have a felony conviction for forgery because I'm a crack addict," she said, shaking her head. "If I get kicked out of the shelter, I'm going to jail. And you know what's weird? I won't even mind going to jail as long as it makes me stay clean. That's how desperate I am.

"I really screwed up," Olivia continued. "I'm not even gay. I'm just needy. I had a fling with that woman because I needed someone to tell me how great I am, how beautiful I am. How sick is that?"

[Monday, September 29]

When Max got out of school this afternoon, I drove the kids into the city to buy a bike for Max's birthday. I was set to drop a sizable chunk of change, and I was irritated by Max's lack of appreciation and enthusiasm. Max wants a shrimpy trick bike. I want to buy him a mountain bike.

"This is going to be your car until you can drive," I told

him, pointing to a black and silver Specialized model that had been wheeled out. "You'll be riding to your friends' houses, to school, around town. Remember how upset you got in Wisconsin when you had trouble keeping up with Seth because your bike was so much smaller? You're going to be glad you didn't get a little circus bike you have to pedal like mad."

Max was not a daredevil. He was a cautious kid. If I thought his interest in trick riding would last longer than his two-week interest in his skateboard, I would have bought it for him, but I know better.

"Okay," Max said, frowning and flipping his hand at the mountain bike. "I'll take this one."

It made my heart glad to buy Max a present he was so thrilled about.

I paid for the bike, wheeled it out of the store, and mounted it on the bike rack behind the Jeep. Max moped and got into the car.

"Don't you have anything to say?" I asked him as we pulled away from the curb.

"Oh yeah, thanks Mom," he said.

Part of me felt sad for not getting Max exactly what he wanted for his birthday, and part of me wanted to smack the little ingrate upside his head.

[Wednesday, October 1]

Today was Max's eleventh birthday. I invited my parents over for dinner, and as soon as they walked through the door, my dad poured himself a stiff scotch on the rocks.

"After today, I'm quitting drinking," he told Charlie, who was having a drink with him. "I'm quitting for a week to see if I can get in this study for a new cancer treatment. The doctor told me to lay off the booze because my liver enzymes are elevated."

"Hey Papa," Max interrupted. "Will you help me build a go-cart?" Max's latest thing is he wants to build a go-cart with Papa because Charlie is as handy as I am.

"Sure, that sounds like a good idea," my dad said. My dad can build or fix anything. "Do you know what you want it to look like?"

"I've already designed it," Max said, handing my dad a drawing of a Cadillac Escalade.

"That looks pretty good," my dad said, folding up Max's drawing and putting it in his shirt pocket. "You'll have to come over and we'll measure it out and figure out what we need."

"What you need to do is stop drinking, old man," I muttered under my breath.

[Thursday, October 2]

"Can I ride my bike?" Max asked when he got home from school. "I want to go down the bike trail and see if there are any Cadillac parts for my go-cart."

Our house is a two-minute bike ride to wooded trails. If you ride one way, you'll pass a parking lot surrounded by warehouses where a local car dealership parks part of its inventory. There are some junk cars they use for parts, and one is a burned-out Cadillac.

"I don't know," I said, leery of letting Max ride the trail by himself. "I don't want you out there alone."

"Oh come on," Max said. "The lot's just five minutes away, maybe not even. I just want to look at the car and come back."

"Okay," I said reluctantly. Up until now, Max has only been allowed to ride his bike around the block. Most of his friends have been riding all over the neighborhood, but I'm paranoid. "Come right back," I said. "Supper will be ready soon."

"I will," Max said and bounced out the back door.

Ten minutes later, Max slammed the door open and slammed it shut behind him. He sat at the kitchen table wheezing.

"Are you okay?" I asked. "Did something bad happen?"

"Two men followed me," Max wheezed. He grabbed his backpack, which he'd left sitting on the kitchen table, pulled out his inhaler, and took two puffs.

"Two men followed you?" I gasped.

Max nodded gravely.

"What happened?"

Max jumped from one detail to the next, but the story was this: Max rode his bike down the trail and headed for the burned-out Cadillac. He rode past an old shed and noticed a homeless man on a bike.

"I nodded and said, 'Hello,' and kept going," Max said. "The man looked at me really weird and unfriendly."

Max said he got off his bike by the burned-out car and as he was examining it, he noticed the homeless man and another seedy-looking guy circling him on their bikes.

"The first man had brown hair, a brown jacket, and he was riding an old brown ten-speed," Max said. "The second man had long gray-and-brown hair, real scraggly, and he was wearing a black jacket with white patches on the shoulders. His bike was an old yellow ten-speed with side baskets on the back that were full of junk. Both of them were white, around forty, I think."

Max said he hopped on his bike and pedaled fast toward home and the men followed him.

"I got up to Fourth Street and there were a lot of people around," Max panted. "I raced across Fourth and when I looked back, the men were gone."

"The people probably scared them off," I said shakily, but trying to appear calm. "I'm calling the police."

Moments later, Max repeated his story to the cops.

"From now on, no riding down the bike trail without an adult, ever," I told Max. "Stick to residential streets around the neighborhood. Got that?"

Max nodded. I hugged him and squeezed him tight.

The first time I let Max ride his bike further than around the block, I let him go down a wooded bike trail peopled with homeless pedophiles.

[Friday, October 3]

I took Max to see the movie *The School of Rock.* While we were watching the scene where Jack Black takes the uptight Joan Cusack character to a bar, plies her with beer, and watches her let her hair down, I began missing being buzzed. I miss that warm happy feeling of not giving a shit and getting crazy.

[Saturday, October 4]

Max wanted a paintball shoot-'em-up party for his birthday, so that's what he got today. I sent invitations to a handful of his friends and after I dropped them in the mailbox, I called my friend, Fay, who is neurotically overly protective of her son, Walter.

"I don't know how you're going to feel about this, but Max wants a paintball party for his birthday," I told Fay's answering machine. "I just wanted to give you a heads-up on the invitation because I just put it in the mail."

The last time Walter was at our house, Max asked, "Can Walter and I walk around the block with my walkie-talkies?"

Max was wearing his police vest and badge. He was holding a note pad and pencil. They wanted to do some surveillance.

"I guess so," I said. "But just on our street. I want you guys back here in fifteen minutes."

Max ran upstairs to tell Walter. Minutes later, Walter appeared.

"I can't go," Walter said. "My mother would kill me."

"My mom said we could go," Max said. "Your mom doesn't have to know."

"No," I said. "If Walter's mom doesn't want him walking around the neighborhood, you're not doing it. I think it's great that Walter is honest and honoring his mother's wishes."

"But you said we could," Max whined.

"Now I say you can't," I said.

"Come on Walter," Max said disgustedly and stalked off.

In the almost ten years that Walter has been alive, Fay has not spent one night away from him. Walter has never had a babysitter other than Fay's mother, who is not even allowed to have him overnight. And Fay bailed on an Oktoberfest party one Saturday night because Walter had been stung by a bee that morning and she needed to continue observing him for a possible allergic reaction.

After I left Fay the message about Max's paintball party, I went out to run errands and pick up Max from school. When I returned home, there was a message from Fay.

"I guess you think I'm a big weenie," she said. "I'll have you know there's a boy over here who is over the moon and can't wait for Max's party."

I was shocked.

"Miss Fay is letting Walter come to my party?" Max asked excitedly. "Yippee!"

I drove Max and a carload of his friends, with the exception of Walter, who is coming with his mother, to an outdoor paintball park. Max and his buddies excitedly pulled on camouflage jumpsuits and protective face masks, and a slump-shouldered pimply teenager handed them paintball guns. After giving them a pep talk about the rules, the teenager stood them in line outside a caged "Mad Max"–inspired industrial wasteland where two teams of boys were already nailing each other with paintballs.

Max and his buddies squirmed with excitement as they watched the boys currently in the cage, except for Kevin. Kevin was standing by himself in a corner swiping at tears, snot dripping from his nose.

"Are you okay, Kevin?" I asked softly.

He nodded.

"Are you sure?"

Kevin nodded again.

"You don't have to go in if you don't want to, you know."

"I'm fine, really," he said, sounding irritated.

"Okay," I said. "But if you change your mind, you can just shoot at targets. There's a target range."

I found a napkin and handed it to Kevin. He blew his nose, dried his tears, and the two of us walked back to the group. The referee inside the cage motioned for Max's group to enter. Max and his friends gleefully ran in, all except Kevin, who was shaking and shuffled in last. The referee checked their face masks and signaled for them to start shooting. The boys ran for cover and hid. No one fired.

"I think you guys need to move around and try to find each other if you want to shoot some paintballs," I shouted into the cage. "Time's ticking. They're going to kick you out when your time's up."

The boys hesitantly began to inch away from their hiding spots and dart behind others. One of the boys tripped over his feet, left the enclosure, and lifted his face mask. It was

Kevin. He was hyperventilating. Tears were running down his cheeks and gooey boogers were dangling from his nostrils.

"Hey Kev," I said. "Let's just watch for a while. The guys will come out pretty soon, and there'll be more chances to try it if you want to."

Kevin nodded.

"Oh," Fay groaned. "He got hit on the hand." Fay was staring at Walter through the fence.

I looked at Walter. His arm was held out slightly in front of him and hot-pink paint was dripping from his fingers. A whistle blew and the boys filed out of the cage. I grabbed Walter as he walked by and looked at his hand. A big red welt was rising on the back of it.

"I think we should get some ice," Fay said, her voice quivering. "You need to put some ice on that Walter. Here, sit down." She wrapped her arms around him and sat him at a picnic table. Walter squirmed out of her arms.

"Mom, I'm fine," he shouted angrily. "I'm fine! Just leave me alone!"

"Here," I said taking Walter's hand. "My freezing fingers are as good as ice." I placed my frigid fingers on the back of Walter's hand and began massaging the welt. After a few minutes, the bruising and swelling went down and Walter walked off to join his friends.

"Mikey got hit in the face," Fay said, her voice quivering. "He's bleeding."

I walked over to Mikey. He had a small spatter-shaped welt on his cheek. A pinprick of blood was next to it.

"You okay?" I asked Mikey.

"I got hit through the mask," he said.

"You what!" I said. "How did that happen? Did you take your mask off in there?"

The referee had warned the boys repeatedly not to move their masks once they were inside the cage. If they did, they'd get kicked out.

"Some paint went through the part where you breathe," Mikey said and showed me his mask. His mask had a huge hot-pink paint splat across the eyes.

"You okay?" I asked.

"Yeah," he laughed. "I just need a new mask."

Mikey sauntered off to the paintball desk to get another mask.

Fay walked over. "You know Kim, Kim the acute-care doctor?" she asked. "She said she sees lots of paintball injuries. A lot of them."

I pictured Fay agonizing over this party for weeks, complaining to anyone who would listen. I looked at Max and his friends. Everyone, including Kevin, was swaggering, acting tough, and feeling like a big shot.

When it was our group's turn to enter the cage again, everyone went in except Kevin. Kevin watched his friends play for a while then pulled down his face mask and ran in. He scurried behind a huge macaroni-shaped metal air duct, ran and dove behind a metal gate, and ran back out.

"You want to shoot at targets?" I asked Kevin nonchalantly. Kevin nodded and I walked with him to the shooting range. I walked back to the cage and saw Walter fiddling with his gun behind a barricade. Ty ran by, saw Walter, and popped Walter in the knee. Walter started crying and shaking his gun in frustration.

Fay looked horrified. The ref blew the whistle and the boys exited the cage.

"I think Walter's more frustrated at his gun jamming than being hurt," I told Fay.

"No, he's really hurt," Fay said and ran over to Walter. She began pulling up Walter's pant leg and he wrestled with her and pulled it back down.

"Mom!" Walter growled. "Leave me alone! I'm fine!"

Fay yanked his pant leg up and pointed to a paintball-sized bruise on Walter's knee. Walter squirmed, yanked his pant leg down, and jumped in line with the rest of his friends for round three. The boys excitedly bantered about their last shooting spree, and Fay looked like she was going to be sick.

"Do you really want to play again?" Fay asked Walter. "You really don't have to if you don't want to."

Walter looked at her angrily. "I want to," he growled.

"How's your hand?" she asked him.

"It's fine," Walter snapped.

"He got hit in the hand?" asked a walleyed teenager standing behind us. "If you get hit on the same spot twice, your skin will explode. Happened to me. Hand just busted wide open."

Fay's eyes looked like they were about to pop out of her head. She walked off and came back with a pair of bright orange gloves. She walked over to Walter and forced the gloves onto his hands.

"I don't want to wear these," Walter complained.

"If you don't wear them, you're not playing," Fay told him. "If you get hit in that same spot your hand will explode!"

The walleyed teen's head bobbed up and down. "Yup, happened to me," he said.

Walter removed the glove and stared at his hand.

"Why don't you just shoot targets?" Fay asked. "Why don't you do that? See if you can perfect your aim."

The boys entered for round three and Walter, staring at his hand and envisioning it exploding, walked toward the targets with his mother. Kevin, however, ran into the cage and started shooting like Rambo. He was having the time of his life. Then Mikey lumbered out of the cage.

"What happened?" I asked Mikey.

"That guy's a jerk," Mikey said motioning toward the ref. "He kicked me out. I didn't even do anything. I was just trying to clear my mask so I could see and he kicked me out!"

"He probably freaked that you took your mask off," I said. "You could have gotten hit in the eye."

I had had enough. When the boys finished their round, I told them it was time for pizza and cake. The boys, elated, began reminiscing about their bravery and shooting prowess while they devoured food. I breathed a sigh of relief, glad the evening was almost over. Boy, would I love a stiff vodka.

[Tuesday, October 7]

I went to a meeting tonight and the woman who gave the lead said, "Someone who's not an alcoholic changes his behavior to meet his goals. An alcoholic changes his goals to meet his behavior."

Everyone except me emitted a knowing "Ah."

"I didn't change my goals to meet my behavior," I said when it was my turn to comment. "My drinking was getting in the way of my goals, so I quit. That just got me thinking, *Maybe I'm not an alcoholic.*"

Everyone except me let out a concerned "Hmmm."

[Thursday, October 9]

My mom called to tell me that my dad had blood work done and his liver enzymes are higher than ever, even though he'd quit drinking for a week. The cancer study didn't want him.

"He's not doing anything to help himself," I shouted. "Nothing, no research, no dietary changes, no exercise. And he's drinking like a fish."

"I know," my mother said, sounding disgusted and concerned.

I recalled my father telling his boating buddies at the harbor, "Fuck it. I'm going to go out with a drink in my hand. We've all got to go sometime. May as well enjoy myself."

[Friday, October 10]

I met Sara for dinner and a meeting. Sara was supposed to pick me up at my house, but she called fifteen minutes late to tell me that she'd locked her keys in her office. I drove to Sara's office, picked her up, and drove her to a second office she shares with another therapist to retrieve a second set of keys. Like I said before, I have my doubts about Sara's effectiveness as a therapist. She's insightful and intelligent, but also forgetful, tardy, and routinely in a medicated fog from her bipolar meds. She's the perfect sponsor for me. After Sara retrieved her first set of keys, we gobbled down dinner, then went to a meeting. Olivia, who was still in danger of getting kicked out of the shelter, was there.

"Instead of reading the Big Book while I was in rehab, I decided to read the classics," she said. "Can you believe I did that? Another time I was in rehab, I got a dictionary out of the library and thought I'd increase my vocabulary instead of reading recovery material." Olivia shook her blond head from side to side and laughed. What a card she thought she was.

After the meeting, Olivia cornered Sara. "Can you believe the way my mind works?" she asked Sara. "There I was reading the classics thinking I was so unique."

"You still think you're unique," Sara deadpanned.

Olivia shut up.

As Sara and I were leaving the meeting, Jane, who runs the recovery group with her girlfriend, Laura, invited me to come to their house for the after-meeting get-together they host every week. Jane has invited me many times and I've never gone, so I figured I'd go this time. I dropped Sara off at her office, where her car was still parked, and drove to Jane and Laura's lovely home on a cul-de-sac. Jane opened the door and her boxer ran up and began sniffing me. He was a cutie and I rubbed his head and back. Jane motioned toward a pile of shoes next to the door.

"If you wouldn't mind," she said. "We do that here. We have slippers for guests if you'd like."

"No, that's fine," I said, taking off my high-heeled black sandals and following Jane into the kitchen, where I found Henry.

"I'm so glad you came," Henry said and hugged me.

"Everyone take a seat in the dining room," Laura shouted.

I looked at Henry, puzzled.

"They're having a meeting to plan the next anniversary party for the group," Henry said.

"Great. The one time I accept an invitation they're having a party-planning meeting. I'm going to go."

"No, don't," Henry pouted. "You go to that meeting. You belong here."

"I don't really want to stick around for this," I said.

"Come on, I'm staying, and I've been coming around about as long as you have," Henry wheedled.

"Oh, all right," I said.

As Henry and I headed for the dining room, I saw Miriam head outside with a cigarette in her hand.

"Where do you think you're going?" Laura yelled at Miriam. Laura is Miriam's sponsor.

"Out to have a quick smoke."

"Not now you're not," Laura said. "Sit down at that table."

Miriam put her cigarette back in her pack and headed toward the table.

I shot Henry a what-the-hell look and Henry frowned and shook his head.

After everyone had gathered at the table, Jane said, "It takes a long time to plan our anniversary party, so we're going to fill our department chair and cochair positions tonight. Let's start with the top positions, party chair and cochair. How much sobriety time should the chairs have?" Jane looked around the table.

A few suggestions were thrown out and it was decided that each department chair should be sober at least six months, but it didn't matter for cochairs.

"I think before anyone is voted in they should announce how long they've been sober, what steps they're working, and how many meetings they attend a week," Laura said. "Who's interested in being party chair?"

"I'll do it," said Derek, who is Henry's sponsor. Derek announced that he's been sober ten months, worked through all the Steps, and goes to meetings almost every day. He smiled at Henry and Henry gave him the thumbs up. Derek was voted in, as was a woman who volunteered to be his cochair.

Next position up for grabs was refreshment committee chair. "Henry can't chair because he's got one month of sobriety, but I nominate Henry for cochair," Derek said. "He's owned several restaurants and catering businesses, so even though he won't actually be the 'chair,' he could pretty much run things."

Henry was voted in.

"Okay, who wants to chair the committee?" Jane asked.

Silence. Everyone looked at everyone else at the table.

After a long uncomfortable several minutes, I figured, *What the hell, I've thrown a lot of dinner parties*. Henry was going to run it anyway.

"I could do it," I said.

"Okay," Jane said. "Would anybody else like to volunteer before we vote on Brenda?" No one did. "Okay Brenda, tell us about your recovery program."

"I've been sober nine months, almost ten. I'm working on the Fourth Step."

Disapproving glances moved around the table. Jane and Laura, the grande dames of the meeting, encouraged their sponsees to finish the Twelve Steps in a month.

"My sponsor is having me go over the Steps with a fine-tooth comb so I get the nuances," I explained.

"I nominate Brenda to be the refreshment chair," Derek said.

Henry, who was wiggling in his seat, said, "I second it."

"Wait," Laura said, standing up. "I didn't even know you were coming to our meeting." She glanced around the table with a panicked look on her face. Laura, an attractive, tall blonde with chiseled features, has that crazy manic-eyed look a lot of women in recovery have. Despite the fact that I've attended this meeting off and on for nine months, she never remembers me.

"I started going to your meeting nine months ago," I said. Laura looked at Jane. Jane nodded her head. "But if you'd rather have someone else chair, fine with me. No one else was offering. I'm just trying to be nice."

Laura looked around the table hoping someone else would offer, but no one did.

A pasty-faced, middle-aged guy with a bad comb-over, said, "Brenda needs to do her Fifth Step. Everyone knows you'll drink a fifth if you don't do your Fifth."

"Her sponsor's got a plan, Reggie," Jane said in my defense. "She's doing what she's supposed to."

Laura and Reggie looked at each other doubtfully.

"Does this mean you're going to come to all of our meetings, make a commitment, and come every week?" Laura asked like a drill sergeant.

I nodded my head.

"Really? You're going to make this commitment to us? You need to be committed to this."

I was quite sure I didn't want to make the commitment, but I'd stepped out on the ledge in front of a bunch of people, so I jumped and said, "Yes."

The people at the table voted me in and I felt queasy. More committee chairs and cochairs were voted in. Jane's boxer walked up to the table and began whining and barking.

"I think one of us needs to take him out," Jane told Laura.

"He's fine," Laura said irritably. "He's just mad because I stuck him in the crate earlier."

Jane shot Laura an unhappy look.

"He chewed up somebody's shoes," Laura huffed. "A pair of black heels."

I pictured the pile of gym shoes and loafers near the door that I'd thrown my sandals on.

"Those would probably be mine," I said.

Jane groaned.

"They're nice shoes, too," Laura said, looking more manic. "We'll pay for them, of course."

I loved those shoes. I'd shopped a long time to find a pair that were sexy and comfortable.

When the meeting was over, Henry sidled up to me and whispered, "I'd ask for a lot of money. They're loaded."

I walked to the shoe pile and picked up a shoe. The other was missing. Jane walked over, looking miserable.

"I'm so sorry," she said. "How much for the shoes? You're not leaving until I pay for them."

I told her how much and she reimbursed me.

"Can I have my other shoe so I can go home?" I asked.

Jane disappeared and came back with a mangled shoe. The heel and back end of the sandal were frayed and disfigured. I slipped the shoe onto my foot and walked to my car. The heel of the mangled shoe gurgled with dog saliva each time I stepped on it.

[saturday, october 11]

We had Van's birthday party today since his real birthday is Wednesday. My parents and my sister and her two kids came over for dinner. It was a gorgeous day, summer-like weather, and the kids drove Van's new motorized Jeep that he got for his third birthday all over the yard. I made vegetarian lasagna and my dad, who thinks he has to have meat at every meal, loved it.

"If you made vegetarian stuff like this, I'd eat it," my father told my mother. "This is delicious." My mother bristled and shot him a dirty look.

I brought out the birthday cake and we sang "Happy Birthday." While I was cutting the cake, there was a loud crash and a loud "Shit!" from the kitchen. I knew Paula had dropped a half-gallon glass milk jug on the floor. I was instantly irritated, even though I'd dropped a jug of milk on the floor and created a huge mess days ago. I reminded myself of this and pushed down my anger before entering the kitchen to help Paula clean up.

"I'm really sorry," Paula said.

"Hey, don't worry about it," I said. "I did the same thing."

A year ago, I would have thinly veiled my irritation, huffed and puffed while I cleaned up, and insisted that it was no big deal while making my sister feel like shit. I am easily irritated and like to fix blame on others. This I've recently recognized. It's something I'm working on.

[Monday, October 13]

I went to a meeting tonight and saw Darcy.

"I have some bad news," Darcy told me after the meeting. "Eve had to move out of her town home and she's living in one of Mel's rental units. She's drinking constantly and totally gone to hell. Mel said the place is a mess and she's sleeping on a mattress on the floor. He went over to check on her and she answered the door naked, completely out of her mind."

I felt nauseated. I wanted to drive over and help Eve, but I knew there was nothing I could do.

[Tuesday, October 14]

Kelly and I met for lunch. As we were eating our salads, she asked, "So, how's the not drinking thing going?"

"I haven't had a drink in almost ten months," I said. "It's getting easier.

"I couldn't quit," Kelly said.

"If you're just having a glass or two of wine every night and occasionally getting crazy with your friends, why would you?"

"Yeah," Kelly said, looking troubled. "You know, if I'm saying I don't think I can quit, maybe I have a problem."

"I'm glad I quit. I feel much healthier. But, honestly, I sometimes miss getting buzzed, partying with my friends."

"I have to tell you, Bren, you were fun to party with. You were the best. You were the most fun person there was to drink with."

"Thanks," I said, feeling warm and fuzzy and hugely complimented.

"My brother hasn't had a drink in four years," Kelly continued. "But he doesn't mind if anyone else drinks in his home. He's there pouring wine for us. He's so cute, such a gracious host."

I knew this was a dig for having the Bacchanal Dinner Club at Ravinia instead of my house. I'd also just called my book club pals and told them I was serving dessert and coffee and tea instead of wine at the book club I was going to host. Everyone liked the idea except for Kelly, who wasn't coming anyway because I was hosting book club on Ryan's birthday.

• • •

I went to the women's meeting I go to every Tuesday night and gave the lead, which I'd signed up for last week. My lead was on acceptance, because I have trouble accepting people and situations as they are. Sara made me read a story about acceptance that claimed that a person's level of serenity is directly proportional to that person's level of acceptance. It said that accepting things as they are and having no expectations are the keys to happiness.

"I have a problem with that," I said. "I think there are things in life you shouldn't accept. If you're in an abusive relationship, you shouldn't accept that. When your kid comes home with an 'F' on his report card, you shouldn't accept that. And this going through life with low expectations, it's a recipe for failure. My high expectations often leave me disappointed and ticked off, but I don't want to aim low and never get anywhere."

I apparently hit a nerve with a lot of women because a lot of commiseration came forth. Then Tanya said, "Accepting a situation doesn't mean you have to be okay with it. You can take steps to change things, but then you need to detach from the outcome and accept how things turn out. You keep doing your best and accept reality. If you keep getting upset over things you have no control over, you have no peace."

I can accept that.

I gave Kat a ride home and told her about my aborted attempt to see Tony Bennett and how I really wanted to drink that night.

"Well no wonder you wanted to drink," Kat said. "You felt it was your responsibility to make everyone feel happy when Reed was being an asshole. Instead of letting him own it, letting it sit out there, letting him be the bad guy, little people-pleaser you took it upon yourself to diffuse it all. That's really stressful. And you wonder why you wanted a drink?"

Kat sighed and shook her head. "You and I are pretty much the same. We're egomaniacs who hang around people who blow sunshine up our asses. We're people-pleasers to keep the sunshine coming."

[Thursday, October 16 – Sunday, October 19]

I flew to Miami and spent a long weekend in South Beach with my high school friend Abby. It was great. We relaxed, laid in the sun, talked about everything from politics to God. Amazing bodies shimmering in shiny stretch pants and bikini tops sashayed past.

One afternoon, as Abby and I were sunning ourselves on the beach, I rolled onto my stomach and found myself staring into two enormous dimpled butt cheeks separated by a G-string.

"Abby!" I hissed, and jerked the back of my head in the direction of the three-hundred-pound woman flipping her beach towel behind me. Abby discreetly motioned with her chin that

I should look again. The woman was running topless, her gigantic boobs bouncing down to the ocean. When she got knee-deep in the water, the woman dove in and resurfaced at waist level. She cupped her hands and began splashing the undersides of her flapping boobs with water.

"You know what?" I said and turned toward Abby, "Good for her. She's enjoying herself and not giving a shit that she's fat and laying next to a couple of skinny bitches."

Abby nodded. "Yeah."

That night, after a delicious fish dinner, Abby and I went to the Delano for drinks by the pool, and I ordered a club soda with lime.

"I forgot you quit drinking," Abby said, looking a little bummed. She and I had a history of getting wasted together as teenagers. "You can't have just one or two?"

"No," I said. "Put one drink in me and I'll keep going until I'm messed up."

"I can't drink like that," Abby said. "I start feeling bad if I have more than a couple glasses of wine."

"That's why you're not an alcoholic," I said.

It's funny because I was a lightweight drinker and drugger compared to Abby in high school. She and I both liked quaaludes and booze, but Abby got way more messed up than I did. Audrey, my constantly buzzed high school drug dealer, can't even finish a beer now. But I'm the alcoholic. This strange twist of fate confounds the three of us. Why am I the drunk? I didn't feel well after a couple of drinks when I first started drinking, but I kept drinking because I wanted to be the life of the party, the fun girl everyone wants to hang out with. I think I pushed myself into alcoholism by continually overriding my body's resistance to booze until it stopped resisting. There's the heredity factor, too, I guess.

Abby and I left the Delano. As we walked back to our hotel,

an attractive elegantly dressed older woman heading in the opposite direction staggered and swerved past us. Her glassy eyes were blank.

"Did you see her?" Abby asked, looking shocked.

"Yeah," I answered, grateful I wasn't walking in that woman's shoes.

[Monday, October 20]

Back at home, I went to a meeting and Gerald, a charming well-to-do old man who used to be a corporate big shot, gave a lead on honesty.

"I was telling an old golfing story, one I've told hundreds of times, and realized the punch line was a lie," Gerald said. "I felt guilty and fessed up to the guy I was telling the story to."

As people took turns commenting, it became clear that most of us had done the same thing, like my story about the biker party where a guy named "Rabbit" got stabbed to death.

The party was at an apartment of a biker I knew named Horatio. He was in the motorcycle club The Outlaws, and I went to high school with Horatio's younger brother, Blake.

Audrey drove me and another friend, Samantha, to the party. Horatio's apartment was on the first floor, and his back door opened onto a fallow cornfield where he'd built a huge bonfire. Inside the apartment, people were dancing to ZZ Top, and Horatio grabbed my arm and started grinding his hips against mine to "Tube Snake Boogie." When the song ended, I walked outside, where people were filling jumbo-size plastic cups at a beer keg.

At some point during the evening, after consuming a lot of beer and weed, I noticed I hadn't seen Audrey in a while. I left the bonfire and went back inside, spotted Samantha sitting on a couch in the living room talking to some biker, and sat down next to her.

"You know where Audrey is?" I asked Samantha.

"Off with some guy doing lines," Samantha said.

"Oh," I said, instantly jealous that I wasn't offered coke.

"They're doing more than that," the biker sitting across from Samantha said. "Last I checked, your friend's car was bouncing up and down."

A back door slammed, and a woman began screaming, "I'm gonna kill her! I'm gonna kill that bitch!"

"That would be Steve's old lady," the biker sitting across from Samantha said. "You might want to get Audrey out of here."

Samantha and I looked at each other, got up, and bolted for the back door. We jogged swiftly through the kitchen past a deranged-looking woman with a carving knife. Another woman was holding the deranged woman's wrist. "Don't do it," the woman was telling the deranged one. "Don't do anything stupid."

"There's the car!" Samantha shouted as we ran through the parking lot.

We ran to Audrey's brown Corolla. It wasn't bouncing, but the windows were fogged up. Samantha and I began beating on the windows. Audrey rolled a window down, and she and Steve blinked up at us. "What?" she asked, sounding annoyed.

"Your friend's girlfriend is on her way out here with a knife!" I shouted. "We have to get out of here!"

"Fuck!" Steve said, quickly zipping his pants and bolting from the car. Audrey moved her seat to the upright position, and Samantha and I hopped in. The mad woman came tearing through the parking lot and Steve grabbed her.

"I'm gonna kill her!" the woman screeched and struggled free.

"Go!" Samantha and I both screamed.

Audrey backed her car out of its parking space, and the mad woman slammed her body against Audrey's car door and pounded her fist against the window. Audrey stepped on the gas and we took off.

"I'm never going to another one of these parties," Samantha said angrily. "Last one I went to a guy got killed."

"Really?" I said.

Samantha turned around in the passenger seat and looked at me in the back seat. "This guy named 'Rabbit' was hitting on me all night. I finally got him to leave me alone and he started hitting on someone else. The woman he started hitting on had a boyfriend. Rabbit and the boyfriend started fighting, and the boyfriend stabbed him. We all got the hell out of there, and when we left, Rabbit was sitting up against a tree bleeding. We found out later he died."

"I guess you should have fucked him," Audrey told Samantha.

We all started laughing, and Audrey lit a joint.

When I began relaying my biker party story, I tacked on the Rabbit murder, and after I told it enough times, it felt like the truth.

• • •

As I was getting ready to pick up Max from school, I got a call from Janie, a cute, little twenty-year-old I met at a meeting months ago but haven't seen since. She told me that since I'd seen her, she detoxed twice, tried to kill herself, and just got out of a treatment facility.

"I was at a place in Florida, one of the few that specialize in mental disorders plus addiction," she said. "I'm bipolar, you know. My parents weren't thrilled about paying $11,000 for it. And now here I am climbing the walls, crawling out of my skin, and jobless. My parents are paying my rent, and I'm having suicidal thoughts again."

"Are you talking to a therapist, a psychiatrist?" I asked.

"Yes," Janie said. "And they don't help much."

"Maybe you should find new specialists."

"I've been through a lot of people already."

"I'm glad you called me," I lied, feeling completely out of my depth. "It helps when I talk about what's going on in my head. There's something about hearing myself say what I'm thinking out loud. It forces me to make sense out of what's pinging around inside my skull.

"Maybe you should look for a job," I added. "A job you don't bring home with you, maybe at a coffee bar or bookstore or something. Get out of your apartment and start feeling productive. I feel like shit if I'm not productive. I go nuts if I have too much time on my hands."

After we got off the phone, I hoped I hadn't said anything to make Janie feel worse.

[Friday, October 24]

I've been thinking about Janie for days. I've been worrying that she killed herself. I should have called her, but I didn't because I don't want to get sucked into her life. I called her today, however. I called several times and each time got a weird automated message that kept telling me I dialed an inaccurate number.

[Tuesday, October 28]

I was hoping to see Janie at the women's meeting tonight but she wasn't there. Deidre gave the lead and announced that she might be going to jail again for thirty months. Deidre is on probation and not supposed to drink, but she's been drinking off and on since her arrest, and her probation officer finally caught her. On November 6, her next court date, Deidre will find out how badly she screwed up.

I don't get it. How can Deidre attend meetings, make insightful pro-sober comments, and keep drinking? The last place I'd want to be if I were drinking is at a meeting. I'd feel like a fraud, nerve-wrackingly uncomfortable. I'd be hanging out with people I could drink with, not sober people. But maybe Deidre doesn't have any drinking buddies left.

"I was feeling cocky," Deidre said. "I was feeling like I could get away with everything. My driver's license was returned to me mistakenly, and I was driving with it until they realized their mistake and took it back. Probation was just a slap on the wrist. So while I was feeling above it all, I sucked down a bottle of rum while I was performing my community service. The next morning, someone from the probation office showed up with a Breathalyzer and I blew a high number even after sleeping. Now I'm facing jail time, and the judge hates me."

I looked at Darcy, who was sitting across the room from me. She was hunched over and silently sobbing. When it was her turn to comment, Darcy wiped away tears and sniffed loudly. "I'm going through a very tough time," she croaked. "I'm single, I've been unemployed for almost a year, I'm running up debt, and I'm scared. I took a part-time sales job, but it's all commission and I'm not even making pocket change. I just came from a bad psychiatrist's appointment. My doctor is unsympathetic about my job situation. He told me I wasn't trying hard enough." Darcy began sobbing again. "I've sent out 200 resumes since I lost my job and I'm looking at losing my house."

After the meeting I sat next to Darcy and hugged her. "I wish there was something I could do," I said. "I'm so sorry."

When I first met Darcy, she was one of the best-dressed, most chic-looking women at meetings. The first time I heard her speak, she said she made good money and was trying to separate her identity from her career because who she was was too wrapped up in what she did. Lately, every time I see Darcy she's wearing sweats and looking puffier and puffier from antidepressants. I left the meeting feeling depressed, and when I got home and began getting ready for bed, the phone rang. It was Derek from the meeting.

"I haven't seen you in a while and I was wondering if everything's okay," Derek said.

"My husband was out of town last Friday night and I was in Florida the weekend before that," I said. "You guys were probably wondering where I was since I volunteered to chair the refreshment committee for your party."

"Laura and Jane are going to talk to you about that for sure," Derek said. Then he changed the subject and told me Henry relapsed.

"I don't know what to do," Derek said. "I'm not sure how I should handle things as his sponsor. I'm getting harsh advice like, 'If he was my sponsee, I'd drop him.'"

"That's pretty heartless," I said.

"I think so," Derek said.

"Aren't we supposed to help people, not tell them to fuck off?" I said. "If people reach out, we're supposed to give them a hand. Frankly, I can't believe some of the control freak shit I've heard sponsors say to their sponsees."

"I know this one sponsor who wouldn't even let her sponsee go out for a cigarette break," Derek said.

"I know you're talking about Laura," I said. "I heard her bossing Miriam around the night of the planning meeting. I have to tell you, I get bad vibes from Laura."

"Yeah, I know," Derek groaned.

"I thought I was doing something nice, volunteering to chair that committee when no one else stepped up," I said. "Then Laura starts grilling me like a suspect. 'I didn't know you attended this meeting,' I mimicked. 'Does this mean you're committed to our group, that you're going to attend every meeting?' I nodded like an idiot. I wish I had told her to go to hell."

"I know," Derek moaned. "They're planning to talk to you about that."

"I don't want to chair that damned committee," I said.

"Really?" Derek said, his voice brightening. "That's what they want to talk to you about. They really want a regular to chair the committee."

"I thought I was a regular," I said. "I don't hit that meeting every week. I have a husband and children and things come up. But I'm there a lot."

"They want you there every week unless you're sick or out of town," Derek said.

"Yeah? Well that's not going to happen."

"They'd like to make Doreen the refreshment chair because she and Gwen both wanted to chair the decorating committee and Gwen got it and there were some hard feelings."

"Good," I said. "Give the position to Doreen. And tell Laura not to call me."

"That wasn't the reason I called," Derek said. "It really wasn't."

It really was, but I like Derek. And I'm thrilled to be off the hook.

[Thursday, October 30]

I hosted my first alcohol-free book club. Earlier in the week, I called my friends to remind them I was making crème brulee and serving tea instead of wine and appetizers. I set the ramekins of crème brulee on my kitchen table, sprinkled them with sugar, and pulled out my blow torch. The doorbell rang and my friends began filtering in.

"I love that little torch," Margaret said as she watched me melt the sugar into sheets of caramelized glass. "Can I try it?"

"Sure," I said, handing over the torch.

Tina and Nosey Rosy had a turn at the torch, then the six of us sat at my dining room table, ate crème brulee with fresh raspberries on top, and drank tea from three different pots: black tea, green tea, and fruity rooibos.

"This is fabulous," Margaret said.

"Yeah," Tina agreed. "I love this. Cloth napkins, silver, china—you outdid yourself, Brenda."

"Thanks," I said, feeling pretty happy. It had been less work and less expensive than serving appetizers and wine.

We began discussing *The Liars Club* by Mary Carr, a memoir about Carr's rocky whacked-out childhood.

"I remember chasing the mosquito abatement truck with my friends as it sprayed insecticide everywhere," Margaret said. "No adults stopped us. They just watched us. Unbelievable."

"I grew up in Levittown, Pennsylvania," Tina began, "and I remember going to the dump for school picnics. What was that?"

Nosey Rosy grew up in a Catholic orphanage and said, "The nuns scared us to death. They told us ghost stories at night so we wouldn't get out of bed. I used to lie under my covers petrified, afraid to move."

"Our children are so fortunate," Tina said.

"But you know we're screwing them up somehow," I said. "Sometimes I wonder what I'm doing or saying that they'll wind up discussing with a therapist."

We drank tea and talked until eleven o'clock. It was one of the better book clubs we've had, I think.

[Friday, October 31]

I met Sara for dinner before picking up Van at my parents' house. My mother had attended Max's Halloween Poem Recitation at school yesterday. Max stood in front of his classroom with a silver garbage can over his head and recited the Shel Silverstein poem, "The Man in the Iron Pail Mask." Then my mom took Van home with her for a sleepover because she wanted to take him trick-or-treating.

"Is Max out trick-or-treating?" Sara asked.

"Yeah," I answered. "He's out with a big group of friends. It's his first year trick-or-treating without me. I'm kind of sad about it."

"They grow up," Sara said.

"He's probably having more fun without me."

"I don't know about that."

"I went to the Spooky Stroll at his school today," I said. "The kids walk around the block in their costumes. It's really cute."

"What's Max dressed up as?"

"A SWAT guy. My mom's probably trick-or-treating with Van right now, but maybe they're done. He's only good for a handful of houses."

"How old is Van?"

"He turned three on the fifteenth. Hey," I said, changing the subject. "I had the weirdest conversation last night."

I told Sara about Derek's call and filled her in on the horrid party-planning meeting I'd gone to. A while back, Sara mentioned she was looking for a receptionist and that Laura applied because Laura wanted to become a therapist. This supports my theory that psychology draws messed-up people who want to fix their own heads.

"Laura was practically frothing at the mouth, grilling me about my commitment to her meeting," I said. "Look at her face. She's totally nuts."

Sara, looking thoughtful, nodded her head. I hope for Sara's sake she didn't hire the loon.

[Saturday, November 8]

I've been practicing yoga for six years, and let me tell you, it's a beautiful thing to practice without a hangover. Lately, I've been practicing with my new friend, Vivian, whom I met at a recovery meeting. Vivian's yoga teacher recently moved, and I invited her to come to class with me. Now we're yoga buddies. The thing that concerns me about Vivian, though, is she's bipolar. I've kind of made a point of steering clear of women who say they're bipolar—which seems to be a quarter of the women I've met at recovery meetings. Sara is bipolar, too, but so far she's been a good sponsor. Vivian, unlike Sara, is intensely loud, opinionated, funny, and sharp as a tack, so I'm pretty sure she's not taking the fog-inducing meds Sara does. I'm kind of waiting for the other shoe to drop.

A few days ago, Vivian invited me to walk a labyrinth with her.

"I'll pick you up at six o'clock on the eighth," she said. "There's going to be a lunar eclipse at seven fifteen. Let's get Indian food and start walking the labyrinth when the moon is being eclipsed."

Vivian said six planets were going to be in some hexagonal alignment, and this alignment would increase communication with God.

"Why don't we ask Darcy to come with?" I asked. "She really needs to get out."

When Vivian showed up at my door, Darcy wasn't with her.

"Darcy bailed," Vivian said. "She said she was feeling under the weather."

"She's depressed," I said. "I bet she doesn't want to spend money on dinner either. Want to split the bill and treat her?" Vivian agreed and I called Darcy. After some minor arm-twisting, Darcy said she'd go out with us. Vivian and I hopped in her car and picked up Darcy. At the restaurant, we ordered food and Vivian looked at her watch.

"It's seven fifteen," she said. "The eclipse is happening right now."

"Shoot," I said.

"That's okay," Vivian said. "Let's hold hands and chant 'Om.' Thousands of people are doing it all over the world."

We held hands in the restaurant and chanted "Om" three times.

After dinner, Vivian drove us to a labyrinth in the backyard of a Catholic church. We pulled into the parking lot and looked at the dark clouds floating across the eclipsed moon.

"This is going to be perfect," Vivian said. "Here." Vivian pulled out a little brown vial that looked like the kind of glass container I snorted cocaine out of. She unscrewed the lid and sniffed it. "Mmmm. Give me your wrists."

Darcy and I offered up our wrists and Vivian rubbed essential oils on them. The oil smelled good.

"Okay now, close your eyes and relax," Vivian said. Darcy and I closed our eyes. "Imagine you are sitting by a stream and the stream is crystal clear." Vivian then asked us to pick our favorite tree and picture ourselves sitting under it.

"What kind of tree did you picture?" Vivian asked when our creative visualization was over.

"I pictured an oak," Darcy said.

"Yeah, that's what I pictured, too," Vivian said. "What did you picture, Brenda?"

"A weeping willow."

"Really," Vivian said, looking at me with interest. "I actually almost picked that."

The three of us got out of the car. It was freezing. Vivian, who was the only one to have walked a labyrinth before (Charlie and I didn't know what to do with the one in Budapest), told us to watch the ground in front of our feet as we slowly snaked our way to the center. We began walking and she told us to clear our minds, be silent, and observe our thoughts. When we got to the center, we were to pause and wait to feel something before walking back out.

As I walked the labyrinth, I quieted myself and waited for profound thoughts. What came was an overwhelming sense of gratitude, and I found myself meditating on the words "thank you." It was incredibly spiritual.

The three of us arrived at the center and Vivian held out her hands, one palm up, one palm down. "Let's stand in a circle around this rose quartz rock here," she said. "Put your hands out so your palms hover below or above the next person's." We stood around the rose quartz with our palms hovering inches away from each other's. "Do you feel the energy?" Vivian asked.

"Mm-hmm," Darcy and I nodded. My palms tickled.

"Now take off your rings, place them on the rose quartz, and ask for healing," Vivian said.

We did that, put our rings back on, and silently began walking out of the labyrinth. Vivian unlocked her car and we got in.

"Well?" Vivian asked.

"That was incredible," I said. "I feel so peaceful and happy right now. Thank you, Vivian."

"I feel cold," Darcy complained. "Can you start the car and get the heat going?"

Vivian started her car.

"You want to go somewhere and get something hot to drink?" I asked.

"I don't have any money," Darcy said.

"I'll buy you a drink," I said. "Let's get some tea."

"Let's go to Whole Foods," Vivian said. "They have really great tea there."

I bought Darcy tea, and she didn't say thank you. She didn't thank Vivian and me for dinner either, and she didn't thank Vivian for driving out of her way to pick her up. Darcy sat in a chair sipping tea looking sorry-assed and self-absorbed. I know she's going through tough times, but I don't want to be around Darcy right now.

[Monday, November 10]

There's a gourmet kitchen boutique in town that offers cooking classes, and Kelly and I attended one this evening. The chef du jour showed us how to make cassoulet and pumpkin crème brulee. Kelly and I were getting hungrier by the minute as we watched him cook. When he finished, we were handed bite-size cups of the cassoulet and a tiny aluminum foil tin of pumpkin crème brulee. It was dinnertime. Kelly and I looked at each other and started laughing.

"I can't believe this," I said looking at the paltry amounts. "How can they charge us thirty bucks, host the class at dinnertime, and not feed us? I've taken other cooking classes and eaten fabulous meals at the end of them."

"We should go to McDonald's," Kelly snickered. She picked up the comment card we got when we walked in and nodded toward the chic-looking woman who owned the shop. “She’s going to hear from me,” she said. “By the way, how’s your dad?”

“It looks like he’s got cancer on his lungs,” I said.

My father had started seeing an oncologist at Evanston Hospital after he found out he was terminal this summer. I wanted my dad to see Dr. Benton at Northwestern because he wanted to start my dad on hormone therapy and get him CT and bone scans right away. But my dad hated Benton because he gave him an honest answer when my dad asked how much time he had left.

“Your father won’t see Dr. Benton,” my mother said after I asked her to convince my dad to switch doctors. “Chevron wasn’t doing anything, so we went back to Dr. Barren at Swedish. He’s the reason we found out your father has lung cancer. He did a CT and bone scan.”

“Why’d you go to Barren?” I shouted.

“What does your father have to lose?” my mother asked.

When my dad was first diagnosed with prostate cancer, a woman from my mother’s church recommended Dr. Barren. Barren told my father he could cure him. He told my father he was the only doctor who could. He told my father not to have his prostate removed or have radiation—which every other oncologist and urologist was recommending.

“You’re going to Svengali,” I shouted. “The guy is bad news.”

“He’s the only one who thinks he can cure your father,” my mother snapped. “At least he has your dad on hormone therapy and did those scans.”

“Dr. Benton would have scanned Dad and had him on hormone therapy months ago.”

“Your father didn’t like him, and he doesn’t want to go to Northwestern,” my mother said irritably. “He doesn’t want to go that far.”

"You don't pick the doctor who's closest," I said. "You pick the doctor who's best."

"One of your father's friends from the harbor told him to see Dr. Barren, too," my mother said defensively. "His wife is a nurse and she worked with Dr. Barren for years and thinks very highly of him."

"Put Dad on the phone," I said. When my father picked up, I said, "I'm worried about your choice of doctors. When a doctor says he's the only one who can cure you, that's bullshit."

"Dr. Barren told me I did the worst things for myself," my dad said, his voice shaking. "He told me, 'You had surgery. You never should have had surgery. You had radiation. I told you not to have radiation. Radiation feeds cancer, makes it grow. That's the bad news. The good news is you're back with me and I'm going to get you going on these hormone pills and hormone shots.' Real nice, huh? I did the worst things for myself."

"That guy is a quack," I said. "He's full of shit. Why don't you go back to Dr. Benton?"

"Because that guy told me if he saw cancer on the bone or CT scans, I had three to five years to live," my father shouted. "How would you like that? I hear him telling me that every night before I go to bed. I'm not going back there. At least Dr. Barren thinks he can do something for me."

"Mom said Dr. Barren thinks the lung cancer is unrelated to your prostate cancer," I said. "She said Dr. Barren is sending you to a surgeon who removes lung cancer when he's not working as a cardiologist. Shit Dad, you want a specialist, someone who does nothing but lungs. You don't want some part-time lung doctor opening you up."

"I don't feel good about that either," my dad said. "But doctor Barren says he can help me. What the fuck? What the fuck am I supposed to do? I'm so fucked up!"

"I'll find you a specialist at Northwestern."

"Evanston," my father said. "I don't want to go into the city. I don't want your mother to have to drive all the way downtown when I'm dying in the hospital."

"Fine," I said.

As good as a martini sounds right now, I'd be ineffective in this cancer nightmare if I were drinking.

[Tuesday, November 11]

Charlie never asks about my father. He doesn't seem to give a shit. Charlie works, brings home a paycheck, and wants to get laid. That's it. He rarely strikes up a conversation, and I can't remember him ever sharing anything personal with me. I've stopped talking to him, and I don't think he's noticed.

[Monday, November 17]

After making phone calls the last few days to find a good pulmonary doctor for my dad, I made an appointment.

"You're going to see a pulmonary specialist tomorrow," I told my father over the phone.

"Hmm," my dad said, sounding concerned and depressed. "Is that what you'd do?"

"Yes," I said. "You don't want to screw around with this. The doctor wants to see your X-rays, he'll probably schedule you for a needle biopsy. We'll figure out what to do from there."

"Let me think about it and I'll call you back," my dad said. He called back a little while later and said he'd go.

I sat down at my computer to work on a story I'm writing for the *Chicago Reader,* profiling the Healing Rooms of Zion. The Healing Rooms is a little storefront operation where evangelicals lay hands on sick people and ask God for healing. I'd thought about asking my father if he wanted to go, but I doubted its effectiveness. A Healing Rooms client I was featuring was dying of cancer, and she'd experienced no breakthroughs. I'd gone as a client myself to see if the Healing Rooms could get rid of my sinus infection before contacting them for this story. I'd wound up calling my doctor days later and getting a prescription for antibiotics. I asked the Healing Rooms healers about their less-than-stellar track record and they told me that doubt or a blockage in either the healer's or patient's connection with God could prevent healing.

The phone rang and it was Fay. There was a lot of noise in the background.

"Where are you?" I asked her.

"Where are you?" she shot back. "We're at Fiona's for breakfast, all except you."

Fiona was having the book club over to have breakfast and donate books to a charity. I'd had it on my calendar for weeks but completely forgot. I didn't want to go. I needed to work on my story, and I was worried sick about my father.

"I'll pop by for an hour," I told Fay.

I brushed my teeth, washed my face, and went to Fiona's looking unkempt. I didn't care. Tina was telling everyone how stressful it was working with an architect to come up with the perfect plans for her new house. Shelly was yammering on and on about the new granite countertops she was installing and how difficult it was to select a new faucet.

"I want a brushed silver finish, but the sprayer that matches the faucet only comes in a shiny finish."

I wanted to scream.

[Tuesday, November 18]

My dad saw the lung doctor today. My mom called after his appointment, which I wasn't at, and told me, "We really liked the doctor. He's a young guy about your age. He has long hair. He looked at the X-rays and said it could be the prostate cancer or an infection. Whatever it is, his lungs are pretty spattered with it. Your father's scheduled for a needle biopsy on Thursday."

[Thursday, November 20]

It's my sister's birthday today. I'd planned to mail her a birthday card, but never got around to it. I'm terrible with cards. Paula and I usually celebrate each other's birthdays by going out to dinner, so I called her to wish her a happy birthday and get a dinner date on the calendar. But as usual, Paula and I couldn't agree on a date. I'd bought Paula a silver and turquoise cross pendant for her birthday when I was in South Beach with Abby. When it became clear dinner wasn't going to happen any time soon, I told Paula I'd drop off her present at our parent's house so she could pick it up on Thanksgiving. Charlie and the boys and I are spending Thanksgiving with Charlie's family.

"I can't talk to Dad," Paula said. "He gets upset and yells at me. It seems like he doesn't want to talk to me. I called him this morning and he was getting into the shower and said he couldn't talk. I called last week and he picked up the phone and right away he said, 'You want to talk to your mother?' So screw it. Just let me know if there's anything I can do to help."

I'd called Paula a couple of weeks ago when our father went back to Dr. Svengali, hoping to get her on my bandwagon and push Dad to see Dr. Benton. I'd called her yesterday as well to tell her about Dad's lung consultation.

"You got him to see a different doctor?" Paula had said irritably. "That was quick."

"He's got to get on this," I said.

"You couldn't get him to go to Northwestern, though, huh? I mean, like you said, it's a better hospital."

"It's a step in the right direction," I said. "The lung doc he saw is affiliated with Northwestern and Dad said he liked him."

"You talked to Dad?"

"Uh, yeah."

"Oh."

Later, I went to a meeting. As I was leaving, my cell phone rang, and it was Eliza, a young woman I'd met at a meeting a couple weeks ago. She was sobbing hysterically. Eliza called me earlier this afternoon. She told me she'd been living at the shelter for seven months, got on a waiting list for a subsidized apartment where she'd be monitored, but when she became friends with another young woman at the shelter named Dashawna, she moved in with her instead.

"We jumped the gun," Eliza told me earlier this afternoon. "Dashawna said she knew some good people we could move in with and save money for our own place."

Those "good" people were a woman and her two twenty-something-year-old sons, one a registered sex offender.

As Eliza cried hysterically, I stood near the doorway of the meeting I was leaving and pressed my cell phone closer to my head.

"You need to calm down," I told her. "I can't understand you."

In between sobs, Eliza choked out that she was calling me from a gas station near my house. "I need a place to stay tonight," she cried. "Can I stay at your house?"

"Uh, hmm, um, yeah, sure," I told her. "I'll pick you up in a few minutes."

Shit, I thought to myself. I hadn't given Eliza my cell phone number. I'd only given her the number to my house. She must have talked to Charlie. I called Charlie.

“What the hell’s going on?” Charlie yelled.

I told Charlie.

“I don’t want you bringing this into my house,” he growled.

“I’ve got to help her out,” I said. “It’s just for one night. It’ll be all right. I think the pie house is still open. I’ll take her there and calm her down before we come home. She’s going to her sponsor’s house tomorrow. Put the kids to bed and don’t tell them anything. They won’t see her until morning. Put sheets and a blanket on the living room couch. She’ll sleep there.”

Eliza was still sobbing when I pulled into the gas station. She plopped her 250-pound butt onto my car seat, and we drove to the pie house.

“Are you hungry?” I asked.

Eliza nodded; her chest heaved as she tried to stifle sobs.

“I’m going to buy you some dinner or pie or whatever, and you’ll stay at my house tonight,” I said. “You’re going to be okay. Tomorrow, we’ll get you to your sponsor’s house, and you two will figure things out.”

Eliza nodded. We pulled into the parking lot of the restaurant and sat there for several minutes, so Eliza could compose herself enough to walk into the restaurant. At the table, we sipped coffee and Eliza ordered dinner.

“I fucked Germaine, one of the guys I’ve been living with,” Eliza said. “Now I’m pregnant, about a month-and-a-half pregnant. I’m working two jobs, and I’m the only one working in the house. I’m paying for everything: their food stamps and everything public aid don’t cover. I’m supporting everyone and not saving a dime. My sponsor gave me nuts, oatmeal, rice crackers, a bag of stuff to keep in my room so I have something to eat. Now my wallet’s missing along with my ID and Social Security card. My bank was supposed to send me a new ATM card because mine was missing, and I called the bank today to find out if they sent it. They told me they sent it two weeks ago.

"I came home from work today, and Germaine was outside. He said, 'Hey, what's up, nigger?' I told him not to call me that. It's disrespectful. He started screaming at me. I walked into the house and as we were walking up the stairs to the apartment, he pushed past me and called me a white bitch fat ass. He went into the apartment and slammed the door in my face." Eliza started crying again. "He wouldn't let me in. He locked me out. I've been locked out for hours and no one will let me in." She began sobbing. "He's been getting ugly and scary ever since he found out I was pregnant."

"Here," I said, sliding a glass of water in front of Eliza. She drank some water and began calming down. "How do you feel about being pregnant?"

"I'm happy I'm having a baby," she said, brightening up. "I know how to raise kids because I raised my nephew for three years while my sister was in jail. My whole family is happy for me and wants me to move back home. They'll help me. I just don't have the financial part of it worked out.

"I'd like to move back home to be with my mom," she continued. "My mom's dying of AIDS. She's been clean for twenty years and they don't know how she got it because she was diagnosed with HIV when I was seven and the last day she got high was the day I was born. My mom only slept with two guys, my dad and this other guy. I'm not sure which one is my dad, but the other guy is dead, so I don't care."

The waitress came by and set a hamburger and fries in front of Eliza. Eliza took a huge bite of her burger and, with her mouth full, said, "When my dad found out my mom slept with someone else, he got so mad he slept with three other women and got them all pregnant. I have two older sisters by my mom and dad, and I have two younger half-sisters and a half-brother by my dad and those women. I didn't even know about my younger sisters and brother until I was in junior high and high school. I found out about one of my sisters after I fooled around with her. My dad felt really bad about that. When he found out we were fooling around, he told me we were sisters."

My mouth was hanging open and I shut it.

"My dad is a great guy," Eliza continued between bites of food. "He's a lot of fun and everyone thinks he's the coolest dad. But I don't think I can go back home because of him. He still smokes pot and PCP. I've been sober since December eleventh, and I'm really trying hard. And that fat ass name. He calls me fat ass, and I don't take that well."

Eliza put her hamburger down. "He's going to court, my dad. He says he didn't sexually molest that girl, but I don't know if I believe him after what he did to me."

"Did he molest you?" I asked.

"Yeah. But it was mostly physical and psychological abuse."

Eliza had the shittiest life and didn't even know it. Her phone rang.

"Finally, it's my sponsor," she said.

Eliza snapped her phone shut. "May says I can live with her temporarily until other arrangements can be worked out."

"Should I take you there now?" I asked hopefully. "May probably has a guest room where you'd be more comfortable. I only have a couch."

"Are you kidding?" Eliza laughed. "I've slept in cars. I can sleep anywhere."

I took Eliza home with me. It was eleven o'clock, and Charlie was still up watching the Blackhawks game. I introduced Charlie and Eliza.

"I'm sorry about freaking you out earlier," Eliza told Charlie.

"That's okay," Charlie said. "Well, I'm going to bed now."

I made up Eliza's bed on the couch, said goodnight, and went upstairs with my purse, which I usually leave downstairs.

[Friday, November 21]

I got up early and was surprised to see Eliza sitting on the couch reading a magazine.

"You want some coffee?" I asked.

"I'd really like to take a bath," Eliza said. "I've always wanted to take a bath in a bathtub like that." We have a huge claw-foot, cast-iron tub.

"Yeah, sure," I said. "I'll run the water for you. You have to start the water really hot to warm up the tub." I filled the bath, adjusted the water temperature a couple of times, and estimated how much water Eliza would displace before I filled the tub to a fairly low level and handed Eliza a towel.

As I spooned coffee into the coffee maker, I recalled Eliza telling me how she's been super horny since her pregnancy. A picture of her masturbating in my tub floated into my head, and I quickly banished it. I went upstairs to get Max ready for school.

"You let your friend Eliza sleep here last night?" Max asked.

Charlie must have told Max about Eliza.

Max had met Eliza exactly a week before. Eliza had called and asked me to take Dashawna to the ER because they thought Dashawna had food poisoning from eating bad mayonnaise. I drove up to the crappy two-flat around the corner that the neighbors all want razed and stopped. "They live here?" Max asked. Max had been advised to steer clear of this building.

"Go up and ring the second-floor doorbell," I told Max.

"If I go up, they're not going to know who I am," Max said.

"You're not going all the way up," I said. "Walk up the front steps, ring the doorbell and get back in the car. They'll come out."

Max rang the bell and, instead of getting into the car,

stood outside trying to get a peek inside the off-limits building. His mouth dropped open when Eliza and Dashawna, who is as overweight as Eliza, waddled out. Eliza squeezed into the back seat and Dashawna, who smelled like a dirty ashtray and ass, plopped into the front seat next to me. I dropped off Dashawna at the hospital, then drove Eliza to the shopping mall where she works. Before she got out, Eliza leaned over and told Max that he looks like Harry Potter, which he hears a lot.

"Thanks," Max said politely.

"How do you know them?" Max asked after Eliza got out of the car.

"They go to the No Alcohol Club," I said.

"Oh. Well, they seem really nice."

• • •

While Eliza was in the bathtub, I poured Max a bowl of cereal.

"Aren't you going to eat with me?" he asked.

"I'm going to take Eliza and Van out to breakfast," I said.

"I wish I could go out to breakfast."

"I wish you could, too, but you don't have time."

I pulled up in front of the school to let Max out. Fay was dropping off Walter and staring through my windshield at Eliza. I waved to her and smiled. Fay waved and shot me a look that said who-the-hell-is-that? I drove off. I checked my rearview mirror and saw Fay watching my car. I turned down a side street and stopped at a stoplight. Seconds later, Fay pulled up next to me and rolled down her window.

"Where're you off to?" she asked.

"Elly's."

"I'm off to get tires," Fay said, trying hard not to obviously stare at Eliza.

The light changed and we both pulled away.

I drove Eliza to the bank after we had breakfast, where she

attempted to straighten out her pilfered checking account. Then we went to the DMV so she could replace her stolen state ID. Eliza's sponsor met us at the DMV and took Eliza from there.

It actually felt good driving Eliza around and helping her out. Aside from stashing my purse in my bedroom, I'd been completely at ease with her staying at my house. I also enjoyed freaking out Fay.

[Tuesday, November 25]

I went to a meeting, and Tracy, who is Deidre's sponsor, told us Deidre is under house arrest until the middle of January. Deidre is wearing an ankle bracelet, and the authorities electronically imprinted her voice. About every forty-five minutes, the department of corrections calls Deidre. If she's not there, she's screwed. If her voice is impaired by alcohol, their computer will pick it up.

"A small group of us has been going over to Deidre's to have a meeting, and she keeps saying how much she wants to drink!" Wisconsin Whitley told me after the meeting. "I can't believe it. After everything that's happened to her and could happen to her, I can't believe it!"

[Wednesday, November 26]

I went to my father's doctor appointment with the pulmonary specialist, Dr. Whistler. Whistler's pretty sure the prostate cancer metastasized to my dad's lungs.

"My cancer doctor is Dr. Barren," my father told Whistler. "You know him?"

Whistler looked my dad square in the eye and said, "You should see the guys downtown."

"Who would you send him to?" I asked Whistler.

"Kevin McCreevy, he's a urologist, and an oncologist by the name of Steve Newhart."

My father's sister, Diane, who's a nurse in California, had suggested my dad see Newhart. One of Diane's friends had been treated by Newhart before she died of cancer, and she loved him.

"I'm going to Florida to go fishing on Friday," my dad said. "Is that okay?"

Whistler looked at my dad with a mixture of amusement and incredulity. "Yeah," he answered. "But get to the doctor when you get back."

"Is this something I have to take care of right away?" my dad asked. "How soon do I have to do this when I get back?"

"As soon as possible," Whistler laughed. "I talked to Dr. Chevron, your former doctor, and he said you weren't being very aggressive. Take care of this. This is advanced."

All along my parents had been telling me Chevron didn't want to do anything. He was the one doctor I hadn't met. Now I began to see the real picture. "Is this something I have to do right now?" I could hear my father asking Chevron. "I feel great. Couldn't I start this later?" I pictured Chevron nodding and going along with my father's wishes. To Svengali's credit, he'd insisted my dad start hormone therapy and get X-rayed.

We walked out of the examining room, and my dad ducked into the bathroom.

"How are you doing?" I asked my mother. Her mouth was set in a tight, thin line. She shrugged. "This is bad," I said. My mom nodded.

My dad popped out of the bathroom and asked me to come to their house.

"Okay," I told him. I got in my car and cried.

My parents and I sat at their kitchen table.

"I'm going to leave you and Paula all my money because I know as soon as I'm gone your mother is going to marry John-John from church," my father joked. John-John is a pathetic gossiping bachelor.

"I don't think Mom wants to saddle herself with another man," I joked back.

"I wouldn't," my mom said.

We all laughed.

"Make an appointment with those doctors Whistler recommended," I said.

"I don't know if I want to go downtown," my father said.

"Did you hear what Whistler said?" I shouted. "You told him you were seeing Barren and he looked you straight in the eye and said, 'See the guys downtown.'"

"Well, this whole thing makes me want to say fuck it and do this," my dad said, putting two fingers to his lips and pretending to smoke.

"That's the stupidest thing I've ever heard," my mother said angrily. "You're not going to start smoking again. I'm not putting up with it. I'm not going to smell it on you and your clothes. I'm not going to stand for it."

"See what I have to put up with?" my dad said to me.

I hung out at my parents' house for five hours. My dad and I reminisced about how he and I used to get on his motorcycle and go horseback riding on the weekends. He reminded me about the time he and his father rescued me from a rain-drenched Seventh-Day Adventist youth campout, and how the three of us sat at a bar—me drinking orange juice and eating cheese and crackers—before driving back home. My dad talked about his childhood and said that at the age of three, he'd tied ropes around his tricycle wheels so he could ride it in the snow.

My dad got a faraway look in his eye and grinned. "Adolph and I had a lot of fun, too," he snickered.

I met Adolph once when I was a kid. Adolph was old enough to be my father's father. When my dad was a child, Adolph had taken him under his larcenous wing because my father's dad was a barfly.

"He taught me how to steal," my dad chuckled. "I used to have a saying, 'If I can touch it, I can own it.'"

"What are you talking about?" my mother asked, walking into the room and catching the tail end of our conversation.

"Adolph," my father answered.

"That degenerate," my mother said, a look of disgust sweeping onto her face.

My father snickered and winked at me.

[Thursday, November 27 (Thanksgiving)]

As of today, I haven't had a drink in eleven months. That was my first thought this morning. My second thought was of my father wasting away, curled up in a hospital bed, dying of cancer just like Martha. I cried off and on all morning, during which time I called Paula and told her about dad's lung diagnosis. We cried together.

"How did Mom and Dad take the news?" Paula asked.

"You know Mom," I said. "She doesn't give much away. But not good. She had a very pinched expression."

"What about Dad?"

"Last night, when I was at their house, he kept getting phone calls from his fishing buddies, the ones he's going to Florida with. He told them, 'I got some bad news. . . . Yep, cancer's on my lungs. . . . But I feel great. . . . Yep, I'm drinking a cocktail right now. . . . I'm gonna beat this damned thing and I'm going fishing and I'm not going to think about it. . . . That's right. . . . Fucking A.' But he got teary a couple of times last night. He's worried he won't get to see his grandsons grow up."

Paula and I wished each other a happy Thanksgiving. My parents are going to Paula's house for dinner. Charlie and the kids and I are going to Charlie's sister, Liz's. I called my mom.

"I can't believe your father's thinking of smoking again," was the first thing she said. "How stupid!"

"He's dying," I said. "It might not make that much of a difference."

"Yeah," she said flatly, "but still."

"He may not be around much longer," I said. "You realize that, right?"

"Yeah, but it's hard," my mom said. "And the doctors don't know what they're talking about. Look at Barbara, your father's cousin. They gave her three months and that was a year ago. The guy who invented this Flor Essence supplement I'm giving your father had lung cancer and he cured himself with it. And look at Lance Armstrong."

I got off the phone feeling completely alone with the ugly reality of my father's prognosis. I made myself some tea and longingly looked at the huge martini glasses on the shelf above my teacups.

Later, at Liz's apartment, I looked at her wine but didn't give much thought to drinking.

Liz's daughter, Amber, was at dinner. I've always had a special spot for Amber, but I haven't seen her in five or six years. The last time was at Max's fifth birthday party. Amber came with her baby daughter, Kiara, and since then, Amber, a drug addict, has had several stints in jail and prison, mostly for stealing credit cards and writing bad checks. Liz has custody of Kiara.

Amber looks like a white girl trying to be black. Her curly long hair is plaited and stuck to her forehead. Her language is mildly peppered with ghetto.

"She actually sounds pretty normal tonight," Liz told me.

"You should hear how she talks sometimes. You'd swear she was a gangsta."

Kiara's father, who is in prison, is African American. The father of Amber's new four-month-old, twenty-two-pound sumo baby, Angel, is a different imprisoned African American. As Amber cooed over fat little Angel, Kiara unhappily watched.

Kiara is having identity issues, Liz said. She's upset about being the only dark-skinned member in her household. Noah, Liz's son and Kiara's uncle, lives with them, and sometimes Kiara says she's white and sometimes she says she's black. She's also not sure if she should call Liz Grandma or Mom.

I remember Amber at the age of ten singing "Satin Doll" one Christmas. Martha taught her the song and she got up in front of everyone and sang it beautifully. She was a gorgeous, smart little girl. Fucking drugs.

[Saturday, November 29]

I went to a meeting tonight and the woman who spoke said, "Instead of half listening to people and formulating an answer while they're talking, I give people my full attention now and don't always have a pat answer."

I'm always half listening to people and coming up with what I think is great advice, and I think most of the time people just want someone to listen.

A bunch of people from the meeting went to dinner at Jimmy's Char House afterward and Playboy Pete asked me to join them. "You should be a jeans model," he said as I turned to sit at the table. "Turn around again, come on." I rolled my eyes at Brent, who was sitting next to me, and we shook our heads.

Women either find Playboy Pete offensive or a harmless hoot. I'm in the latter camp. Playboy Pete and his stupid jokes somehow make me feel normal again, like I'm not hanging out with a bunch of alcoholics. He reminds me of my dad's old cronies and he makes me laugh.

[Monday, December 1]

I made appointments for my dad with the urologist and oncologist that his pulmonary doctor recommended. My dad gets back from Florida on Thursday, and on Friday he's seeing Svengali.

I called my mom and told her about the appointments. "You need to get the slides of Dad's prostate biopsy and take them to these doctors," I told her.

My mother groaned. "I suppose," she sighed disgustedly.

I went to the grocery store and bought ingredients for a Christmas cookie exchange I'm going to tomorrow, but I was too depressed to make the cookies. I called Fiona instead and told her what was going on with my dad.

"Have you told Fay what's going on?" Fiona asked.

"No," I said, feeling irritated because Fay rarely asked about my father, and when she did, she didn't listen. She tends to be absorbed in her own little world and prattles endlessly about her children. "Fay is kind of hard to talk to sometimes."

"Well, Fay's got a lot going on, too," Fiona said. "Ron lost his job and they're all freaked."

"Oh, no."

"Yeah. He was let go right before Thanksgiving."

[Tuesday, December 2]

I made nine dozen butter pecan cookies and took them to Tracy's house. My expectations were low because I didn't think a bunch of recovering addicts would bring anything good, but it was one of the best cookie exchanges I've been to. Tracy served a delicious turkey tetrazzini, and we had a goofy white elephant grab bag.

Iris, a woman I've seen at a few of the Tuesday night meetings, and I started talking. I'm not sure how we got on the subject, but Iris began telling me about her brother's suspicious death back in 1963. Iris said that after her mother died, her widower father had had a hard time raising the kids, and Iris's brother, Joe, a troubled teen, was kicked out of Catholic school, then public school, and finally sent to a Catholic ranch for wayward boys on the Montana/Wyoming border. Joe was there three months before he turned up dead.

School officials told Iris's family that Joe was mending fences when the truck he was riding in flipped over, killing him. The story bothered Iris. She had repetitive dreams about her brother lying on a slab in the morgue.

"I had one of those dreams on the anniversary of Joe's death," Iris said. "He was lying on the slab and opened his eyes. I asked him, 'How did you die?' and he said, 'The God-damned faggot did it.'

"I started digging around," Iris said. "There was no accident report and no fatal truck accident reported in the newspapers. I spent months trying to track down my brother's death certificate. I was told it had been filed in a different county than the county the school was in. I called the funeral home where his body had been prepared and convinced the funeral director to send me the certificate, which turned out not to be a certificate at all. It was nothing but a slip of paper saying who the deceased was, with no other information. There was no coroner's report, no time of death, no accident report.

"The priest who ran the ranch is dead now," Iris said. "Died in a plane crash. One of the promotional points for the ranch was that it had an airstrip and the boys could learn to fly a plane. The priest would take boys on weekend trips and fly them in the plane to conventions to raise money for the ranch. God knows what happened to those boys during those trips. Alumni of the ranch have come forward and filed lawsuits against the ranch for sexual abuse, which the ranch has quietly settled.

"That priest had boys on board when he crashed the plane," Iris continued. "Everyone was killed. The ranch sanitized that, too. But when I was poking around, I found the coroner's report and the priest's blood alcohol count was high.

"It kills me that the ranch is still open," Iris said. "The place is like a shrine to that fucking priest. There's even a statue of him. I want to get that place closed down. I just don't know how to go about it."

Tracy poked her head into the great room where Iris and I were talking. "Come into the kitchen and grab the rest of these cookies," she said. "Almost everyone's gone and there are a lot left. Take them home or I'm throwing them out."

Iris and I followed Tracy back into the kitchen, where Stella and Tanya were loading up on more cookies. Stella was telling Tanya about her recent relapse.

"My friend and I were out trying to find more crack," Stella was saying. "We were combing this bad neighborhood and stumbled into a dealer we didn't know." Stella started laughing hard. "We bought fifty dollars worth of what turned out to be crunched-up saltine crackers."

"I got sold grass clippings instead of pot on my honeymoon in Maui," I said. "Charlie and I were driving the Road to Hana and a couple of guys were standing on the side yelling, 'Smoke.' I made Charlie stop—he didn't want to—and I smoked some awesome weed with those guys. I bought a bag and when Charlie and I were back in our hotel room, I discovered it wasn't even dirt weed; those assholes had sold me grass clippings."

"I used to be a coke dealer and I had a kilo go missing on me," Iris said. "I was lucky because my supplier was understanding and chalked it up to a business loss. About a year later, a friend of mine was helping me move and we found it stuffed between towels in a closet. God, did we have a party."

"I have one for you," Tracy said. "One night, some friends and I were sitting around my coffee table doing coke. My wasted husband was passed out on the couch. We'd just dumped an eight ball out and I was about to do a line when Ken woke up. He snatched the rolled-up bill out of my hand and said, 'I'm going first.' He bent over the mirror and sneezed a huge sneeze, blowing coke everywhere. He laughed and passed out on the couch again."

Tracy folded her arms across her chest and got a far-off, pissed-off look on her face. The incident happened more than ten years ago, but Tracy is still very ticked off about it.

[Friday, December 5]

I picked up Max from school, took him to Walter's birthday party at Chuck E. Cheese, bought some tokens for Van, and played a few arcade games with him before he ran off to climb around in the slide maze. I spotted an empty booth, sat down, and called my mom to find out how my dad's appointment with Svengali went.

"We gave Dr. Barren the report from the needle biopsy and he said, 'What did you go to this guy for? He's a nothing little pulmonary doctor. This report tells me nothing. I don't know what kind of cancer this is. Why didn't you go to the guy I told you to see? You just wasted valuable time. Go and get this done like I told you to.' I know you've been trying to help, but we're going to stay with Dr. Barren and do what he says. So thanks for your help, but we're done with running around."

I sat in the booth, stunned. My mother had just told me to piss off. Ron, Fay's jobless husband, walked into Chuck E. Cheese and sat in the booth behind me. We sat sideways with our legs stretched out in front of us separated by the booth back.

"How are you?" Ron asked.

"Eh," I said shrugging. "You?"

"Eh," he said and laughed. "The upshot of being unemployed is it's freeing. It's allowing me to open my mind and look at all sorts of options around the country, but Fay's freaking. She doesn't want to leave her family."

"We're spiritual beings having a human experience," I said.

Ron looked at me like I had rocks in my head. "Did you hear that from one of your yoga friends?" he asked. We laughed.

Fay was shooting me a "what's wrong?" look while running around doling out game tokens to Walter and his friends. I felt guilty not helping her, but I had to keep an eye on Van.

As the boys and I were leaving the party, Fay asked, "What's going on?"

"Just more Dad stuff," I said.

"You wanna get together for coffee tomorrow?" she asked.

"Yeah," I said. "How about after my yoga class?"

I took the boys home and after they were in bed, Charlie, who'd been in San Francisco since Wednesday, arrived home. Charlie and I lay in bed in the dark and I finally told him what was going on with my dad, even though he didn't ask.

"I just know they're going to cancel those appointments I made," I said. "They're going to stay with that freak and they don't want me butting in."

Charlie lay silently. He moved his hand over to my hip and I turned away, curled up in a rigid little ball, and lay awake thinking about my father and resenting Charlie for being nothing but horny.

[Saturday, December 6]

I worked out a lot of my anger and resentment in yoga, then met Fay for coffee. As I told her about my dad and Svengali, my anger came surging back.

"I always thought you do a needle biopsy first and if you can't get a good sample, you do surgery," Fay said.

"Svengali has my parents' minds bent," I said. "He's scared them to death. He actually told them he's the only doctor who can cure my dad. He yelled at them for wasting precious time seeing other doctors. He cursed my dad out, swore at him, for getting a second opinion. This is a nightmare and my hands are tied. My parents basically told me to fuck off."

"You should write them a letter or send them an email pointing out all the red flags this doctor is waving," Fay said. "Even though you've told them your worries, it's often effective to look at them in writing."

I drove back home and began stewing about how my mother huffs and puffs any time I ask her to get slides or CT scan reports, or to do anything that requires a little work. I decided if she wants me to piss off, I'm going to piss off.

[Sunday, December 7]

The phone rang and I was surprised to hear my mother's voice.

"Your father came back from Florida with a lot of mahi-mahi and wants you to make it on Christmas Eve," she said. "Do you want to talk to him?"

"Yeah," I said.

She handed the phone to my dad.

"Did you have a good time on your trip?" I asked.

"I had a great time," he said. "Had a lot of fun. You know

that Christmas fish you make? I've got a lot of mahimahi, and I'd like you to make it Christmas Eve."

"That recipe is for sea bass," I said. "I'm not sure if it'll work with mahimahi. I'll check it out. One way or the other, I'll make your fish."

"Good."

"You know, I hope you're still going to see those doctors at Northwestern," I said. "It's really important to hear what they think. Keep those appointments, Dad. I'm begging you."

"I suppose so," he said.

I breathed a sigh of relief. "Thank you," I said. "Why don't you put Mom back on the phone so I can make sure she gets all the right stuff for your appointments."

My dad handed the phone to my mother and she agreed not to cancel the doctor appointments. "Make sure you track down the slides of the prostate biopsy," I told her.

My mother sighed disgustedly. "I guess," she said. "I don't know why I have to do all this running around. I think all of these doctors stink. I don't think any of them know what they're doing or that any of them care."

[Tuesday, December 9]

I was up until eleven last night making lemon drop cookies for the cookie exchange with book club tonight. My family is now up to its ears in homemade Christmas cookies. Yum!

We were discussing the book *Keeping Faith* at book club and, as usual, our conversations veered off topic. Nosey Rosy, who was pretty lit, loudly made herself the center of attention.

"I was watching Dr. Phil," she announced. "There was a couple on his show who had two kids, and Dr. Phil told the husband that the wife had two full-time jobs taking care of those kids. I called my husband," Rosy continued, waving her finger at everyone sitting around her, "and I told him, 'I have three full-time jobs! Three full-time jobs!'"

It was typical Rosy. I pray I was nothing like Rosy when I was drunk. It's often said that the flaws that annoy you in others are flaws you have yourself. It makes my skin crawl to think people looked at me like I was looking at her.

I got home around eleven thirty and Sturgis, my sweet old dog, was acting weird. He was panting anxiously and pacing by the sliding glass door that leads to our backyard deck. I let Sturgis out and he stayed in the backyard for twenty minutes, which is unusual for him. He pretty much comes right back in as soon as he finishes doing his business. When Sturgis came back in, I followed him as he slowly limped upstairs on arthritic legs. I love that dog. It makes me so sad to think of him dying, too.

[Wednesday, December 10]

Charlie got Max out of bed this morning and found a bloody spot of urine on Max's bedroom floor. I looked at Sturgis panting on our bedroom floor. After taking the boys to school, I drove Sturgis to the vet. On our way into the office, Sturgis took a bloody whiz on the sidewalk. He never pees in the house or on the sidewalk. We walked into the building, and Sturgis lay at my feet as I talked to the receptionist. After a couple of minutes, Sturgis got up and I noticed a bloody smear on the floor. An older couple sitting in the waiting room with their cat noticed, too.

"Oh, the doggy cut himself," the old man said.

"He's peeing blood," I said, making a worried face.

"Me, too," the old woman said.

A veterinary assistant came out from behind the counter and handed me a small plastic cup and asked me to get a urine sample. I took Sturgis outside and he immediately lifted his leg and let out a stream of blood-clotted urine before I could get the cup under him. We walked around the yard and Sturgis lifted his leg here and there marking territory. Each time he lifted his leg, I stuck the cup under his penis but not much came out. What did come out sprayed erratically, mostly on my hand and coat, but I did manage to get a couple of drops into the cup.

"Here," I said handing the cup to the assistant with my blood-and-urine spattered hand. The assistant frowned and tried to suck up a clot off the floor with a syringe. I walked Sturgis into an examining room. The vet felt all over Sturgis's body and took him in the back to see if he could get more urine out of him with a catheter.

"I'm going to snake the catheter into his bladder, inflate it with air, and take some X-rays," he told me.

After twenty minutes, the vet walked back in with Sturgis.

"I took two X-rays," he said with a grim look. "The first one wasn't good. You can't see anything. The second one . . ." The vet clipped the X-ray to a light panel. "See this whole area?" He traced a blob on the X-ray with his pen. "That's his bladder. And see this?" He pointed to a small triangle in it. "That's what we were able to inflate, which leads me to believe the rest of the bladder is tumor. I had a really hard time running the catheter up. I kept hitting obstructions and I couldn't get past the prostate. Your dog is thirteen years old. I could put him under and try to get a better picture, but I'm pretty sure what I felt is a tumor around his prostate that entered his bladder."

"How sure are you?" I asked.

"Seventy-five, eighty percent sure," he said. "There's not much we can do."

"I want you to put him under and get a better picture," I said. "I want to know what's up there."

"Okay, you can bring him back tomorrow," the vet said.

"What about now? We're here now."

"Uh, yeah, I could do it during my lunch hour."

I hugged Sturgis and gave him a kiss before the vet led him out and into a back room. I walked out of the office, sat in my Jeep, and cried. I called Charlie.

"The vet said he'd call around one o'clock with the results," I sobbed. "But it seems likely I'll have to put Sturgis down."

I was supposed to go to the hospital this afternoon with my parents to meet the surgeon Svengali recommended. I drove home, called my mother, and told her I couldn't make it.

At noon, I called the vet to see if there was any news and a veterinary assistant told me the vet was able to get a smaller catheter into Sturgis's bladder and there was no tumor; Sturgis just had a severe bladder infection that could be treated with steroids and antibiotics.

I was a wreck, but a happy wreck. I picked up Sturgis a few hours later, took him home, made dinner, and began eating with the kids. Charlie was going out to dinner with his boss, Neil, whom we'd had dinner with in Savannah. While the kids and I were eating, the phone rang.

"Neil would really like to see everybody, so I'm bringing him over," Charlie said. "We'll be there in half an hour. We'll just stay for a little bit, then head out for dinner."

About a month ago, Charlie told me Neil was flying in for meetings and asked me to make a nice dinner for him tonight. The appointment with the surgeon came up, and I asked Charlie to take Neil out to dinner instead.

"The house is not picked up for company," I said. "Neil will see a mess."

"Uh, that's okay," Charlie said. "See you in a bit."

Bastard! I thought as I quickly picked up the downstairs but not the upstairs. Half an hour later, Charlie and Neil were at the door. As soon as Neil walked in, Van invited him up to his room. Neil smiled and shrugged and followed Van upstairs where the beds were all unmade and the hamper was overflowing. I didn't give a rat's ass.

Charlie got home at ten thirty, pumped up with wine and ready for action. He grabbed my ass and said, "Hey baby, I have to get up early tomorrow. Neil and I have to be at a meeting downtown at nine."

"You said only Neil was going to that meeting tomorrow," I said.

"Neil wants me to go now."

"You know I have to be downtown at nine," I yelled. "I have to be at Northwestern for my dad's doctor appointment! You knew that."

Charlie stood there with a sappy look on his face saying nothing. I pushed past him and called Liv and asked if I could bring Max to her house before school. She said yes. I crossed my fingers and hoped Van's preschool wouldn't mind if I dropped Van off two hours early. I went to bed and turned my back on my horny prick of a husband.

[Thursday, December 11]

The preschool let me drop Van off early, and I drove downtown to the urologist's office. My parents and I were taken into an examining room and Dr. McCreevy, an attractive guy in his early forties, walked in.

"What brings you to see me?" he asked my dad with a friendly smile.

My dad told McCreevy his medical story and told him he was seeing Svengali.

"Dr. Barren told me he could cure me and no one else could," my dad said.

McCreevy raised his eyebrows, gave my dad a you've-got-to-be-kidding look, took a deep breath, and put a hand over his mouth to pull down his smile.

"Dr. Barren told me not to see any other doctors, to stick with him and I'd be fine," my dad continued.

McCreevy tipped back in his chair and groaned. I held out my arms, met my father's gaze, and said, "See? Do you see how he's reacting?" I turned to McCreevy. "My dad went to Dr. Barren after he found out he was terminal. Dr. Barren told him, 'You just did the two worst things: You had surgery, I never would have done surgery, then you had radiation, and radiation feeds cancer. But the good news is you're back with me and now I can take care of you.'"

McCreevy shook his head, rubbed his face, and groaned again.

"Do you see?" I said to my dad. "Look at the doctor."

"That's just wrong," McCreevy said, still shaking his head. "You did the right things."

My dad told McCreevy about the invasive biopsy Dr. Barren still wants to do and the needle biopsy he already had done. "Dr. Barren screamed at me for seeing that other doctor and getting a needle biopsy," my father said. "Yesterday, I saw the surgeon he wants me to see. I'm scheduled for a biopsy on the sixteenth and I'll be in the hospital for two days."

McCreevy looked at my dad's needle biopsy report, which said "suspicious for prostate cancer."

"I want you to take the biopsy slides to our top cytologist," McCreevy said. "If she says it's prostate cancer, it's prostate cancer. If she doesn't know, no one would know and you'll have to have the other biopsy. But why have it done if you don't have to?

"Up until now, you've done all the right things," McCreevy assured my father. "But now you need a quarterback to manage things for you, you need a good oncologist."

"I've got an appointment to see Dr. Newhart on Monday," my dad said.

"Great," McCreevy said. "He's a really good doctor. Get the CT scans of your lungs for Dr. Newhart."

We walked out of McCreevy's office and my mother hugged me.

"Thank you for being persistent," my mom said. "I feel really good about this. I like him."

"Me, too," I said. I closed my eyes and sent up a silent, "Thank you, God!"

[Friday, December 12]

Max must be eavesdropping on my phone conversations. Out of the blue, while I was cooking dinner, Max said, "I never knew you had a drinking problem, Mom. It never seemed like it to me."

"Well," I told him, "it runs in our family. Papa is an alcoholic. His father was an alcoholic. Grandma Martha was an alcoholic. Dad's dad was an alcoholic. You're going to have to be very careful when it comes to alcohol. I quit because I didn't like the way I was drinking and I didn't want things to get bad."

"Oh," Max said and thought for a moment. "But Dad's not an alcoholic."

"No. Sometimes it skips people."

"Oh," Max said and left the kitchen.

This time I didn't think, *Maybe I don't have a problem,* and I smiled at this small sign of growth.

After dinner, I went to a meeting and Eliza was there. She looks good and seems happy.

"My sponsor found me a room to rent and I have to walk to catch the bus for work," Eliza said. "I've lost weight and feel healthier."

I gave Eliza a big hug and told her to call me if she ever needs help. Life's going to get a lot tougher once that baby is born.

[Saturday, December 13]

Charlie made dinner while I was at a meeting. He cooked the frozen lobster tails I bought a couple of months ago and was pulling them out of the broiler when I got home.

"We didn't have any breadcrumbs, so I made my own," Charlie said proudly.

I was impressed. We sat down and Charlie served up the lobster.

"How are we supposed to eat this?" Max asked.

I looked at my plate. Partially translucent meat protruded from where the tail had been connected to the body. The breadcrumb mixture was sitting on top of the shell, and the shell had not been split open.

"You didn't split the shell?" I asked.

Charlie began to fidget irritably.

"How many times have you had lobster when the tail wasn't split open?" I asked. "The breadcrumbs. What purpose do they serve sitting on top of the shell? They're supposed to be on the meat, you know, so you can eat the breadcrumbs and meat together. Didn't you read the recipe?"

"Yeah," Charlie said angrily, fidgeting even more. "But the recipe didn't say anything about opening up the tail."

I got a serrated knife and began sawing through Max's tail. I pulled out a chunk of meat that was half cooked. "Didn't you thaw these before broiling them?"

Charlie angrily got up, snatched our plates, and put the lobster tails back in the broiler. When he returned the tails to our plates, the meat was still not cooked. I shut up and picked at what I could.

"The parts I can eat taste good," I said condescendingly.

Charlie scowled.

"I can't believe the cookbook didn't say anything about opening up the tail," I said. I got up and retrieved the cookbook he'd used. "Here, it's right here." I pointed to a long paragraph in the middle of the recipe. There was also a diagram showing how to prepare a lobster.

"That's for a full, live lobster," Charlie said.

"Yeah, but it shows you what to do with the tail," I said.

Charlie blanched. "I can't believe you pulled out that cookbook," he said. "I never would have done that to you."

"I never would have cooked the lobster like that and lied," I said.

The look on Charlie's face screamed, "Bitch!" He began slamming things as he cleared the kitchen. I started feeling bad. After all, he had tried to cook a nice dinner.

"I'm going to start calling you Little Emeril," I said in a joking way, hoping he'd laugh.

Charlie shot me a look that said, "Drop dead."

"Bam!" I shouted.

Charlie laughed.

"Thanks for cooking dinner," I said. "It did taste good," I lied.

Charlie scowled and started to say something.

"Bam!" I shouted again.

He laughed, thank God.

[Monday, December 15]

Max stayed home sick with a wicked strain of the flu. Poor guy had to take care of himself for an hour because I had to leave for my dad's oncology appointment at eleven thirty, and Charlie, whom I talked into taking half a vacation day, couldn't get home before twelve thirty.

When I got to Dr. Newhart's office, my parents had already been led to an examining room and a nurse escorted me to them. Minutes later, Dr. Newhart walked in and my dad repeated what he'd told McCreevy.

"I had my prostate removed then radiation and Dr. Barren told me those were the two worst things I could have done," my dad told Newhart.

"That's bullshit," Newhart yelled.

My dad laughed and looked relieved. I knew at that moment Newhart was going to be my dad's doctor.

"The cytologist is pretty sure the lesions on your lungs are prostate cancer," Newhart told my dad. "The lesions are very small and there are many on both lungs. A surgical biopsy of one lesion out of many would not tell us much more, so cancel your biopsy. I'll do another CAT scan in a couple of weeks to see if the hormones are shrinking the lesions. We'll go from there."

By the time we walked out of Newhart's office, it was time for an early dinner. My parents took me to an Italian restaurant around the corner.

"I like this Newhart," my father said apprehensively. "I just hope I'm doing the right thing. Dr. Barren says he can cure me."

"Dr. Barren is a lying sack of shit who shouldn't be practicing medicine," I said.

"We weren't going to tell you this," my mother said, "but when we went to see Dr. Barren the last time, he called you an idiot and told us not to listen to you."

"He made me promise not to see any other doctors," my dad said. "He took my hands, looked me in the eye, and made me promise."

"Your father looked like he wasn't going to promise anything," my mother said. "But Dr. Barren kept holding his hands and staring your father in the eye until he said yes."

"We should report this guy," I said, anger twisting my gut.

I put my face in my hands for a moment and just breathed. "You don't know how hard I've been praying for you to leave Svengali."

[Tuesday, December 16]

Max was still very sick: fever, congestion, body aches. I called his school. Lots of kids were out sick. I babied Max, waiting on him hand and foot, and in the evening passed him over to Charlie and went out to dinner with Emily and a few of the Door County chicks.

"Donna has blood plasma cancer," Emily told me when we made dinner plans. "Her prince of a husband told her he was having an affair and wanted a divorce the day she was diagnosed. She started cancer treatment and the treatment caused her to have a stroke. Now she's legally blind. But through it all, I have never heard her cry or complain. She's amazing. Instead of being resentful, she's glad she's alive. Instead of being upset that she's blind, she's happy she can see a little and still see her kids."

Out of us all, Donna was the most upbeat person at dinner. If Emily hadn't told me she was blind, I'd never have known. Not once did Donna bring up her crappy circumstances. If I were Donna, I'm pretty sure I'd be crying in my beer.

[Saturday, December 20]

Max was sick all week, leaving snotty tissues everywhere. But now that he's better, Van came down with the flu.

I bought tickets a month ago for Charlie, Max, and myself to see the Joffrey Ballet perform *The Nutcracker* tonight, and Van is supposed to sleep over at my parents house. I called my mom and asked if she'd mind coming to our house to watch Van.

"I don't want you to get sick, but I really don't want Dad to get sick," I said. "You should be fine if you don't kiss Van and you put him to bed early. I feel bad asking you to watch him. If you don't want to, I'll understand."

My mother, of course, said yes. She came to our house, and Charlie, Max, and I drove downtown. We went to Prairie for dinner, and while we were having soup, I called my mom to see how things were going. I wasn't worried about Van, I was worried about my father giving my mom a hard time for being at my house when she should be home with him. My mother had already put Van to bed and was lounging on the couch reading a book, but as I suspected, my dad was being a dick. My father had spent the day hunting with his friends in southern Wisconsin. When he got home, he realized he'd forgotten his house keys and was angry that my mother wasn't home to let him in.

"Your father called in a foul mood, swearing like a sailor," my mother said. "He was especially mad because he'd practically driven past your house on his way home. He drove here to get my keys, scoured your pantry for booze, and got even madder when he couldn't find any. He found your cooking sherry and polished it off. He just left."

"What an ass. I'm so sorry, Mom."

"Eh, it's okay," she said. "Hopefully he'll be sleeping when I get home. He's always sorry in the morning."

When I hung up, Charlie asked, "Your dad?" I rolled my eyes and nodded.

Our food arrived and the waiter placed the pork chops Max ordered in front of him. The chops came with a red currant sauce and were topped with crunchy bits of sweet potato. A square of cheesy grits sat off to the side. Charlie got the mixed grill and I got beef tenderloin topped with grilled onions and mushrooms. Max eyed my plate.

"I thought I was ordering what you have, Mom," he said.

"Don't you like yours?"

Max shook his head. "I don't like the sauce."

"You want to switch?"

Max nodded. "That's what I ordered."

"No, you ordered the pork chops, but I'll switch with you."

We exchanged plates. Max scraped away the onions and mushrooms and dug into the tenderloin. For dessert, he had a hot fudge sundae, and Charlie and I split a piece of sweet potato cheesecake with caramel sauce and fresh berries.

The Nutcracker was beautiful. The dancers were spectacular. The scenery and costumes were gorgeous. And Max hated it. He began sighing loudly and checking his watch toward the end of the first half. The only upside for him was that he was wearing his suit. Max loved wearing his suit. He even asked to go to church just so he could put it on.

"Come on, let's get a Coke," Charlie told Max when the intermission lights went on.

"Will you hand me my jacket, Mom?" Max asked. "I don't want to look like the manager of Osco Drug." I looked at Charlie and we burst out laughing.

During the second half of the ballet, Max's sighing and watch-checking was constant. The family in front of us was having the same problem. Their son, who appeared to be about thirteen, got up three or four times during the second half and disappeared for long periods of time.

While we were driving home, Max said, "I don't know why you thought I would like that. I hated it."

I laughed. I couldn't help thinking that if I had been drinking, I would have ripped into Max for being a little ingrate. Instead, I was laughing.

"Yeah, I don't know what I was thinking," I said.

[Sunday, December 21]

Charlie and I decided not to get each other much for Christmas. We were going to save money, just get each other token gifts. But when the December issue of *Harper's Bazaar* came out in November, I saw an ad for a watch I wanted. The steel wristband on my Kenneth Cole watch comes apart all the time and falls off my arm. The watch I want has an over-sized face with diamonds instead of numbers, has a leather wrist strap, and comes in hot pink or robin's egg blue. I showed Charlie the ad.

"I know we decided to get each other inexpensive gifts for Christmas," I began, "but I'd really like this watch."

I learned on my thirtieth birthday, almost ten years ago, that I had to tell Charlie exactly what I wanted to avoid disappointment. I'd told Charlie I didn't want a big party on my thirtieth, so he planned nothing. As my birthday got closer, I told him I wanted to do something nice, just the two of us. Charlie booked a room downtown at the Hotel Nikko. We had cocktails at the bar and took a cab to Shaw's Crab House for dinner. When our taxi pulled up in front of the restaurant, Charlie turned to me and said, "I don't have any money." I paid for the cab. After dinner, the waiter placed our check on the table, and Charlie fished out a gift certificate my sister had given to us for Christmas and paid the bill with it. He then said he was too tired to go anywhere but back to the hotel, so we hailed a cab, which I paid for, and Charlie passed out in our hotel room. I spent the next hour in the bathroom scrutinizing my drunk naked body for signs of age while knocking off mini bottle after mini bottle of vodka from the mini bar.

A month ago, when I told Charlie I wanted the watch and handed him the magazine, he looked at the ad, snorted disgustedly, and chucked the magazine onto a side table. Last

Sunday, while we were at church, my watch fell off my arm, hit the floor at Charlie's feet, and I was unable to put the band back together. Days later, Charlie asked, "Do you have any thoughts on what you'd like for Christmas?"

"Yeah," I snorted sarcastically. "You know my broken watch? If you don't get me the watch I want, I'm buying it for myself."

"Do you still have the ad?" Charlie asked sheepishly.

"The magazine is in our bedroom somewhere."

Tonight, I decided to ask Max which color he thought I should get and began leafing through the magazine looking for the watch ad.

"Dad must have ripped it out," I told Max.

"Why do you always blame Dad for everything?" Max asked.

"I don't," I said defensively. "He probably ripped it out because he's going to order it for me."

Charlie walked into the room.

"Did you rip the watch ad out of the magazine?" I asked him.

Charlie left the room and came back with the page. I gave Max an I-told-you-so look and handed him the ad.

"Which color?" I asked Max.

"Pink," he said. "It's your favorite."

Back in November, I told Charlie I wanted the blue one. "You know," I said, "I believe I would prefer pink." I looked up at Charlie and he looked panicked.

"You may not have a choice," Charlie said. "I think they shipped it." He disappeared.

"At least it'll be a surprise on Christmas: blue or pink," I told Max.

I called my mother and thanked her for watching Van last night.

"You know, forty-two children in Illinois have died from

the flu," my mother said. "I saw it on the news. They say you can be contagious for six days after symptoms subside."

I can always count on my mother for the worst news. Max had a wicked sinus infection several years ago that landed him in the hospital for a couple of days. After his release, I had to take Max to his pediatrician for two painful injections of the antibiotic Rocephin—one in each thigh. Before Max's appointment, my mother called to tell me she'd seen a documentary on an Indian boy who'd received antibiotic shots in his thighs and now crawls on all fours because the injections deformed his legs.

"I've been a basket case worrying about Max's infection, and now you tell me this crazy shit?" I howled. "I wouldn't share that story with my worst enemy."

I knew better than to worry about the injections crippling Max, but when I took him in for his shots, I asked his doctor about the hideous side effects my mother warned me about. Max's doctor put her hand to her mouth and tried not to laugh.

I knew better than to worry about Van keeling over from the flu, but when I called Liv to tell her Van and I wouldn't be at her Hanukkah party tomorrow night because he's sick, I told her what my mother said about the flu being deadly contagious even after the person seemed well. I was thinking about keeping Max home, too.

"I'll call Max's doctor tomorrow and let you know what she says," I told Liv.

[Monday, December 22]

I called Max's doctor and told the nurse what my mother had said about the flu. The nurse stifled a laugh.

"Tell Grandma that just isn't true," she said. "If your child has been fever free with no fever-reducing medication for twenty-four hours, your child is not contagious."

I called Liv and told her Charlie and Max would be at her Hanukkah party tonight.

"Why don't you and Charlie tag-team?" she suggested. "Have Charlie come for a while, then you come?"

When Charlie got home from work and began getting ready for the party, I mentioned Liv's idea.

"I don't want to go at all under those circumstances," Charlie said testily. "You just go. I really don't mind staying home."

Passive-aggressive asshole. Fucking martyr. When I had asked Charlie what he wanted for Christmas, he sourly said, "Nothing. There's really nothing I need."

"How about a hair shirt?" I asked. "You'd get a lot of use out of that."

Charlie snickered. "I could use a new gym bag and a pair of gym shoes. But that's it." We were standing in the kitchen and Charlie was pouring himself a cup of coffee. I saw the one lone plastic travel mug we owned in the cupboard behind him. Charlie had lost all of our stainless steel ones.

"I know," I said, "I'll get you travel mugs for Christmas."

"Doesn't that just sum it up," Charlie said. "You get an expensive watch and I get coffee mugs."

"And the hair shirt," I said.

• • •

"Take Max to the party tonight," I sighed. "I socialize more than you do, just go."

I got out the chopped liver I'd picked up from Kaufman's Deli in Skokie, scooped it into a nice crystal serving bowl, and stacked the Hanukkah presents I'd wrapped on the table. "There you go," I said. Charlie picked up the liver and presents, and he and Max left for the party.

I put Van to bed and popped open a bottle of nonalcoholic sparkling wine I'd purchased for Christmas Eve. I took my champagne glass out on the deck and had a smoke. It felt like old times, me standing out there drinking and smoking. I spent a lot of time doing that. I'd even convinced myself it was healthy: Smoking got me outside looking at the stars and breathing fresh air, even in the most frigid weather. But it felt weird this time. I don't want to smoke and drink on my deck and get messed up every night. I was standing in my old groove. I stubbed out my cigarette and walked inside.

[Tuesday, December 23]

Charlie and Max got home from the Hanukkah party around eleven last night. There was a plate loaded with Hanukkah dinner that Liv had made up for me in the refrigerator and a plate of Hanukkah cookies on the kitchen counter.

"We had a great time," Charlie said.

"Good," I said.

"The kids played dreidel, we read the Hanukkah story, lit candles, opened presents," Charlie rattled off. "The kids played like crazy and the adults ate and drank like crazy."

"Liv tap danced," Max said. "She put on her tap shoes and went to town. Seth was embarrassed."

"What about Reed?" I asked.

"He was going like this," Max said. Max rolled his eyes and looked away.

"Yeah, I can picture it," I said. "But Liv's a pretty good tap dancer."

"Did you ever tap dance?" Max asked. "Oh, wait, Nana didn't let you dance."

"Nope, couldn't dance," I said. "Adventists don't dance. It's one of their rules. I wanted to take ballet, and I'd put classical music on and dance around the house once in a while, but that was it."

Max frowned. "That Nana."

"It was a great party," Charlie said again. "A lot of fun, great food. There's a plate for you."

"I saw it," I said irritably. I was thinking, *I'm so glad you had a great time with the friends I made, the chopped liver and gefilte fish I ran to Skokie to purchase, and the presents I shopped for and wrapped.*

I went to a meeting later, and during my drive back home, decided to celebrate my upcoming fortieth birthday with a yoga party for my girlfriends. Surprisingly, I've been feeling happy about turning forty. I look young, I'm in good shape, and I'm grateful to have lived this long. Life is good. However, I'm not sure I should mingle my sober friends with my non-sober friends. On one hand, I think it would be interesting, but on the other hand, the "How-do-you-know-Brenda?" question is sure to come up.

I began making scalloped potatoes and pumpkin crème brulee for Christmas Eve dinner. I scalded the milk and cream, placed ramekins of liquid crème brulee into a roasting pan half full of water, and slid it into the oven. I started thinking about what Renee had said at the meeting earlier.

"I don't know when it happened, but I don't feel weird anymore," Renee said. "I don't feel like a freak lurking on the fringe of things. I can participate in everything and have a good time."

That's how I feel. Renee and I got sober about the same time. Maybe it takes a year for life to feel normal again.

Tracy had said, "I have to babysit my personality. I spend a lot of time every day trying to have the right thoughts and the right responses. About the only time I'm not working on it is when I'm grocery shopping—and God help me if someone bumps my cart."

I thought about the time a guy cut me off while I was driving and I yelled, "Douche bag!" with Van in the back seat of my car. A couple of minutes later, Van sweetly repeated, "Douche . . . bag?"

Charlie walked into the kitchen. "I'm going to bed," he said.

"I've been home with sick kids for weeks and working my tail off to get ready for Christmas," I complained.

"I was going to take Max to open soccer tomorrow," Charlie said. "Why don't you take him instead, get out of the house?"

"Are you insane?" I shouted. "Tomorrow's Christmas Eve. People are coming over at three. I'll be busting my ass. Like hell. You're taking Max to soccer."

I was proud of myself for not calling Charlie a douche bag.

[Wednesday, December 24]

My plan was to have dinner cooked by three, leave the food warming in the oven, take everyone to church for the four o'clock Christmas Eve service, come home, eat, open presents, and have dessert. Thank God Van has been feeling good and fever free for twenty-four hours. Paula and her family and my parents arrived, and everyone but my father was dressed for church. My dad was wearing corduroy pants, a flannel shirt, and moccasins.

"I'm not going to church," he snickered and poured himself a stiff Maker's Mark. "I'm gonna stay here and take a nap."

I looked at him and shrugged.

"I've been hunting since five this morning," he added.

I put my mother's food in the oven to warm and set my sister's appetizers aside. As we were getting ready to leave for church, I saw my father eyeing Charlie and Max in their suits and ties.

"Looks like Brenda's got her men in line," he sneered.

"Yep," Charlie said cheerfully.

"If I'd known everyone was going to be wearing a tie, I would have worn one, too," my dad said, looking guilty and left out. He walked into the TV room and lay down on the couch. "Why don't you leave Van here with me?"

"Van wants to go to church," I said. "They have a fun kids' room at church and he's looking forward to bringing Riley there."

"You want to stay home with Papa?" my dad asked Van.

"No, I'm going with Riley," Van said.

My father shrugged and took a belt of his drink.

After the service, my sister began serving appetizers. I took the food out of the oven and began grilling the fish. My father started teasing Riley. He took away the blanket that Riley drags around like Linus.

"Give that back!" Van yelled, sticking up for his cousin.

"I'll give it back if you come over here and give me hugs," my father told Van and Riley. Van and Riley wouldn't hug him and my dad stomped out of the TV room and poured himself another stiff drink in the kitchen.

"I don't even know why I'm here," my dad shouted. "The kids don't want anything to do with me. The only one who's my buddy is Max. He's the only one who's going to keep getting the tree houses and motor scooters!"

My sister and I made Van and Riley hug their jackass of a grandfather and things calmed down. The rest of Christmas Eve was fine.

After my family left and the kids went to bed, I wrapped my last few presents and stuck them under the tree. I wasn't drunk and tired. I wasn't going to lie down on the couch, pass out, and wake up at two in the morning with "White Christmas" blaring from the TV. It felt good.

[Thursday, December 25]

I woke up Christmas morning without a hangover. Charlie got me the watch I wanted, in blue. It's beautiful. I'm glad it wasn't the pink one. He also got me a laptop computer and a wireless keyboard and mouse. He really outdid himself. It's the first time Charlie got me big presents for Christmas. We never buy each other big-ticket items. I felt guilty for under gifting. I gave Charlie a pair of Nikes, an Under Armor gym bag, a package of sexy underwear, and two travel coffee mugs.

After breakfast, I checked email. My editor at the *Chicago Reader* loves my Healing Rooms story. Cool. We went to Charlie's brother's house in the afternoon and spent the holiday with Charlie's family. Not once did I want a drink. It was a great day.

[Friday, December 26]

"When you tell people you're an alcoholic, it's the type of thing people don't forget," Brent said at the meeting. "It's like saying, 'I murdered someone.'"

"No," Jane disagreed. "People forget all the time. People I've told still offer me drinks. It's really not that big of a deal. It's more in your mind than anyone else's."

"It's all about you, Brent!" Gwen shouted. "It's all about you!"

"Shut up, Gwen, and do us all a favor," Brent retorted.

Gwen, not the least bit rattled, began her comments: "When I got sober, I announced it to the world. The first words out of my mouth when I met someone were, 'Hi, I'm Gwen, and I'm an alcoholic in recovery.' Eventually, a friend pulled me aside at a party and told me to stop it, it was embarrassing. But it was such a release."

Brent looked at me and rolled his eyes.

A middle-aged guy said, "My boss was on the cover of *Parade* magazine as the subject of a story on depression. Now everyone knows she battles with depression and takes medication for it, but she's hugely respected. On the other hand, that story opened the door for another woman I work with to start telling people about her depression, and oh my God, the stuff she tells you. When I see her coming I run the other way."

After the meeting, I told Brent about the yoga party I'm going to throw for my birthday and asked him what he thought about mixing sober and nonsober friends.

"If you get a bunch of recovering alcoholics together, they're going to talk about recovery," Brent said. "They can't help it. The cat will be out of the bag."

"Maybe I'll just invite my normal friends, if you can call anyone normal," I sighed.

[Saturday, December 27]

Today, I haven't had a drink in one year. That blows me away. I didn't want to quit forever. In the back of my mind, I planned on taking a nice long break, maybe a year, but I didn't think I'd last this long. I looked at sobering up as an adventure, something new and different to do, a journey into self-awareness, and it's been that and a lot more. I'm happier, more useful. I feel better physically, mentally, and spiritually. I don't want my drinking life back. I hope I can stay sober.

[Wednesday, December 31]

I took Max to a soccer tournament and ran into Kelly at the complex.

"Hey Bren, what are you doing here?" she asked.

"What do you think?" I answered, sounding more snotty than I wanted to. It's New Year's Eve, and I've had a bug up my butt because Kelly didn't invite me to her annual New Year's Eve party.

"What are you doing for New Year's?" Kelly asked.

"Nothing," I said, sounding defiant.

"Isn't it great?" Kelly said. "I'm looking forward to doing nothing. I had that Christmas party and decided that was it."

"I kinda figured," I lied.

"I've gotten calls from people wondering if I'm having a party," Kelly said. "I wonder if people are mad at me thinking I'm blowing them off?"

"Maybe," I said, suddenly feeling bad.

Kelly left, and I felt petty and small. Damn it. I'm no better than she is when it comes to juvenile jealousy.

Charlie and I took the kids out for a New Year's Eve dinner. Later, we watched the New Year's countdown on TV. I felt lame and unpopular. As I watched the sweaty, pie-eyed people shouting "Woo, woo," from downtown bars, I started feeling superior. I'm glad I'm not one of those people.

[Thursday, January 1]

I woke up without a hangover.

[Saturday, January 3]

Max and I worked in a soup kitchen in the basement of a church. Max handed out cafeteria trays and I dished out salad. Most of the clients were homeless men, and I was amazed at how few of them wanted vegetables.

"How about some salad?" I'd ask. "It's good for you."

The men would shake their heads, raise a hand over their plates, and grab lunch meat and cheap white bread. A few women filtered in and, toward the end, a family of five came in for dinner. Max handed the family trays. One of the boys was about Max's age, and Max watched him closely. On our way out, as Max and I walked to our car, Max looked troubled.

"How do people become homeless?" he asked.

"Lots of ways," I said. "Some people are mentally ill and can't support themselves. Some are alcoholics and drug addicts. Sometimes families get in trouble when the dad or mom gets sick and can't work. They run out of money. The family you saw tonight is having tough times."

"I don't want to talk about it anymore," Max said.

I hugged Max and kissed the top of his head.

[Sunday, January 4]

I compiled the notes I'd written during previous attempts to do my Fourth Step: "Made a searching and fearless moral inventory of ourselves." Then I did my Fourth Step. I listed everyone I resent, my bad behavior toward them, and categorized my fears under those resentments. Every resentment, supposedly, is based in fear. I used to think that was a crock of shit until someone explained that fear falls into two categories: fear of something I have being taken away, or fear of not getting what I want. The people I resent are my mother, my sister, and Charlie. And now that I've looked at my bad behavior toward them and the fear behind my behavior, I'm going to have to make amends to them. Not looking forward to that.

[Saturday, January 10]

I feel like an enormous baby. I did my Fifth Step with Sara, "Admitted to God, to ourselves, and to another human being the exact nature of our wrongs," and blubbered most of the way through it.

"You have a lot of work to do where your mother is concerned," Sara told me. "You can start by praying for her health, happiness, and prosperity every day." She gave me the same advice for my sister.

"I think it's strange that your father isn't on your resentment list," Sara added.

"My father and I scream at each other, make up, and move on," I said. "We say what we want to say to each other and apologize when necessary. I don't have resentment with him. With my mother, sister, and Charlie, I don't have full-out honesty. I've held a lot in."

"You're ready to do your Sixth and Seventh Steps," Sara said.

In bed, I read the Sixth and Seventh Steps. Step Six: "Were entirely ready to have God remove all these defects of character." Well, I'm not entirely ready. Some of my defects, such as stretching the truth here and there, have served me well. It scares me, the thought of turning my defects over to God. Manipulating situations has felt necessary. I don't know if I'll ever be entirely ready to do this. Just the other day, I stole a bisque-colored handle off a toilet at the hardware store because the handle on the toilet they sold me a couple of years ago broke. I felt guilty about it, but damn it, they'd sold me a faulty product and I'd have to jump through hoops to get the right handle the right way.

Step Seven: "Humbly asked Him to remove our shortcomings." An old man once told me, "If you're not willing to have God remove your defects of character, be willing to be willing. That's the place to start. Being willing to be willing will get you far." I closed my eyes and prayed, "God, I'm willing to be willing. And please take things slow with me. I don't think I can handle a drastic change. But I'm willing to be willing. Amen." I opened my eyes and felt relief, peace, and happiness.

I read Step Eight: "Made a list of all persons we had harmed, and became willing to make amends to them all." I'd listed the people I'd harmed during my Fourth Step, and I'm willing to make amends to them. I read Step Nine: "Made direct amends to such people wherever possible, except when to do so would injure them or others." I'll have to discuss this with Sara.

[Sunday, January 11]

I went to a yoga/meditation class this morning and saw Vivian there. She and I went out for coffee afterward.

"Nancy disappeared for seven days right before Christmas," she told me.

Nancy, Vivian's seventeen-year-old daughter, has been in recovery for almost two years.

"No," I said, feeling sick to my stomach.

"Yeah," Vivian said. "She went on a coke binge with a girlfriend and two guys. Right before Christmas, Nancy saw her stepbrother, my husband's oldest son. He sexually abused Nancy when she was younger and seeing him again whacked her out. I'm going crazy. My ex-husband, Nancy's dad, called and told me, 'Nancy wants me to meet her and bring seven hundred dollars to a pancake house because she owes some really bad people money.'"

"Fuck," I whispered.

"She just wanted the money for drugs," Vivian said. "I told him not to bring the money, that I'd meet him at the pancake house. I pulled into a parking space way in the back of the parking lot and waited. I watched Nancy park and walk into the restaurant where my ex was waiting. As soon as Nancy was inside, a girl and two guys got out of her car and started cleaning it out, throwing stuff in the garbage Dumpster. I called the police. As soon as the police showed up, I got out of my car and started confronting Nancy's friends. 'What are you throwing out, drugs? Officers, you have my permission to search this car. It's my car. I know this girl, but I don't know these two guys. I bet they're over eighteen and have been aiding and abetting a seventeen-year-old minor I reported missing a week ago.' While the cops were dealing with those three, I walked into the restaurant. Nancy's face fell when she saw me. I told her, 'You're getting in my car, going to the hospital, getting drug tested, and going into treatment.' That's where she is now, in treatment."

"Oh Vivian, I'm so sorry," I said.

"I'm thinking we should take a meeting to her," Vivian said. "Will you go with me?"

"Yeah."

[Tuesday, January 13]

The phone rang. It was Vivian.

"Hey, you want to take a meeting to Nancy tonight?" she asked. "I already asked Darcy and she said yes."

"Count me in," I said.

Vivian picked me up after dinner. Darcy was already in the car. We drove to the treatment facility and Vivian parked and turned around in her seat. "Nancy got into trouble," she said. "She lost all of her privileges."

"What happened?" Darcy asked.

"She got some stupid tattoo, her boyfriend's name on her right shoulder blade," Vivian said. "Getting tattooed in here is against the rules. She got in trouble for that, then narced on the girl who gave her the tattoo, then got into a fight with her."

Vivian got out of the car. Darcy and I stared at each other, then followed Vivian into the facility. Nancy was sitting in the waiting area. An obese white girl with skinny blond braids all over her huge, round head stomped over. She was wearing athletic pants with one pant leg pushed up over her thick, dimpled knee. A gang thing.

"I tole you I ain't gone let you run," the fat girl screamed at Nancy. "I tole you. I know watch yo plans be and I ain't gonna let you. No. You ain't runnin'."

Nancy stood up. The fat girl got in Nancy's face. She continued to scream at Nancy and backed Nancy down the hall away from Vivian. Vivian trailed after them. Darcy and I looked at each other.

"What the fuck?" I silently mouthed.

"Get the hell out of here!" Vivian screamed at the fat girl. "Get the fuck out of my way, now!"

The fat girl disappeared, and Vivian and Nancy stood in the hallway whispering heatedly to each other. The fat girl reappeared and began harassing them again. Vivian pulled Nancy into a small room off the hallway and told the fat girl, "Get the fuck away from us!" The fat girl kept spewing the same gibberish, but finally lumbered away.

A mousy young social worker who appeared to be about thirty walked into the waiting room. She'd been lurking in her office off the waiting room until things cooled down before making an appearance.

"Thanks for bringing a meeting to us," she told Darcy and me. "I just have to warn you, a lot of the girls might ask you to be their sponsor."

The fat girl reappeared and began screaming at Nancy from the doorway to the conference room. A twitchy skinny girl walked into the waiting room and began spookily pacing. The mousy social worker pretended not to notice anything that was going on. Vivian and Nancy pushed past the fat girl and walked into the waiting room.

"Okay, let's do the meeting," Vivian said wearily and directed Darcy and me into a lounge area. Several minutes later, ten girls filtered in and sat down. All of them were wearing sweat suits with one leg pushed up over the knee. The first few girls to talk said they just smoked pot once in a while and drank a little.

"I don't know why my mother sent me here," one of them said. I looked at the homemade gang tattoo on her calf and thought, *No good reason, I'm sure.*

Nancy sat across the room from me. The upper half of the wall behind me was an expansive window that looked out onto the hallway. Nancy kept shifting her gaze between the floor and the window behind me. About halfway through the meeting, she looked up, began shifting nervously in her chair, and walked out of the room. I looked behind me and saw the fat girl who'd been screaming at Nancy. I looked at Vivian. She continued listening to the girl who was speaking and tried to look unruffled.

The girl who was speaking was the girl who'd gotten in trouble for tattooing Nancy. "Yeah, I know it was some of me, I shouldn't have done it," she said referring to the tattoo. "But I'm always careful about the needle. No one shared. I don't do that. I know better. My mom, she did heroin. She was sick. I don't want to get into all that. My little brother was born sick. When my mom died, my older brothers blamed me. My mom was in a hospital bed at home very weak, very sick, couldn't feed herself. I gave her a drink of water and she choked on it and died.

"I've tried to kill myself," she continued. "If anything happens to my little brother, though . . . I raised him. If anything happened to him, I don't know . . ."

I looked around the room at the tough girls pretending to be fearless. I felt like crying. When the meeting ended, a slightly chubby Latina gangbanger named Martina asked me to be her sponsor.

"I'm here mainly for running away and sleeping around and gangbanging," she told me. "I used to be skinny, but my mom put me on Depo-Provera for birth control and I gained a lot of weight when I went off it. I don't have a drug problem. I drink and do drugs once in a while, and yeah, when I do them I do them to excess, but that's normal. I just need a sponsor to get to the next level."

"Here's my cell number," I said, writing it down for her. "If you want to, call me."

The spooky skinny chick was still pacing the halls as we walked out of the meeting. The fat chick was still yelling, "I ain't gone let you run!" Vivian directed Nancy, Darcy, and me to a small lounge. Nancy started to cry.

"That girl runs things here," she sobbed. "All that shit she's talking, it's an act. She's going to make me run tonight to create a diversion so she can do something. It's all gangbangers in here with the GDs (Gangster Disciples) on one side and all the other gangs on the other. And the girls are all ho-ing each other."

"This place is dangerous," I told Vivian. "These girls have seen people killed, beaten the shit out of people. I wouldn't have my kid here."

"You'd take Nancy out tonight, wouldn't you?" Vivian asked.

"I know she was on the run doing messed-up things," I said. "But this place?"

"You'd take her out tonight, wouldn't you?" she repeated.

"Do you think any good is going to come of her being here?" I asked.

"You'd take her home tonight, you would."

"Yeah, I would."

The four of us went to Nancy's little cell of a room, packed her up, and left. Vivian dropped off Darcy and stopped for gas. As Vivian was fueling up, Nancy started bragging about the week she was MIA.

"We were doing piles of coke and taking whole boxes of Coricidin," Nancy said.

"You were taking boxes of cold medicine?" I asked.

"The kind in the purple box gives you a trippy effect," she said. "You have to get the ones in the purple box. They make you hallucinate."

"Really."

"We were crashing at people's houses, hotels, and one night I think I was raped," she said matter-of-factly. "My three friends didn't know where I was, but they ended up at the same house I was at. Some guy told them he fucked some bitch in the bathroom. They found me in there on the floor. My lips and my nails were blue and I was barely breathing. I remember slipping in and out and thinking I was dying. I remember my girlfriend saying, "I'm sorry. I'm so sorry I have to do this." There was a warrant out for one of the guys, so they couldn't take me to the hospital. My girlfriend kicked me in the stomach until I threw up. When my mom found me, I was dirty and my side was all swollen."

"You know how fucked-up that was, don't you?" I asked, incredulous of her braggy tone. "You were raped. You almost died on a filthy bathroom floor. Instead of taking you to a hospital, your friend kicked you in the stomach. No one gave a shit that you were dying."

Nancy didn't say anything. After a while I said, "How can you take a box of Coricidin? I can't take that stuff. I feel like I might die if I have one or two."

"What color was the box?" Nancy asked.

Vivian got back into the car.

"Red," I answered.

"Oh God, those will kill you," she said. "No, you have to take the ones in the purple box. Those are the good ones."

"Brenda doesn't want to take Coricidin to get high!" Vivian screamed at Nancy. "What the hell is wrong with you?"

"No, no, I just meant," Nancy stammered.

I was beginning to wonder if I'd done the right thing in encouraging Vivian to take Nancy out of treatment. I'd been calling Sara, who runs an outpatient treatment center for adolescents, and she finally called me back. I told her we'd just taken Nancy out of that facility and Sara said, "Good. That's a really bad place. You wouldn't put your kid in there unless you were court-ordered to."

I told Sara, "I gave Vivian your cell phone number. She needs to get Nancy in your program."

"That's fine."

"She'll call you when she gets home."

"Good," Sara said.

I just wanted to hug my kids and put this shit behind me.

[Wednesday, January 14]

I drove to Henry's house to take him to lunch and discuss how he's going to cater my yoga birthday party. I'm having doubts about Henry catering it, however. Henry has back problems, recently began walking with a cane, and can barely turn his head, but he insists he wants to do it. I rang Henry's doorbell and his father answered. Henry quickly materialized and introduced us. I helped Henry to the car and while we were driving, he said he lives with his parents, Leslie, a very nice obese woman whom I've seen chauffeuring Henry to meetings and waiting for him in the car (Henry's driver's license was revoked), and his mentally disabled brother, Davin.

"It's a madhouse," Henry lamented. "My mother is on medication and whacked out. The other day she tried to cook breakfast and lit her robe sleeves on fire. And my mentally disabled, 300-pound, thirty-seven-year-old brother is getting scary. He's hearing voices and talking to them. That's why I moved back in with my parents. I was afraid Davin was going to kill them. Now I'm afraid he's going to kill me. He sneaks up on me and I never hear him even though he's enormous. He says—and he talks like Billy Bob Thornton in *Slingblade*—'Hey man, I'm sorry. I'm sorry for what I did. I told them I'd never hurt you because you're my brother.'

"I told Davin's doctor about this and about how I've been waking up to find Davin hovering over my bed," Henry continued. "His doctor told me to put a bolt on my bedroom door, so I did. But no one in my family is taking this seriously. They all think Davin is completely harmless."

"Wow," I said. "I don't even know what to say."

"No shit," Henry said.

Henry and I arrived at the yoga studio where I'm having my party. I showed Henry around, and he eyeballed the layout and told me where the tables should go and regaled me with a list of yummy appetizers.

"I'll print up a price list for you, then you can choose," he said as we drove back to have lunch. "I catered the governor's ball in Kentucky, you know."

"Really?" I said, doubting this was true.

"That's where I'm from," Henry said. "My family has been in the restaurant business for years. We have investments in several restaurants. We have exclusive rights for catering events here," he added as we pulled into the parking lot of Hackney's.

We walked into the restaurant, and the waitstaff all knew Henry, which made me feel better, but guilty for doubting him.

"Have you ever eaten at Bacchus Nibbles?" Henry asked while we were eating.

"I had dinner there with my aunt when I was still drinking," I said. "They have a great wine list."

Henry gave an eye roll of ecstasy. "Did you have their house wine?"

"No, we ordered a bottle."

"There's no need to pay for an expensive bottle there," Henry said. "Have you ever had their house wine?"

"No."

"You should."

Henry's comment made me queasy, and the look on my face must have portrayed it.

"I mean, you know, you should have," Henry stuttered. "Not that you should have some now."

I'm really not feeling good about Henry catering my party.

[Saturday, January 17]

I went to one of those come-to-my-house-and-buy-something parties at my sister's home. I'd been invited to three of these things this week: a basket party, a candle party, and my sister's home décor party. I figured I should at least attend Paula's. I walked into Paula's house, loaded up a plate with appetizers, sat down, and listened to the sales pitch. When the spiel was over, I paged through my décor catalog three times looking for something I liked and wouldn't feel fleeced purchasing. I came across a set of mixing bowls for forty dollars and asked the rep if I could see them. She walked away and came back with bowls that looked like you'd find in a dollar store. It was the first time I went to one of these shindigs and didn't buy anything. I would have forced myself to purchase the bowls if no one else was buying, but the woman was writing up sale after sale.

[Thursday, January 22]

Karen was supposed to host book club tonight, but she called this morning and cancelled.

"My dad's dying," she said. "The prostate cancer's killing him. He's in assisted living now and he can't swallow, he can't wet his own lips, he's in intense pain. I just can't do book club."

I remembered Charlie's mother, Martha, lying in her hospital bed, skin and bones, dying of lung cancer. I felt hollow inside. "If there's anything I can do, if you need help with the kids or anything, let me know," I said.

"Thanks," Karen said, sounding like she was about to cry.

I began leafing through one of my cookbooks to find my favorite cassoulet recipe to make and take to Karen's. I thought about my dad and what's in store for him. I'm so scared.

[Saturday, January 24]

I talked to Martina this afternoon. She called me last Tuesday and left a message saying she'd read the addict literature I encouraged her to read and was ready to talk about it. I tried calling her back several days in a row, but the phone just rang and rang. When I saw Vivian at yoga, she told me, "They mostly have the pay phone turned off. It's only turned on certain hours of the day." So today I called during good phoning hours and got Martina.

"Did you get anything out of the book?" I asked.

"Three things," Martina said. "Number one, you don't have to be a skid row drunk to be an alcoholic. Number two, you don't have to drink every day to be an alcoholic, you can go for long stretches not drinking. Number three, alcoholics usually get messed up every time they drink. I get messed up every time I drink."

"Me, too," I said. "Do you think you have a problem?"

"Yeah, probably, but I don't see how I can stop doing drugs and drinking. They're part of my lifestyle."

"What lifestyle?"

"I'm in a gang, the Maniacs," she said. "The gang's by my aunt's house, which isn't close to where I live with my mother, but I run away a lot. I go missing for days. I go by my aunt's and hang with my gang. That's why my mother sent me here. My mom's forty. When she was younger, she was in a gang. She isn't anymore. Hasn't been for the last twenty years. Gangs were everywhere back then, too. Everyone my mom knew was in one."

"Does she know you're in a gang?" I asked.

"No, but my aunt does. I don't think she told my mom."

"So you're going back to your gang," I said. "Why don't you stay away from your aunt's, get out?"

"I told them I wanted to get out, but the way I got in, I'd have to do a violation to get out," Martina said. "I'm not ready to go to jail for the rest of my life. They said they would cover for me, but I'm not going to trust that."

"What did they say you had to do?"

"I can't really say."

"Kill someone?"

"Yeah."

"How did you get in?"

"I got really drunk one night. I don't remember nothing until the next morning. But when I woke up, this guy wanted me to have sex with him. I said no and he said I had to. He said I became part of the gang last night and I'd slept with all these guys. Now it was his turn."

"Can you talk to your mother?"

"Yeah, we talk," she said. A lot of noise erupted and it sounded like a fight at the treatment center. "Yeah, yeah," Martina said to someone. "I gotta go," she told me.

I felt depressed and went to a meeting. The guy who spoke said he drank because he didn't want to grow up. I can completely relate. Drinking allowed me to cut loose, feel free, forget my responsibilities. I still fondly remember feeling that way. I have to make myself remember the hangovers, the memory loss, the dangerous driving, the responsibilities staring me in the face when I sobered up. It's funny how easily I remember the good times and have to work at conjuring up the bad. I can love sobriety one day, then think about drinking the next.

[Tuesday, January 27]

I sent Henry a down payment for the food. I still feel uneasy about him catering. He's not great at returning phone calls, I think he's exaggerated his credentials, and he's probably drinking. I'm crossing my fingers.

[Saturday, January 31]

I went out to dinner with Vivian. She told me Nancy ran away again.

"I wasn't home when she took off, but Kayla was," Vivian

said, referring to her ten-year-old daughter. "Nancy and her friend, Michelle, the girl she ran with last time, and two guys, I don't know if they're the same guys, looted my house. They took Nancy's electric guitar, the new camera we bought her for her photography class, my vacuum cleaner, the new PlayStation we got Kayla for Christmas. Kayla was so scared, poor thing. Nancy also took the curtains out of her room and moved into some flophouse where a bunch of druggie kids live. I tracked down Michelle's mother, she's an alcoholic drug addict, and she reluctantly told me where the girls were living, sort of. She didn't know the name of the street or the house number, but she told me the house was beige and gave me rough directions. I called the cops and told them I wanted to press charges against Nancy for theft. A cop and I drove to the neighborhood and knocked on the wrong door, but the people who lived there told us about a house where a bunch of kids were living. Nancy spent the next two nights in a psych ward and went back to the treatment facility we yanked her out of. I gave her a choice of facilities and she chose that one. That episode we saw when we were there? That was staged for our benefit."

"They staged that?" I asked incredulously.

Vivian shrugged. "She as much as admitted it, and she wanted to go back there. I told her, 'You're good. I hope Hollywood is ready for you.'"

A week and a half ago, Hope and I had gone to yoga class and picked up Nancy after her group therapy session with Sara. As Vivian was driving me home, Nancy asked if she could smoke in the car. Vivian said no and started lecturing her on how bad smoking is. Nancy told her, "I'm young. I can get away with it. I'll worry about it when I get older."

I flashed back to when I was in high school sitting in someone's basement smoking pot, drinking beer, and chain smoking. Without thinking, I mentioned it and said, "I remember thinking, *I'm going to have to quit this when I get older, but I'm going with it now.*"

"Well, I'm still seventeen," Nancy said.

I immediately regretted opening my mouth.

"I knew Nancy wasn't done," Vivian said, sipping her water. "Remember that last drink you had to have? We all had to have that last one."

"I didn't think she was done either," I admitted. "She was bragging about almost dying the night we took her out of that treatment home. And the night we picked her up from group therapy, she was talking about being young and able to get away with abusing her body."

"Yeah, and I remember what your response was," Vivian said.

I cringed. "I remember it, too," I groaned. "I'm so sorry. I regretted saying that as soon as the words left my mouth. I may as well have told her, 'You've got time. Keep getting fucked up.' I'm such an idiot. I'm so sorry, Vivian."

"You didn't make her go out and use again," Vivian said. "Nancy went and did that all by herself. She wanted to."

"Yeah, but what I said didn't help. If someone had said that to me when I was seventeen, I'd have perceived it as a green light."

"If someone wants to stay sober, you can't say anything wrong, and if someone doesn't want to stay sober, you can't say anything right," Vivian said.

I nodded but didn't believe her. I fucked up big time.

[Monday, February 2]

I called Henry to find out how the catering plans were going as well as how he was feeling. The day we'd had lunch, Henry told me he was going to have X-rays to find out why he was having back and neck pain.

"My doctor detected a mass on my spine near my neck and he's pretty sure it's cancer," Henry said haltingly. "They think I have cancer in my stomach and liver, too." Henry choked and stopped speaking for a moment. "I'm on interferon and insulin for my diabetes, and it's too difficult to give myself shots. My father's been giving them to me and his hands shake and it's painful." Henry began weeping.

"God, Henry, is there anything I can do?" I asked. "I give Max and myself allergy shots. I can give you injections. I don't know. I'm so sorry."

"I want to go bowling," Henry said in a teary voice. "My family doesn't think I'm up to it and they won't take me."

"How about Wednesday?" I said. "I'll come over, give you your shots, take you bowling?"

"Okay," he said weakly.

"I'm looking forward to pinching your ass when I give you that shot," I joked.

Henry giggled. "Don't say anything about how ill I am at the Friday night meeting," he said. "I haven't let Derek know how sick I am. I haven't let my family know either."

"You should tell your family," I said. "At least tell one of your brothers. You've got six siblings. There's gotta be one you can tell. Don't carry this alone. Wouldn't you be upset if someone in your family kept information like this from you? I'll get the food for my party catered from Sunset. It'll be easy. So don't worry about that."

"No," Henry said firmly. "I don't want to hear that. Catering your party is the one thing I'm enjoying. It's a good diversion. I'm doing it."

I was hoping Henry would pass on my party. I'm worried

he's going to mess it up. Henry is a drama queen who would be telling everyone about his cancer if he had it. Shit. Every way I look at this I'm worried.

[Tuesday, February 3]

Today is Charlie's birthday. He's forty-one. I gave him a kiss and wished him a happy birthday before rolling out of bed.

"Could you let Ernie out about one o'clock this afternoon?" Charlie shouted up the stairs as he was eating breakfast. "Judy and Dennis have to go to a funeral and won't be around to let the dog in the yard."

"Yeah, okay," I shouted down.

As I poured myself a bowl of cereal, Charlie told me they would leave the back door open so I could let their dog out. He kissed me good-bye and left. I whisked the kids off to school and began writing a story for *The Daily Herald* about a hockey school that teaches lessons on plastic ice. I banged away at the story until three o'clock. I picked up Max from school, picked up Van from preschool, took Max to his eye doctor appointment, drove home, and sang "Happy Birthday" to Charlie. We gave Charlie his presents, a new ski jacket and sweater, and piled into the car to take Charlie to one of his favorite steak houses for dinner. The car was facing our next-door neighbor's house.

"Oh shit!" I said. "I was supposed to let Ernie out, wasn't I?"

"Yeah," Charlie said. "I told you this morning."

"Shit," I said again.

It didn't look like Judy and Dennis were home yet, so I got out of the car and tried to open the side gate to their backyard. Deep snow covered the sidewalk and I couldn't open the gate.

I got back into the car and drove down the alley. I got out of the car and as I was about to open their back gate, their kitchen light flipped on and I could see Dennis. "Shit," I muttered and got back into the car.

"Well, there's nothing you can do about it now," Charlie said. "Let's just go to dinner."

I drove to the steak house. "Of all the people to forget to do a favor for," I moaned. "They cleaned up our yard when we were out of town during that microburst. They water our plants and take in our mail when we're out of town. I'm such a schmuck!"

"Yeah," Charlie said, nodding his head and snickering.

"I wonder if I should say something or pretend I let him out?" I said. "What if I pretend I let him out but Ernie peed all over his cage? What if he was so happy when they came home that he peed a river?"

"Are you going to dwell on this all night or are we going to enjoy our dinner?" Charlie asked.

We ordered drinks and appetizers and I continued to stew. Charlie looked at me and shook his head. "Come on," he said. "Can we enjoy ourselves?"

"I've got to call them," I said.

I called and Dennis answered. I began apologizing profusely.

"Well, he's okay," Dennis said testily. "But that's really hard on the kidneys."

I got off the phone and felt better having confessed. But I was still bummed.

"If you don't put a smile on your face, I'm going to paint one on," Charlie said. I put on my happy face and hoped it was convincing. Now I'd made Ernie cross his legs all day and ruined most of Charlie's birthday dinner.

[Wednesday, February 4]

I bought a bucket of dog toys for Ernie and set them on Dennis and Judy's front porch. I called Judy at work and apologized some more.

"Oh, Ernie was fine," she laughed. "The only reason we asked you to let him out was because of the snow, we didn't know how long it would take us to get home. When we let him out, he didn't even go that much."

So Dennis had put the screws to me. I couldn't blame him. He'd done all that chain sawing and clearing of my yard after the microburst and I didn't let his dog out.

Martina called. "I don't think I'm an alcoholic," she said. "I don't think about booze or drugs and I don't want them. My sister's husband called and said, 'I bet you miss drinking. Here, I'll chug a beer for you.' I could hear him chugging it but it didn't make me want it. It's just that when I get together with my friends, it's what we do. I drink until I black out. I know that's a bad sign, but I'm not an alcoholic."

Minutes after I got off the phone with Martina, Kelly called.

"Ryan has a soccer game the night of your party," she said. "So I don't think I'll be able to make it. I was thinking maybe I could take you out to lunch instead."

"Okay," I said, irritated.

"Are you angry?" Kelly asked, sounding kittenish.

"No," I said, lying.

"Well, his soccer game is from five thirty to six thirty. Maybe I could come by after."

"If you want. Everyone's showing up at six, but the yoga probably won't start until six fifteen, six thirty. You could hop in late or show up for food."

"I'd like to make the class if I can," Kelly said.

"I'll put a mat by the door for you. If you can make it, make it. If not, have some dinner and cake."

Kelly is doing a little tit-for-tat thing. Last April, when Kelly was turning thirty-nine, her friend Candy threw a wine-tasting party for her and I was just three months sober. I blew off her party to work at a homeless shelter and took her out to lunch instead.

[Friday, February 6]

Karen's father died. I picked up Nosey Rosy and Fay and we drove to the wake.

"I asked Kelly if she wanted to come, too," Nosey Rosy said. "But she said, 'No, wakes aren't my thing.'"

"Oh, they're totally my thing," I said sarcastically. "I'm sure everyone loved going to Kelly's mother's funeral."

After spending a little more than an hour at the funeral home thinking about how my dad was going to die next, I drove Rosy home and on the way to Fay's, Fay said, "I can't believe Kelly didn't come to this. You show up for your friends. 'I'm not into it,' or whatever it is she said, my God."

Fay got out of the car and I drove to the Friday night meeting. Derek pulled me aside afterward and told me he was concerned about Henry.

"He's drinking and not going to meetings, and he's losing his eyesight," Derek said, shaking his head. "All this other medical stuff he says is going on, I suspect he's lying, and I'm not the only one who thinks so. Lila (another regular at the Friday night meeting) thinks so, too. It just doesn't add up. He's very evasive about what's actually wrong with him. One minute he's crying, and the next he's giggling. He's sketchy about what the doctors say and what they're doing. I know he really likes you and looks up to you, so maybe you could convince him to get to some meetings."

"At the risk of sounding selfish," I said, "Henry is catering my fortieth birthday party tomorrow night and if he fucks it up, I'm going to kill him."

"Things could go bad," Derek said.

[saturday, February 7]

I woke up feeling giddy and nervous about my party. I sent up a prayer, turned my party over to God, and felt okay.

A couple of hours before my party, I put a case of wine and two mega packs of bottled water in coolers and threw them in the back of my Jeep. I went to Caribou Coffee and picked up an urn of coffee and the fixings. Carly and Joyce, my two yoga instructors, and Carly's husband helped me carry the stuff upstairs into the studio.

My sister was the first to arrive, followed by a steady stream of twenty-five friends, a quarter of them recovering addicts. I'd gone back and forth over whether or not to invite Jill, a nonrecovering alcoholic who has a knack for offending people, but ultimately invited her. Jill walked in. I don't know what she was on, probably a combo of weed, speed, and alcohol, but she was jittery, loopy, and loud. Bonnie, my straight-laced sister-in-law, arrived seconds behind her.

"We know each other from high school," Jill squealed. "Remember me? Remember me from high school?"

"Yes," Bonnie said, looking like she'd just sipped sour milk.

I walked away to greet more friends and Jill trailed after me. "I think we used to be good friends," Jill said, referring to Bonnie.

"Really?" I replied.

At six thirty, everyone but Kelly had arrived and we began practicing yoga. Carly began moving us through a sequence of poses, and about thirty minutes into it, Kelly showed up. I gave Kelly my mat and unrolled another for myself and took a spot up front next to Carly. The session ended with everyone relaxing on their backs in Savasana. I got up and snuck out to help Henry bring in the food.

Jill, who apparently bailed on the yoga early, walked over to me and asked, "Is your caterer blind? Who's the guy out there with the cane? Whoever he is, he smells like a brewery."

"Shit," I said, walking briskly to the reception area. Henry was standing in a corner, weaving in place. His eyes were half-mast. I walked over and hugged him. He reeked of vodka. "Where is everything?" I asked.

Henry's mouth began moving but nothing came out. Finally, he said, "Everything is downstairs in the van. You wouldn't believe the day I had."

I glanced around and saw Vivian and Emily chatting near the reception desk. "Will you guys help me?" I asked, trying to conceal my panic. "My caterer is fucked up."

"Yeah, we can see that," Emily said. "Tell us what to do."

Vivian, Emily, and a few more of my friends went downstairs and began bringing up food and tables. More of my friends began helping arrange the tables and spread linens. I was acutely aware that Henry had disappeared. I walked out of the studio and into the reception area and began dragging the coolers in. I opened the lids.

"Is that wine?" Lea, one of my recovery friends asked in a wavering voice. Her eyes were glued to a cooler full of chardonnay bottles.

"Yeah," I said and winked. "But it's not for you or me." I put my arm around her and we laughed.

My friends and I began unwrapping the platters of food.

The food looked fabulous. Marinated asparagus spears wrapped in prosciutto, sugar snap peas and water chestnuts wrapped in marinated beef, baked brie topped with dried apricots and slivered almonds, fruit and cheese kabobs radiating out of a huge pineapple, jumbo shrimp, marinated vegetables, finger sandwiches of herbed cheese on pumpernickel. Leslie, the woman who lived with Henry and drove him to meetings, was rearranging generous slabs of chocolate bark that had gone askew on the enormous chocolate-mousse-and-fresh-raspberry birthday cake Henry had made for me.

"Henry's messed up," I whispered to Leslie under my breath.

"It's not what you think," she said. "He worked his butt off. He's not well. And this was more work than he remembered. Everything that could go wrong today did, and he's in a lot of pain. I told him, 'Whatever you do, don't take a pain pill. Promise me you won't.' But he did. We got here early, but he passed out and I couldn't wake him."

"I'm so sorry, Leslie," I said. "This day was hell for you, wasn't it?"

Leslie nodded and looked like she was about to cry.

"Well, it's over now and the food is incredible," I said and smiled. "Everyone is raving about it. And that cake, oh my God, I've never seen a cake look that delicious." Leslie smiled. "Go get yourself some food and relax."

The party was a hit. As I visited with my friends, I saw Henry standing by one of the food tables taking compliments. He had a big smile on his face and was talking animatedly. He looked sober as a judge. I don't know how he pulled it off, and I didn't care. I was relieved. Emily walked over and began raving about Henry and his food. Then Kelly cut in.

"I've got to go, Bren," she said, cocking her head to one side and putting on a sad face. "I promised Ryan I'd read him stories at nine o'clock and here it is nine thirty."

"Uh-huh," I said. "Well, thanks for coming." Asshole.

Sara approached me. "Was that Kelly?" she asked.

"Yep," I said.

She gave me a knowing smile. "It looks like Henry wet his pants," she said.

I shot a quick look over at Henry, but the table he was standing behind obscured his crotch.

"He's making excuses about spilling on himself, but I don't know how anyone could have spilled on themselves in that precise way," Sara said.

When I got home, Charlie was watching *Saturday Night Live*.

"How'd it go?" he asked.

"There were a few rocky moments, but overall it was great," I said and filled him in on the details. I went upstairs, changed into my pajamas, and crawled into bed feeling grateful and happy.

[Sunday, February 8]

I'm forty. Charlie and the boys made me breakfast in bed and sang "Happy Birthday." Max gave me a special writing pen and a hardcover journal. I got up and went to a yoga class.

On my way back home, I began thinking about my party and my interesting, beautiful friends. Deidre was ankle bracelet free and off house arrest. Vivian was blissing out in yoga poses momentarily forgetting about her messed-up daughter. Darcy was smiling and laughing, something she doesn't do a lot of anymore. Liv, my rock-solid friend throughout my first year sober, was contorting herself into bizarre shapes even though she hated yoga. Kelly was, well, Kelly. And poor Eve, I pictured her passed out on her mattress.

Charlie had flooded our backyard last week, turning it into

an ice rink, and Max was skating. I put on my skates, and Max and I practiced hockey stops. "Let's see who can spray more ice," Max challenged. He won. Charlie appeared with a picnic tray and set down lunch. Max and I sat on a snowbank next to the ice and ate sandwiches and drank hot chocolate. It was a glorious sunny day. The sky was brilliant blue. The snow was glittering like diamonds. I hugged Max and kissed him. Then I sent up a prayer and thanked God for my life.

• • •

[Monday, June 18
(four-and-a-half years sober)]

The phone rang at one in the morning. I opened my eyes and lay in the dark listening to it ring before Charlie picked it up from his bedside table.

"It's your mother," he said, passing me the receiver.

I knew what she was going to say.

"Your father died," my mother whispered.

"I'm coming over."

I reached over Charlie and hung up the phone. A dull ache crawled into my heart and expanded, becoming painful. Tears ran down my cheeks and I started sobbing. Charlie periodically rubbed my back.

An hour later, I slid into my car and drove away feeling numb.

My father began moving slowly last summer, mindfully, like a man who hurt. My mother began driving him to his doctor appointments. "How do I get to the doctor's office?" she asked the first time she drove.

"Dad knows," I said. "He knows the Loop like a cartographer."

"He doesn't remember."

My dad's doctors found a tumor in his brain that fall. The tumor was removed, but tiny flecks of cancer remained spattered throughout his gray matter. When my dad recovered enough, his brain was radiated. My father shuffled into my sister's house on Thanksgiving looking like dead man walking.

I made my dad an appointment with an acupuncturist and Qigong master. My father teetered into Dr. Deng's office, his skin gray, eyes hooded. Deng rubbed his hands together and pressed his palms to my father's body. He poked my dad full of needles. He turned the lights off and played a meditation tape. My father would have called this voodoo bullshit if he weren't so sick. When Deng flicked the lights back on, my father's cheeks were pink and his eyes had the old mischievous spark. For the next few months, my dad visited Deng three times a week. And during that time I became obsessed with death.

I wanted to convince myself that there was life after death, but I feared I was just deceiving myself. I watched the movie *21 Grams,* which claims that at the moment of death, the body loses twenty-one grams of weight, the weight of the soul. It made me feel better until my friend, Tad, told me it was a crock of shit.

"Google Duncan MacDougall," he said. "The idea for that movie was based on his research. He weighed dying people and reported that their bodies lost weight when their souls left, but his research was bad and he was discredited."

I googled MacDougall, an early twentieth-century physician who weighed six people dying of tuberculosis. MacDougall placed his patients' beds on an industrial scale that was gram sensitive and observed and recorded weight loss—twenty-one grams being the average—when they died. But because he observed only six patients, their weight loss varied, and the exact moment of death was (and still is) difficult to determine, his research was tossed out.

"Life is a slimy sucking eddy of despair with false moments of hope in an ever-darkening universe," played in my head. My childhood friend, Carolyn, recited that line a lot after she got knocked up and had a baby at seventeen. I began thinking about drinking all the time. I may have laid in bed with a vodka bottle if my kids weren't forcing me to get up. And since I had to get up, I began going to meetings at seven in the morning. No one hits meetings at seven in the morning unless they're desperate to get their shit together. And day after day my addict peers screwed my depressed head on a little straighter.

My friend, Tracy, began having a close-friends meeting at her house once a month and, one night in February, I let fly that I doubted there was life after death and I didn't think God existed. "Life feels like too much work sometimes," I said. "I'd be fine if it ended." Afterward, Tanya pulled me aside.

"You need to get the book *Closer to the Light* by Melvin Morse," she told me. Morse, an emergency room doctor, had documented the near-death experiences of children. The kids all had similar out-of-body experiences, and it gave me a lot of hope.

A package arrived from Tanya a few days later containing *Embraced by the Light* by Betty Eadie, another book about near-death experience. I re-googled MacDougall. I decided that just because his work wasn't up to scientific snuff, it didn't mean he wasn't onto something. I found it interesting that no scientist since has attempted to reconduct his research, and I suspected it was because, as Morse said in *Closer to the Light,* his colleagues thought he was a whack job.

I walked into a health food store and asked for supplements to combat depression.

"Vitamin D," the clerk said. "The only way you get vitamin D naturally is from the sun, and you're not getting any in February." I began popping large doses of vitamin D.

Maybe it was the vitamin D, maybe it was because I'd regained hope, maybe it was a combination of the two, but whatever, I emerged from my black hole with a vengeance and made a reservation to camp at the Grand Canyon in the summer.

Van and I had taken rock-climbing classes, and I was certified to belay. I decided my family should climb while we were in the canyon, so that spring I began searching the Internet for pre-canyon climbs at Devil's Lake, Wisconsin. I called a guide, told him what I wanted to do, and he started laughing.

"I'm sorry I'm laughing," he said, "It's just that I'm in Arizona right now, and I'm about to pick up a Girl Scout troop from your town and take them into the canyon tomorrow. Wild, huh? You know, I'm thinking I'd like to take my girlfriend here this summer. If you want, I'll work out a really nice deal for you. It would just be me and my girlfriend and your family. Usually, I take large groups. I'll call one of my guides and have him email you pictures. We'll hike into Havasu, an Indian reservation at the west end of the canyon, not the national park. I've hiked all over the world, and Havasu is one of my top two places."

I looked at one gorgeous photo after another of waterfalls, crystal-clear pools, canyon walls, and lush foliage, and booked the trip. I also booked a weekend climb at Devil's Lake. I shut my computer down and went to my parents' house. My father was complaining about his expensive thrice-weekly acupuncture and Qigong appointments that insurance didn't cover.

"You have something better to spend your money on?" I asked him. "You walked into Deng's office looking like a zombie and now you're doing great, considering."

"I asked Deng, 'Where are you going on vacation with all the money I'm paying you?'" my dad said. "He started laughing. Little bastard is always laughing. Laughing all the way to the bank. I told him I was cutting my visits down to twice a week, and he didn't like that. Told me it wasn't a good idea. Not a good idea for him."

My father cut his visits down to once a week soon after that. Maybe the cancer was just running its course, maybe it had to do with cutting down on acupuncture and Qigong, but my father dropped weight, became unable to walk without assistance, and was in pain all the time. He stopped seeing Deng altogether.

I'd been regularly taking my father out for lunch and car rides, and one warm day in early May, I helped my dad into my car, opened the sunroof, and drove him to the harbor so he could see his boat. His friends had taken his boat out of dry dock and put it in the water so he could try to sell it. We stopped at the bait shop. I helped my dad out of the car, and he put his arm around my shoulders and we slowly walked in. The man behind the tackle counter looked up and went back to checking inventory. "Larry," my dad said. The man looked at my father blankly. "It's me, Jerry." Shocked recognition swept onto the man's face.

"Jerry," he said. "I knew you had cancer last summer but . . . you look like shit. Here, let me get you a chair."

Larry pulled two chairs out and we sat next to the tackle counter. My dad and Larry chatted briefly, and Larry watched sadly as my father and I limped out the door. We drove to the harbor, and I pulled my car up next to the iron security gate that opened to the pier where my dad's boat was docked.

"I want to get on my boat," my father said.

"I don't know," I said. "You can barely lift your feet. How are you going to climb in?"

"Fine," my dad growled. "I won't get on my fucking boat."

I felt guilty, like maybe I should get him on one more time. I began trying to think of ways to get him on his damn boat without us toppling into the water when a friend of his appeared at his window.

"Jerry," Hal said solemnly. "They told me I have prostate cancer, too."

"I'm sorry to hear that," my dad said. "Do they think you can beat it?"

Hal shrugged forlornly.

"I'm very sorry," my dad said. "Look at me." Neither of them said anything for a moment. "You're going to have to move, Hal," my father said. "I'm going to be sick." My dad opened the car door and vomited on the pavement.

"Bye, Jerry," Hal said and slumped away.

"Let's go," my father whispered, wiping his lips.

My father wasn't up for car rides soon after that. I began taking him outside to sit in his backyard, but by the end of May, he couldn't do that either. My mother hired hospice, and a hospice worker put a hospital bed in the middle of my parents' living room. Two days later, my father was unable to get out of bed. I emailed Todd, the climbing guide, and told him I was probably going to have to cancel our trips. Devil's Lake was days away, Havasu two weeks away. But my dad was still hanging in there when Devil's Lake rolled around, so we went. I showed my dad pictures of our camping trip when we got back and brought the kids to visit him. Now that my kids were out of school for the summer, I was bringing them to see my dad every day. My mom would often take Max and Van to play miniature golf, and I'd exercise my dad's legs and arms and feed him Jell-O. My dad was heavily medicated, and sometimes he was lucid, sometimes not.

"I'm going to cancel our trip to the Grand Canyon," I told my sister one afternoon when we were both sitting in my parents' kitchen. It was June fifteenth and we were scheduled to leave for the canyon in six days.

"I don't think you should," Paula said. "A hospice musician was just here playing guitar and singing for Dad. She said she'd seen people like Dad hang on for a month or more."

"Really?" I said, looking through the kitchen door at the back of my father's hospital bed and the crown of his bald head. "Dad just asked me, 'How long am I going to be stuck like this? You don't know what I'm going through.'"

I told my dad to ditch his sick body when he was ready. I reminded him of the near-death-experience books I'd read and told him about. "Most people didn't want to return to their bodies," I said. "They went someplace really good." My dad closed his eyes and smiled.

My father and I had discussed what I'd come to believe about life after death many times out of earshot of my mother.

"You'll sleep in the ground until Jesus comes," my mother routinely told my father, sticking to her Adventist views. "I'm not afraid of dying because I won't know anything. The next thing I'll see is Jesus."

Rotting in the ground for years was little comfort to my father. He liked my thoughts on death a lot better.

"You should go on your trip," Paula said. "You can keep in touch until you start hiking down. If you need to turn around and fly home, that's what you'll do."

The pastor from my mother's church anointed my father's head with oil the next day. It was Saturday, the day before Father's Day. The kids and I showed up shortly after the pastor left.

"Paula and her kids are coming to see you tomorrow," I told my dad. Noises were agitating him now, and I knew four children would be hard on him. "Would it be too much if we all came?"

"I think so," my dad said.

"Then we won't come," I told him.

It was the last time I saw him alive.

• • •

I sent up a prayer as I drove to my parents' house in the dark. "If you could let me feel something, anything, to let me know my dad is out there, I'd appreciate it," I whispered. I whizzed down the empty road, slowed down as I approached the red light at the entrance ramp to the highway, then stepped on the gas and blew off the light. I started laughing. My father would have sped through the light, too. Maybe it was wishful thinking, but I felt a presence in the passenger's seat next to me. "Thank you," I whispered.

I pulled in front of my parents' house behind a huge white van. I walked in the house and hugged my mother. She introduced me to a social worker who had just signed my father's death certificate.

"Two men from the funeral home are here," my mom said. "They're outside in that van. I asked them to wait until you got here."

"I'll leave you two alone," the social worker said and walked out of the living room into the kitchen.

I walked over to my father's gaunt ivory-colored body. One skinny arm was partially raised. His mouth was slightly open. His eyes were visible through thin slits. I felt no connection to his body at all. He had left it.

The social worker asked my mother if she should ask the guys from the funeral home to come in, and my mother said yes. The social worker suggested that my mother and I go into the kitchen so we wouldn't see my father's body being bagged and hauled out. After everyone left, my mother and I sifted through my father's belongings until the funeral home opened. At lunch, my sister joined us and helped select flowers, then I went home and Paula stayed with my mother. I sent a few emails asking friends to pass on information about my father's funeral and went to bed.

[Tuesday, June 19]

My cousin and old drinking buddy, Mike, flew in from California. He put his stuff in Max's bedroom, and we sat outside on my deck with a bottle of tequila, a container of orange juice, and a bucket of ice. Mike poured himself a drink, and I licked my lips as he drank it. I wanted one bad. I grabbed the orange juice and poured seltzer water in it and had that instead. By the time Mike was on his eighth drink, I was hugely happy I wasn't messed up like him. I kissed him on the cheek and went to bed, but Mike stayed up and drank.

[Wednesday, June 20]

My family met at the funeral home an hour before the wake started. We sat in the parlor with my father's body and Mike, gripping a rocks glass filled with ice and bourbon, made frequent trips to the Lincoln Town Car he'd rented to freshen his drink. *Fuck it,* I thought. I sat next to Mike and started to tell him I wanted to go out to his car when two guys from my 7:00 a.m. recovery meeting walked in. One of them was Kent, my new sponsor.

Kent had become my sponsor when my relationship with Sara got weird. I had started writing *Diary of an Alcoholic Housewife* and Sara didn't like it. She had asked me to write her bipolar/alcoholic story. I started teaching yoga and she didn't like that either. "We don't do things without checking with our sponsors first," she told me.

Not wanting a puppet master but feeling conflicted, I went out to lunch with Playboy Pete and asked him what he thought.

"When you don't know what to do, do nothing," Pete said.

"Really?"

"Turn your problem over to your higher power and do nothing until the answer comes."

"Cool," I said. "I like that."

A week later, I told Sara I felt disconnected from her and needed to find a new sponsor.

"Oh," she said, sounding surprised. "I'm sorry to hear that. But, well, I think you need to do what you need to do. I wish you well. You know you can still call me if you want to."

"Thanks," I said. "You've been great in so many ways."

My relationship ended with Vivian after I told her I was going to teach yoga, too. Vivian wanted to be a yoga teacher as well and was in a training program. I hadn't entered a formal training program yet, but I'd been practicing for years, been encouraged to teach by fellow yogis, and was presented with the opportunity to teach. I invited Vivian to dinner at the Indian restaurant she, Darcy, and I had eaten at to pick her brain about liability insurance. I sat at a table and waited for her for twenty minutes, then called to see if she was coming.

"I'm almost there," she snapped. "If you're hungry, eat without me."

When Vivian showed up, she threw her bag on the floor, slammed down on her chair, pulled a three-ringed binder out, and shoved it across the table at me. She opened it to the section on insurance, and I started jotting information into a notebook.

"That notebook is too nice," she said, snatching the notebook from me and pushing it down the table. She dug around in her backpack. "Write on this," she said, thrusting a dented piece of loose-leaf notebook paper at me.

My phone rang. It was Charlie calling to tell me that Sturgis, my sweet old senile dog, had wandered out of the yard and couldn't be found.

"I have to go," I told Vivian, grabbing my stuff, slapping a wad of cash on the table, and bolting. I drove around my neighborhood looking for Sturgis. I called the police, and they told me a veterinary clinic near my house had picked him up and put him in a kennel for the night.

Vivian called the next day to apologize for her bipolar behavior and ask about my dog, whom I sadly had to put down months after that. I accepted her apology but was done with Vivian. Had we been lifelong friends, I would have put up with her crap. I felt bad, but we hadn't been friends long enough for me to do that. I ran into Vivian only once after. We were at a meeting and she pulled me aside. She told me she left her husband and had moved in with a psychic who was a much older gay woman.

"I'm done with men," Vivian said. "I think I'm a lesbian." Then she told me her daughter, Nancy, was still using.

When I asked Kent to be my sponsor, he said, "Hmm, I'm going to have to ask my sponsor about this." A day later, Kent said yes. It's unorthodox for a woman to ask a man to be her sponsor, but Kent was the sanest, most spiritual person I knew. When Kent walked into my father's wake with Ethan, a recovering crack addict who liked hookers, my heart sank. There went my drink. But the next second I was flooded with gratitude. They'd saved me. I got up and gave both of them a big hug.

Kat walked in. My friends from book club arrived with the exception of Kelly. Joel had left Kelly for another woman and, after many miserable months, Kelly started dating. She was in Napa Valley with her new boyfriend. More of my girlfriends showed up. Deidre, who still couldn't stay sober, gave me a big bear hug. The place was packed and I was relieved I wasn't drunk. I caught sight of Hope and Audrey, who were talking to Mike. Audrey had divorced Nehemiah and moved back to Chicago. When she saw me looking at her, she walked over. "Your cousin is really messed up," she whispered. Audrey partied with Mike and me when we were much younger, and she and Mike had gotten intimate once. Mike was propping himself up against a wall and swaying. Liv, Reed, and Seth walked in. Seth, who'd gone to my parents' north woods cabin with us two summers in a row, glanced at my dad in his coffin. Liv teared up and Reed kissed my cheek.

When the last of the 300-plus guests left, I told Charlie I was going to drive Mike and his rental car back to our house. At home, Mike cracked open a new bottle of bourbon.

[Thursday, June 21]

"I hear you're leaving for the Grand Canyon tomorrow," my cousin Peter said at my father's after-funeral lunch.

"Yeah," I answered. "I'm glad to be getting out of here. We're looking forward to it."

"Max isn't," Peter said with a grin.

"Yes he is," I said.

Peter shook his head and chuckled. "He just told me, 'We're driving 2,000 miles to a big hole in the ground.'"

"You're bullshitting me."

"I'm not," he said, laughing. "Go ask him."

I pulled Max aside.

"I'm not thrilled about camping in a stupid hole for five days," Max admitted.

"But we're all looking forward to this," I said.

"You're looking forward to it. Not me or Dad."

"Dad doesn't want to go either?"

"Ask him."

"I can't believe you're calling the Grand Canyon a hole in the ground," I said stalking off.

Driving home I said to Charlie, "Max tells me you don't want to go to the Grand Canyon."

"I want to go," Charlie said. "I'm just not sure I want to camp down there."

"It's the trip of a lifetime," I said.

"I'm sure it will be great," Charlie said.

"A trip of a lifetime for you," Max said.

When we got home I began packing up the car, grateful I had something to do other than cry. Mike showed up a short time later with a bottle of tequila.

"Do you have to do all this now?" Mike asked. "I could push my flight back a day or two."

"Got to go," I told him. "We're on a tight schedule."

Late that night I sat on the deck with Mike, who was sloshed. "Thanks for coming," I told him and kissed him on the cheek. "My dad really loved you. I love you, too. I have to go to bed now. I'm about to collapse." I gave him another kiss and left him to drink.

[Sunday, June 24]

We woke up in Frisco, Colorado, and drove west through the Rockies into Utah and headed east. The ride through the Rockies and eerie windswept desert monuments was stunning. The landscape was swallowing me, and I loved it. I looked at the map and noticed a skinny gray road in the southeast corner of Utah that was a fairly straight shot to where we wanted to go. I directed Charlie, who was driving, to its rock-and-dirt entrance.

"This has got to be it," Charlie said. "But I don't know."

"Let's ask at that general store we passed," I said.

An older woman and a teenage girl running the store looked out the window at our Trailblazer, which we'd bought after selling the Jeep. It didn't look like another person was around for miles.

"You got four-wheel drive," the woman said. "You'll make it. It'll shave half an hour off your trip and it's a pretty drive."

"Do people use it?" I asked. "In case we get in trouble?"

"Oh, cowboys take that road all the time."

We drove back to the dirt road and took it. We bumped along, twisting and turning, grinding up steep inclines, inching down declines, and sidling up to cliffs and rock formations. It took two hours to get down the gorgeous but boulder-strewn road, and by the time we crossed the Arizona border and pulled into a gas station, it was pitch black. We fueled up and headed for Flagstaff.

[Monday, June 25]

Our guide called and said he and his girlfriend, Amanda, were running late.

"You're unlikely to see us before ten," Todd said. "Meet us at the trailhead. We'll sleep in our cars and start hiking down around three, three thirty. We want to start before the sun comes up and avoid hiking in the heat as much as possible. Eat a huge dinner tonight because you'll need the fuel."

We left downtown Flagstaff and drove through brown barren land to the Grand Canyon National Park. As we entered the east gates I asked a Native American woman collecting entrance fees if the dirt road at the south rim would take us to Havasu. Todd had told me not to take that road, which was direct, because it didn't go through. He told us to take the roundabout three-hour way instead. But having taken the unbeaten path through Utah, I felt like maybe we could handle it. The woman looked at me like she wouldn't mind sending me down the bad road but gruffly said, "No, you can't get through."

We wound our way through the park, pulling over at scenic overlooks. The kids and Charlie, thank goodness, were awestruck. We exited the west gate, stopped at a gas station to fill our water bottles, ate a big steak dinner, and headed for Havasu. We drove up a stretch of Route 66 dotted with neon signs for tiny motels before entering total darkness. Eventually, we turned onto a road that ended at the trailhead in sixty miles. Charlie began driving at a snail's pace. Mule deer, cattle, and jackrabbits jumped onto the road, eyes glowing in our headlights. At eleven we pulled into the parking lot. It was surprisingly packed with cars. We drove slowly along the canyon wall, lighting up people sleeping in their vehicles and shoving gear into backpacks. We turned around at the end, headed back, and Todd appeared in our headlights. He directed us to a parking spot next to his car, and we unloaded our gear into bags that would get tied onto horses that would bring down our heavy stuff. Max and Van unrolled their sleeping bags and went to sleep in the back of the Trailblazer. Charlie and I reclined the front seats, opened the sunroof to the stars, and slept in the soft breeze blowing through the windows.

[Tuesday, June 26]

Todd knocked on our car at four in the morning. We lugged six large duffle bags to a beat-up semi-truck trailer the Havasupai use as an office and stood there for a moment in the muted gray light.

"I hope they know to put these on the horses," Todd said. We started down the switchback trail carved into the canyon wall. The trail was alternately steep and flat, powdery and rocky, wide and narrow. Half an hour into the hike, Charlie let out a howl.

"I turned my ankle on a rock," he wheezed. "It's okay. It's a little sore. No big deal."

I felt zero sympathy. I'd bought hiking boots that hit above the ankles for the kids and myself at Todd's suggestion. I'd told Charlie to do the same, but he purchased a low-cut pair. Amanda gave me a strange look as I stood there looking like a hard-hearted bitch, and she stooped to help Charlie.

We hiked on before stopping at two enormous horizontal slabs of red rock jutting out of the canyon wall, one above the other, and ate a breakfast of sandwiches between them. We continued down, and the canyon walls grew taller and taller as we descended. The sun peeped over the edge of one wall and turned the canyon into a brilliant show of light and shadow. I raised my eyes and said, "Thank you." Turning to Max I said, "Isn't this awesome?"

"Yeah, Mom," he answered sarcastically. "It's just great."

We hiked on, periodically taking rest and water breaks. The sun rose higher and the temperature grew hotter. After five hours, a stream appeared and the desert became dappled with green trees and vines. We descended a steep area and Charlie, who'd been bringing up the rear, shouted, "Aw fuck!" I turned to see Charlie lying on the ground grasping his shin and hugging his knee to his chest. He was moaning loudly.

"Was it a scorpion?" Todd asked, rushing to Charlie.

"I twisted my ankle again," Charlie hissed. "The same one."

"Oh," Todd said, looking mildly irritated. "The way you're holding your leg, I thought a scorpion got you."

I stifled my urge to kick Charlie and gave the boys a drink of water. After much panting and gasping, Todd found Charlie a walking stick and we began hiking again. At ten thirty, we arrived at Havasu Village: a dilapidated town of shack-like homes and paddocks full of skinny horses. There was an office where hikers checked in, a run-down general store, and a shabby, overpriced café. While Todd and Amanda checked us in, we walked to the café for a second breakfast. A helicopter was noisily hovering nearby. When it landed, Max yelled, "Mom! The guy who plays Kiefer Sutherland's father on *24* just got out of that helicopter!"

"Cool," I said, glad he was psyched about something.

"Why couldn't we take a helicopter?" Max complained. "Or at least horses. Our supplies are riding down on horses but we have to hike? Don't you think there's something wrong with that picture?"

I walked away from Max and ordered Indian fry bread, French toast, and Cokes in the café. We hiked for an hour more and arrived at camp by noon. Todd looked through the heaps of duffle bags, backpacks, and rucksacks piled next to the horse corral, but our tent, food, and clothes weren't there.

"I'm sure our stuff will turn up," Todd said. "Why don't you guys go hang out at the falls. Amanda and I'll get a campsite. I'm going to go tell the guys running the horses about our bags."

We followed a small wooden sign pointing to Havasu Falls and stood, awestruck, at the wide swath of water cascading over a red cliff before crashing into a crystal-clear pool that pushed into myriad smaller pools. We took off our hiking boots and wool socks. The water was the perfect temperature of icy. We carefully made our way around the rocky edges of the surrounding pools, and I squeezed Van's hand as water gushed between our legs and yanked at them. Many of the pools had shallow edges with deep swirling whirlpool centers. The boys began pushing and shoving each other into the gentler water, and by the time we walked back to the corral, they were soaked. It was three o'clock and our bags were still missing. Charlie began wringing his hands as he looked at our dripping boys.

"I'm sure they'll show up," Todd said. "I'll take you to our campsite."

"Wait," I said, watching a train of horses heading down. "Our stuff might be there."

Ten minutes later, the horses clomped into the corral and Todd scanned their packs as they entered. "They're here," he shouted.

We set up camp, washed in the stream that ran next to it, and Todd and Amanda cooked pasta primavera.

Before crawling off to bed, Todd said, "I used to sleep on the ground without a tent. The guys I hike with are hardcore. You're a wimp if you sleep in a tent. But the last time I was here, a scorpion crawled into my sleeping bag and stung me. I got pretty sick. Snakes have slithered into my sleeping bag, too. I sleep in a tent now. Shake out your sleeping bags before you get in them and zip your tents up tight and you'll be fine."

Max stared at me.

"What?" I said.

"You're trying to kill us," he deadpanned.

"That's my plan."

[Wednesday, June 27]

Todd cooked pancakes for breakfast, rigged a rope harness for Van, and we set off hiking for Mooney Falls. We reached a cliff and began winding our way down to the falls. Hugging rock, groping for finger holds, and snaking around to a cave, we lowered ourselves down the cave's narrow passage before walking out onto a small rocky platform facing Mooney Falls. Todd pulled the rope harness out, fastened it around Van, and clipped Van to a safety line. I began lowering myself down the side of a vertical cliff on a weathered wooden ladder lashed to the rock, then used iron footholds and a crude chain railing jammed into the rock. Van descended next, and Todd clipped Van's safety line to the chain railing. Todd descended after Van, followed by Max, then Charlie, then Amanda. Van and I would climb down several feet, stop, and Todd would unclip Van's carabiner and move it down the chain. Mist from the gushing waterfall sprayed us as we descended. When we reached the bottom, we stripped down to our bathing suits and I looked up the steep cliff we'd just come down. *I'm a bad mom,* I thought.

We jumped in the water, swam through outer pools, and stopped at one that fed into a stream. I sat on the edge of the pool basking in the sun, my legs dangling in the water, and watched Max and Van wading in the stream, scooping tadpoles and minnows into water bottles. I felt happy and free, and my family was along for my ride whether they liked it or not.

We spent hours swimming from pool to pool and hiking along the stream. We ate trail mix and granola bars and eventually headed back. We climbed the metal ladder chained to the canyon wall near the base of Mooney Falls, then pulled ourselves up using footholds in the rock aided by the dangling chain. We reached the flimsy wooden ladder roped to the canyon wall, climbed it, and continued up through the cave and eventually hit the flat trail back to camp.

"Wow," Todd said. "You guys are brave. A lot of people wouldn't have done that. What did you think?"

"I'm questioning my fitness as a mother," I said.

"You should," Max blurted.

"But I'm thrilled we did it," I added. "It was fabulous."

"Good," Todd said. "Now that we know we can make this, we'll hike to Beaver Falls tomorrow. We have to hike back down to Mooney Falls to pick up the trail, which is a challenging four miles. The trip there and back should take about seven hours.

"Great," Max muttered. He trudged back to camp watching lizards skitter across our path. "I wonder if I can catch some of these guys and sell them on eBay."

[Thursday, June 28]

We woke up early and ate oatmeal and bagels and hiked back to Mooney Falls. We hiked along the stream, left it, and entered a swath of canyon carpeted in thick thigh-high vines. We began hiking through them, and Todd began stomping his feet and told us to do the same.

"Why are we doing this?" Max asked.

"To scare away rattlesnakes," I answered.

"Thanks for taking us on a vacation where we're constantly risking our lives," Max said.

"We shouldn't have a problem," Todd said. "Snakes don't want to see you as much as you don't want to see them. It's when you surprise them that you run into trouble." Todd slowed his pace and began hiking next to me. "With me in the lead, I'll take the first snake bite."

"If anything happens to you, we're screwed," I said.

"There's a snake bite kit in the bottom compartment of my backpack," Todd said. "It's a syringe device with a suction cup on the end. Right after a bite, you attach the suction cup to the bite and pull back on the plunger. It sucks out the poison. I tried it out to see if it works and it does. It left me with a welt."

"Hey," Charlie shouted. "Look up there."

Two desert buckhorn sheep were roaming the cliffs along the canyon wall to our left. We continued on and entered a hilly area covered in vines and canopied by trees. Todd began clapping his hands in addition to stamping his feet. I assumed he was doing this to prevent snakes from dropping out of trees on us.

We hiked out of the vines and back into desert landscape and came to a stream. We grabbed our hiking sandals out of backpacks Todd and Charlie were carrying and put them on.

"We'll leave our sandals on when we have to cross a stream more than once during a short period of time," Todd said. "Otherwise, we'll change back into our socks and boots because your wet sandals will start to chafe your feet."

A number of our water crossings entailed climbing over slick downed trees, navigating around swift currents, hiking through deep water with Van riding on Todd's back, and picking our way over slippery rocks. Out of the water, the trail sometimes became dangerously powdery soft, giving away under our feet. So Todd had to find alternate routes over and around steep cliffs covered in sheep scat and spiny cacti.

"We're a bunch of lemmings following Todd," Max muttered.

"What was that?" Todd asked.

"Max thinks we're a bunch of mindless animals about to follow you off a cliff," I said.

Todd laughed hard and we hiked on.

"Great vacation," Max grumbled. "I'm sick of hiking. I just want to go home."

Charlie was huffing and puffing behind me. "Van is exhausted," Charlie wheezed.

I turned and looked at Van. Van looked like he could hike for days.

We reached Beaver Falls in four hours. About fifteen people besides us had made it there from camp. A group of college-age guys were climbing up the sides of the falls and jumping off into the water below. We dove into the water and swam for a while before putting on our boots and hiking back.

"I hate this," Max hissed. "I hate hiking. I hate this vacation."

"The only way to grow is to push beyond your comfort zone," I told him. "You can have a mediocre life or an exceptional life. You get a mediocre life by staying in your comfort zone. What we're doing here is huge. I'm really proud of you and Van."

I looked at Van, my little outdoorsman, happily hiking along. If I hadn't pushed out of my alcoholic comfort zone, I wouldn't be here torturing Max right now.

[Friday, June 29]

I woke up at dawn, grabbed my yoga mat, and hiked to Havasu Falls. I began a series of sun salutations facing the cascading water, its pounding vibrations reverberating through me. I started crying and lay down on my mat and wept. I miss my father. I'm petrified I might die just like him. And like my dad, I want to grab life by the mane and ride it hard—except sober.

I used to think alcohol and other drugs were the way to living large. Using them made me fearless, allowed me to throw up my arms and scream "Wheee!" until they turned me dull and stupid. I was drinking to escape things that pissed me off, bond with friends, celebrate good news. My anesthetized life was a pathetic shadow of what it is now.

Henry and Eve are still drinking and in sad shape. Eve shows up at meetings once in a while looking haggard and unhappy. And the last time I saw Henry, he was in a hospital bed proving that alcohol and diabetes don't mix.

Sometimes, when I'm speeding down the highway, wind whipping through my hair, I still fantasize about smoking a joint and drinking a beer. Then I remember Deidre, whose husband and sons recently checked her into rehab and changed the locks on her house so she couldn't come home after one of her binges.

I can't envision my life getting as bad as Henry's, Eve's, or Deidre's. But I'd climb into that same bullshit façade I used to live in. I see Kelly at our son's soccer games with her new boyfriend. They put on the same public displays of affection she and Joel used to. Kelly and I will occasionally go out to lunch, and she always makes a point of telling me how happy she is.

When I finished crying, I sat on my yoga mat facing Havasu Falls. A feeling that I was connected to something much greater than myself filled me. I rolled up my mat and began walking back to camp. We're hiking out of the canyon at sunset. My kids are going to have to dig deep to hike all night. But when we climb out of the canyon at dawn, I hope they see they're made of strong, extraordinary stuff.

ABOUT THE AUTHOR

Brenda Wilhelmson has written for the *Chicago Tribune, Chicago Reader,* and Advertising Age's *Creativity.* When she isn't writing she teaches yoga and plays cowgirl on her horse, BlackJack. She and her husband, Charlie, live near Chicago with their two sons, Max and Van. This is her first book.

Hazelden, a national nonprofit organization founded in 1949, helps people reclaim their lives from the disease of addiction. Built on decades of knowledge and experience, Hazelden offers a comprehensive approach to addiction that addresses the full range of patient, family, and professional needs, including treatment and continuing care for youth and adults, research, higher learning, public education and advocacy, and publishing.

A life of recovery is lived "one day at a time." Hazelden publications, both educational and inspirational, support and strengthen lifelong recovery. In 1954, Hazelden published *Twenty-Four Hours a Day,* the first daily meditation book for recovering alcoholics, and Hazelden continues to publish works to inspire and guide individuals in treatment and recovery, and their loved ones. Professionals who work to prevent and treat addiction also turn to Hazelden for evidence-based curricula, informational materials, and videos for use in schools, treatment programs, and correctional programs.

Through published works, Hazelden extends the reach of hope, encouragement, help, and support to individuals, families, and communities affected by addiction and related issues.